Jane Austen
& Company

BRUCE STOVEL

Jane Austen & Company

Collected Essays

NORA FOSTER STOVEL | EDITOR

Gutteridge
BOOKS
An Imprint of The University of Alberta Press

Published by

The University of Alberta Press
Ring House 2
Edmonton, Alberta, Canada T6G 2E1

Copyright © 2011 Nora Foster Stovel

LIBRARY AND ARCHIVES CANADA CATALOGUING IN PUBLICATION

Stovel, Bruce
    Jane Austen & company : collected essays / edited by Nora Foster Stovel ; introduction by Juliet McMaster ; afterword by Isobel Grundy.

Includes bibliographical references.
ISBN 978-0-88864-548-7

    1. Austen, Jane, 1775–1817—Criticism and interpretation. 2. Humorous stories, English—History and criticism. 3. Novelists, English. I. Stovel, Nora Foster. II. Title. III. Title: Jane Austen and company.

PR4037.S77 2011   823'.7   C2011-900339-2

All rights reserved.
First edition, first printing, 2011.
Printed and bound in Canada by Houghton Boston Printers, Saskatoon, Saskatchewan.
Copyediting and Proofreading by Lisa LaFramboise.

No part of this publication may be produced, stored in a retrieval system, or transmitted in any forms or by any means, electronic, mechanical, photocopying, recording, or otherwise, without the prior written consent of the copyright owner or a licence from The Canadian Copyright Licensing Agency (Access Copyright). For an Access Copyright licence, visit www.accesscopyright.ca or call toll free: 1-800-893-5777.

The University of Alberta Press is committed to protecting our natural environment. As part of our efforts, this book is printed on Enviro Paper: it contains 100% post-consumer recycled fibres and is acid- and chlorine-free.

The University of Alberta Press gratefully acknowledges the support received for its publishing program from the Canada Council for the Arts. The University of Alberta Press also gratefully acknowledges the financial support of the Government of Canada through the Book Publishing Industry Development Program (BPIDP) and from the Alberta Foundation for the Arts for its publishing activities.

Contents

VII	*Preface*	
	NORA FOSTER STOVEL	
XV	*Acknowledgements*	
XVII	*Introduction*	
	JULIET MCMASTER	

1   *Tom Jones* and the *Odyssey*

21 *Tristram Shandy* and the Art of Gossip

35 "Female Difficulties"
    Charlotte Lennox's The Female Quixote *and Frances Burney's* Camilla

55 *Waverley* and the *Aeneid*
    Scott's Art of Allusion

75 Jane Austen and the Pleasure Principle

95 Asking versus Telling
    One Aspect of Jane Austen's Idea of Conversation

117 "A Contrariety of Emotion"
    Jane Austen's Ambivalent Lovers in Pride and Prejudice

129 Once More, with Feeling
    The Structure of Mansfield Park

145   Comic Symmetry in Jane Austen's *Emma*

163   "The Sentient Target of Death"
          Jane Austen's Prayers

181   The Genesis of Evelyn Waugh's Comic Vision
          Waugh, Captain Grimes, *and* Decline and Fall

203   Traditional Comedy and the Comic Mask in Kingsley Amis's *Lucky Jim*

221   *Afterword*
          ISOBEL GRUNDY

225   *Works Cited*

☙ Preface

NORA FOSTER STOVEL

BRUCE STOVEL was a true scholar. His scholarly life began early with reading the classics, which he studied at the University of Toronto Schools. As a teenager, after a summer spent baling hay on a farm near Kincardine, Ontario, not far from the summer cottage his parents rented at Inverhuron, he set off hitchhiking, his suitcase filled with Latin and Greek texts. When he returned from his road trip, his mother asked him what he had learned: "I learned that people are pretty nice," he replied.

Bruce remained devoted to Homer's *Odyssey* and *Iliad* and Virgil's *Aeneid*, frequently teaching them in courses on comedy and tragedy at Yale and Dalhousie universities. His essays on "*Tom Jones* and the *Odyssey*" and "*Waverley* and the *Aeneid*: Scott's Art of Allusion," included in this selection of his scholarly articles, are evidence of his continuing interest in classical texts and his belief in their relevance to English literature.

When, the year before his death, we travelled for a month in Italy, where I had been teaching at Cortona, the destination he especially wished to visit was Sicily, in which his readings of classical authors had inspired interest. Sicily did not disappoint: for centuries a colony of various imperial powers, it boasted remnants of Etruscan, Greek, Roman, Norman, Byzantine, and Spanish cultures.

Bruce was a humanist who believed in a liberal arts education and loved literature. Although he appreciated literature in general and claimed that he could teach any literary period, given sufficient time to prepare, his major literary interest was Jane Austen. He read Austen early, but his interest in her work did not become serious until some years later. While pursuing his doctorate at Harvard, Bruce was specializing in the Renaissance. We developed a system whereby he would read aloud while I washed the dishes after dinner. To be fair, we tried it both ways, but either he was the better reader or I was the better dishwasher, for we settled into that comfortable pattern. We soon found that no writer was as delightful read aloud as Jane Austen. Her balanced syntax, precise diction, and ironic wit were unmatched. (After our daughter was born in New Haven, we bought an automatic dishwasher, but, because it interfered with our after-dinner reading of Austen, we sent it back.) At Harvard, Bruce had been planning a dissertation in the Renaissance and was attempting to decide among Spenser, Sidney, Shakespeare, and Milton, when he realized that he could not fight it any longer: after reading all of her novels aloud twice, he had to write his thesis on Jane Austen.

After completing his PHD magna cum laude at Harvard, Bruce taught as assistant professor at Yale University. One of his ideal teaching assignments was a course on comedy, which allowed him to teach Austen, among other favourite authors of comic fiction, including Henry Fielding, Laurence Sterne, Evelyn Waugh, and Kingsley Amis, essays about whom are included in this volume. Yale offered courses with the catchy monikers "Problems in Poetry" and "Problems in Fiction." When someone asked me what Bruce was teaching, I replied, "Comedy." "'Problems in?'" he inquired. "No problems," I responded. "Just comedy."

When we came to the University of Alberta, Bruce's interest in Austen was raised to new heights by our colleague Juliet McMaster, who has generously contributed the introduction to this volume. Together, they founded the Edmonton chapter of the Jane Austen Society of North America in 1992 and convened the next year a JASNA conference at the Chateau Lake Louise that was, simply put, a triumph. Bruce began attending the annual general meetings of JASNA in 1987, when the text was *Pride and Prejudice*. After he telephoned from Santa Fe, the conference site, to tell me that he was having the best time he'd ever had, I began to present papers myself, moonlighting in Austen studies, as it were, just to be companionable. (One year, when we were both presenting papers at JASNA, we each received electronic messages inviting us to introduce the other and asking us to arrive early to meet the speaker and glean the necessary information for the introduction!)

Bruce considered Austen the consummate comic author. In his essay on "Jane Austen and the Pleasure Principle," he quotes the German poet Friedrich von Schiller—author of the "Ode to Joy" that provides the libretto for Beethoven's famous chorale—arguing that "comedy is superior to tragedy." Bruce declares that Austen's "vision is comic," and her novels are "odes to joy." His interest in Austen scholarship centred on his insight into comic structure, an interest that provides the focus of his essay on "Comic Symmetry in Jane Austen's *Emma*" and his last essay, "Once More, with Feeling: The Structure of *Mansfield Park*," both included in this volume. Bruce's essays on Austen, especially *Emma*, frequently focussed on the idea of friends becoming lovers. Having enjoyed the privilege of having Bruce as my best friend for forty-five years, I am particularly fond of those articles. His essay on "'The Sentient Target of Death': Jane Austen's Prayers" seems ironic, since he himself proved to be that very sentient target of death of which Charlotte Brontë speaks in her deprecation of Austen. Two other essays by Bruce on Austen—"Secrets, Silence, and Surprise in *Pride and Prejudice*" and "*Emma*'s Search for a True Friend"—have been collected in *Jane Austen Sings the Blues* (2009), a book published (including a CD of blues music produced by our son Grant and his blues-show co-host, Graham Guest) through the generosity of the University of Alberta Press, in Bruce's honour.[1]

Bruce was that rare creature, a genuinely good man, generous to a fault. His intrinsic goodness is reflected in "Jane Austen and the Pleasure Principle," where he argues that "Austen considers that the greatest pleasure lies in following duty and obligation." In her novels, he argues, "pleasure and moral choice happily coincide."

A lover of conversation, Bruce co-edited a collection of essays entitled *The Talk in Jane Austen* (University of Alberta Press, 2002), based on a conference on that same topic co-convened with Juliet McMaster at Jasper Park Lodge in 1999. His paper on "Asking versus Telling: One Aspect of Jane Austen's Idea of Conversation" is reprinted from that collection. It highlights his Socratic method of teaching, based not simply on lecturing, but on asking searching questions intended to inspire students to think for themselves.

Bruce frequently taught undergraduate and graduate courses on Jane Austen at the University of Alberta. He particularly enjoyed teaching courses that compared Austen's novels with their cinematic adaptations. One year, he invited his graduate seminar to our home for a pot-luck supper, after which he showed them the BBC *Pride and Prejudice* miniseries made famous by Colin Firth's fully dressed dive into a river.

In recognition of his contribution to the university, the University of Alberta's Bruce Peel Special Collections Library dedicated to Bruce's memory a first edition of *Pride and Prejudice*, with a handcrafted case commissioned by the Friends of the University of Alberta, a charitable organization to which Bruce contributed. After this was reported by one of Bruce's former students in the University of Alberta daily student newspaper, *The Gateway*,

Director of Special Collections Jeannine Green reported that they were swamped with people, including many first-year students, wanting to read *Pride and Prejudice* in its original edition.

Bruce frequently taught courses in the eighteenth century and in the Augustan Age. After his sudden and unexpected death from an undiagnosed heart condition only six months after his retirement as professor emeritus at the University of Alberta, family and friends, colleagues and students contributed over fifteen thousand dollars to endow the Bruce Stovel Memorial Prize in Eighteenth-Century Studies.

Bruce particularly enjoyed teaching Restoration comedy and frequently had his students act out key scenes, much to their delight. Once, as we were going through airport security, perhaps on our way to a JASNA conference in the USA, an official plucked out a sharp paring knife from the book-filled briefcase that Bruce never travelled without. When the official asked him what it was for, Bruce replied that his students had been acting out a scene in which one character brandishes a knife!

Bruce taught a full-year course in the English novel at the University of Alberta for many years, until the Department of English, in its wisdom, elected to eliminate all full-year courses. In this course he could teach most of his favourite English novelists, including Samuel Richardson and Fanny Burney. No sooner would he complete the academic year in April than he would begin to reread *Clarissa*. He usually taught Austen's *Emma* in that course and often taught *Pride and Prejudice* in the first-year historical course, which ranged from Beowulf to Virginia Woolf.

Bruce co-taught a graduate seminar on eighteenth-century women novelists with our colleague Isobel Grundy, then our Henry Marshall Tory Professor of English, who has kindly contributed an afterword responding to Bruce's essays. In that course, they taught Samuel Richardson's *Clarissa*, Charlotte Lennox's *The Female Quixote*, and Frances Burney's *Camilla*, as well as Austen's *Emma*—authors and texts represented by the essays in this volume.

After being editor-in-chief of the *McGill Daily* in his sophomore year, a privilege normally reserved for seniors, Bruce was a newspaper reporter for the *Montreal Star* and Canadian Press during his undergraduate years. He frequently greeted friends with the query, "What's your news?" He enjoyed imparting news as much as receiving it. One of his favourite T-shirts from the Chicago Blues Festival sported a logo from Sonny Boy Williamson's song: the front read, "DON'T START ME TALKING," and the back continued, "I'LL TELL YOU EVERYTHING I KNOW."

Though never malicious, he enjoyed gossip and admired Patricia Meyer Spacks's work in that area. At the celebration of his life held at the University of Alberta Faculty Club the week after his death, attended by over three hundred people, our daughter Laura recalled that, when, as an Honours English student, she would visit her father, she rarely got as far as his office before she heard his voice chatting amiably with a colleague in the hallway. He was always happy to mentor or supervise new colleagues or graduate teaching assistants and was always in great demand to do so. His essay on "*Tristram Shandy* and the Art of Gossip" conveys some of that lively interest in people, conversation, and the exchange of information.

I recall hearing Bruce chuckling in his study as he reread for the umpteenth time the works of Evelyn Waugh, and he also read Waugh's novels aloud to me. I recall the delight with which he recounted to me Waugh's suicide attempt recorded in his journal. Waugh descended to the seashore at night. As proof of his intentions, he did not take a towel, but had checked the quotation from Euripides about the sea washing away all human ills for the suicide note that he left with his pile of clothing. After swimming out to sea, however, he ran into a school of jellyfish and was forced to turn back. Stung, he ascended the hill back to the future. So, it seems appropriate to include here Bruce's essay on one of his favourite texts, "The Genesis of Evelyn Waugh's Comic Vision: Waugh, Captain Grimes, and *Decline and Fall*."

Another of his favourite comic authors was Kingsley Amis, and *Lucky Jim* was without doubt his favourite Amis novel. He could hardly read it aloud to me without collapsing into laughter, especially in describing Jim's "Sex Life in Ancient Rome" mask. It seems fitting, then, to include his essay on "Traditional Comedy and the Comic Mask in Kingsley Amis's *Lucky Jim*."

Teaching was very important to Bruce, and he won all the teaching awards the University of Alberta had to offer—the Students' Union Award for Leadership in Undergraduate Teaching (SALUTE), the Faculty of Arts Teaching Award, and the Rutherford Award for Excellence in Undergraduate Teaching. It is therefore appropriate that the publication of this collection was made possible, in part, by the generosity of several University of Alberta administrators. Their support, along with the contributions of other individuals and organizations, is recognized in this volume's acknowledgements.

When I prepared to publish *Divining Margaret Laurence: A Study of Her Complete Writings* (2008), I planned to dedicate it to Bruce because he had been so helpful in reading all the chapters and advising me about revising them. I didn't tell him my intention, however, because I wanted it to be a surprise. Unfortunately, he didn't wait for it. He did, however, read the acknowledgements, which concluded by my thanking Bruce, our daughter Laura, and our son Grant, for their unfailing love and support. Preparing Bruce's essays for this collection, like *Jane Austen Sings the Blues*, has been, in part, my way of thanking Bruce for being such a model husband, father, colleague, friend, and helpmeet, because I know he would never have done it for himself: he was much too modest.

NOTE

1. I actually began to prepare *Jane Austen & Company* before *Jane Austen Sings the Blues* as a work of mourning and as a way of continuing my conversation with Bruce, which had been cut so tragically short.

∞ Acknowledgements

I WISH TO ACKNOWLEDGE the invaluable assistance of the following offices of the University of Alberta, without which the publication of this volume would not have been possible: Carl Amrhein, Provost and Vice-President (Academic); Lorne Babiuk, Vice-President (Research); Colleen Skidmore and Jerry Varsava, at the time Acting Dean of Arts and Associate Dean of Arts, respectively; and Susan Hamilton, Chair of English and Film Studies. I also want to thank Ron Betty, Secretary-Treasurer of the Friends of the University of Alberta; Elaine Bander and Renée Charron of the Jane Austen Society of North America, Canadian division; and both Bridget Toms, President of the Edmonton chapter, and Elizabeth Marshall, former President of the Calgary chapter of JASNA.

I wish to acknowledge the following journals for permission to reprint essays: *The Dalhousie Review*; *Eighteenth-Century Fiction*; *ESC: English Studies in Canada*; *The International Fiction Review*; *Man and Nature: Proceedings of the Canadian Society for Eighteenth-Century Studies*; *Persuasions: The Jane Austen Journal*; *Thalia*; and *Transactions of the NorthWest Society for Eighteenth-Century Studies*. I also wish to thank the following editors and publishers for permission to republish essays from their editions: Juliet McMaster, co-editor of *Jane Austen's Business: Her World and Her Profession* and *The Cambridge*

Companion to Jane Austen; Colin Gibson and Lisa Marr, editors of *New Windows on a Woman's World: Essays for Jocelyn Harris*; and the University of Alberta Press, publishers of *The Talk in Jane Austen*.

I also want to thank Linda Cameron, Director of the University of Alberta Press, and her excellent staff: editors Peter Midgley and Mary Lou Roy, designer Alan Brownoff, and marketers Cathie Crooks and Jeff Carpenter. I also wish to thank my Graduate Research Assistant, Beth Gripping, who checked the documentation, and Lisa LaFramboise, who copyedited the collection. I also want to thank my esteemed colleagues, Juliet McMaster and Isobel Grundy for their introduction and afterword, respectively. Finally, I wish to thank my family for their encouragement and support.

∞ Introduction

JULIET MCMASTER

"LUCKY JIM is neither a satire nor high-spirited farce,...but, like its eighteenth-century progenitor, *Tom Jones*, absorbs satire and farce into a broader comic structure and vision." So writes Bruce Stovel in the last piece in this volume. These essays were published in different venues over a number of years, and with no design, one must assume, of their being published together after the author's untimely death. But the sentence neatly connects the last essay with the first, the end with the beginning, and also announces an overarching theme for the collection, of "comic structure and vision." Inevitably I feel mournful in reading again the work of a lost friend and valued colleague; but this reader at least can be buoyed up by a critical vision that delights in the ridiculous, celebrates carnival, festivity, love, and happy endings, and lingers over laughter. Stovel allows us to inhabit what he calls "the holiday world of comedy."

This is a collection about the novel, clearly Stovel's favourite genre, and the essays are arranged in chronological order, not as he wrote and published them, but as the works he engages emerged, from the eighteenth to the mid-twentieth century. We have no treatment of *Clarissa* here, nor of *Tess of the d'Urbervilles* or *Jude the Obscure*. Stovel clearly prefers those novels where "we are all hastening together to perfect felicity," as Jane Austen wrote archly

(*Northanger Abbey* 250). It is her comic irony, and that of Fielding, Sterne, Waugh, and Amis, and not the tragic irony of Hardy, that is the dominant music here. And Stovel's style has its own felicities to lighten and delight. His prose is a pleasure to read. We hear of lucky Jim's "ever-erupting volcano of inner revolt" and Waugh's "triumph over his wish for easeful death"; and we can relax with a treatment of gossip as "a playtime of the mind." Picking up on Fielding's metaphor of human nature as the principal element on his bill of fare, Stovel winds up his essay on *Tom Jones* and the *Odyssey* by showing how both have indeed been "dishing up for our entertainment that very human nature." Such supple stylistic turns make for criticism that aspires to be as light, bright, and sparkling as the novels it engages.

"It is their depiction of a just and harmonious world that makes us think of the *Odyssey* and *Tom Jones* as comedies," Stovel claims. And though not all of us read those epic journeys as humorous—and according to Fielding's own poetics of comedy in the preface to *Joseph Andrews*, the lost *Margites* was Homer's comic epic—Stovel's alignment of the two narratives, with their persistent thrust towards the nuptial bed and a fortunate conclusion, is a case that convinces. Where one is inclined to cavil, Stovel humorously highlights the differences, too: "Sophia has only two men who want to marry her, Blifil and Lord Fellamar, while Penelope has 108."

A buried footnote modestly mentions that "Translations [from Horace's *Ars Poetica*] are my own." Unlike most literary scholars today, Stovel is clearly steeped in the classics and knows his way around Homer and Virgil almost as well as around Sterne or Austen. But unlike the compulsively quoting Baron Bradwardine of *Waverley*, Stovel wears his learning lightly and is never solemn or pedantic. For me, his essay on "*Waverley* and the *Aeneid*: Scott's Art of Allusion" is perhaps the most revealing, as it is the most unexpected. With deft quotation of parallel scenes and issues, he brings the two works together and demonstrates how the recurring allusions, even or especially Bradwardine's quotations that so exasperate many readers, adduce deeply to the whole meaning of *Waverley*. His argument recalled my own impatience, back in my school years, with that eternally "*pius Aeneas*." Back then, to me, the constantly gnashing Turnus was so much more appealing than Aeneas, the passionate Dido so much more sympathetic than dutiful Lavinia. Now it is a revelation to recognize just those sentiments in my own students in their response to the characters of *Waverley*: Fergus Mac-Ivor, they contend, is so much more romantically attractive than boring old Edward Waverley, and fierce Flora puts dowdy Rose Bradwardine in the shade. Stovel's persuasive parallels clarify both works: "*Furor*, or frenzy, is the great enemy of Aeneas's rational dedication to public good; it is, socially, the primitive code of honour, based upon courage in physical combat; psychologically, it is being ruled by raging emotion." Turnus is Virgil's exemplar of *furor*, like Fergus Mac-Ivor and his Highlanders, and however charismatic, these characters lead to chaos and destruction. But in their heroes Aeneas and Waverley, both Virgil and Scott provide "a hero whose story embodies the whole history and nature of the society he founds," writes Stovel. Scott's learning and classical allusion are not introduced for mere ornament or showing off: "instead, like Fielding or George Eliot or Joyce, he uses allusion as an artistic device," asserts Stovel. The same might be said of Stovel's own classical knowledge.

Bruce Stovel was a brilliant teacher, and his essays demonstrate one aspect of the successful teacher in their structural orderliness. One learns in the classroom that to announce enumeration is to get pens poised for note-taking. *Tristram Shandy* and gossip, we learn, "have the same subject, substance, purpose, structure, narrative situation, style, and tone. I would like to develop each one of these resemblances in turn." And sure enough, the following paragraphs go through each aspect. "Rhetorical questions come in many forms in the novels [of Jane Austen]," we hear in the essay "Asking versus Telling"; and in due order we go through the *leading* question, the *Socratic*, the *brow-beating*, the *pleading*, and down to the *abject* question, as they appear in Austen's six novels, with examples of each. Likewise, in the essay on *Lucky Jim*, we are reminded of the "four characteristics of traditional comedy:…the happy ending, the use of festivity, the mood of play, and the pervasive comic irony." You don't lose your way in these essays: if you hear of seven pillars of wisdom, seven pillars you will get. With an elegance that belongs with a fully-thought-out argument, one is led lucidly through the parts to grasp the whole.

Given this strong sense of order and fine ear for rhythm, it's not surprising that Stovel provides in these essays a developed vision of the novels as finely tuned working organisms; and structure is an element of fiction that Stovel is particularly good at illuminating, whether it is the grouping and parallel sequence of books in the *Odyssey* and *Tom Jones*, or the recurring and unfolding plot developments in *Mansfield Park*.

Bruce and I worked together on two conferences on Jane Austen: one on *Persuasion*, the annual gathering, six hundred strong, of the Jane Austen Society of North America in the stunning setting of Lake Louise; and the other on The Talk in Jane Austen, again set in the Rocky Mountains. (On those invigorating but often stressful occasions, he was always the person who would cheerfully take on the toughest jobs, such as grant applications, transport arrangement, and sweet-talking disgruntled delegates.) It is in the cluster of papers on Jane Austen that I hear Bruce's voice most clearly. This is appropriate enough, considering his subject of "Asking versus Telling"—part of the "talk" we were investigating at that conference. I too have worked on the speeches in the novels, which I have always considered the plums in the pudding. By a kind of comedic necessity, his essay on asking progresses from questions on any subject under the sun on which information may be sought towards that crucial question that constitutes the proposal of marriage. Love and courtship in Austen's novels have been my territory, too; and in that essay I hear resonances of many a corridor conversation of times past.

A version of "The Sentient Target of Death: Jane Austen's Prayers" was included in the volume Bruce and I co-edited after the Lake Louise conference, *Jane Austen's Business: Her World and Her Profession*. It's one of his best things on Austen; and just as his knowledge of the classics informs his essays that link *Tom Jones* to the *Odyssey* and *Waverley* to the *Aeneid*, so his deep familiarity with both Johnson, especially in his devotional pronouncements, and the *Book of Common Prayer* echoes through his close study of these brief and often overlooked pieces of prose, informed as they are with the rhythms of the Bible and the Prayer Book. Stovel's "three ways in which [Austen's prayers] might illuminate the novels" require close listening indeed. The most interesting to me is the second: the prayers "reveal to us the sins to which Jane Austen felt she was most inclined." He shows how she clearly felt some guilt for her judgementalism, her restless impatience at the shortcomings of others—a trait she shares with her own heroines Elizabeth Bennet and Emma. Considering the sensitivity of his reading of the individual's self-knowledge in the communal prayer, it's hard to accept the dismissive reading of these prayers in the new Cambridge edition of Austen's works: there the prayers are dismissed as "utterly conventional" and relegated to an appendix, as possibly not by her at all.

Dickens and Thackeray, Brontë, George Eliot and Henry James receive passing mention among the essays, but the great Victorian novelists do not figure in Stovel's criticism, though he taught them regularly. He leaps from Jane Austen's "Divine comedy," the vision of a world that is ultimately "good, just, harmonious, and [where] all will turn out well in the end," to the more rambunctious and chaotic comedy of Waugh's *Decline and Fall* and Amis's *Lucky Jim*. Perhaps most Victorian novelists are too seriously reflective to lend themselves to his comedic approach.

But Stovel is thoroughly at home with Waugh. Here he provides a nicely managed exploration of the "meeting-point between biography and fiction"—following through the connections between the character Grimes in *Decline and Fall*, "one of the world's great rogues," and the real-life original, who was a shameless pederast. In examining these connections of Waugh's life with his fiction, Stovel demonstrates the startling transformations of comedy: the pederast's confession becomes "a richly comic incident"; Waugh's own aborted suicide attempt as narrated at the end of his autobiography, when his bid to drown himself is foiled by a jellyfish, is rendered as "a comic triumph of life over death."

Amis's lucky Jim, with his bagful of comic masks to deploy on a variety of occasions, allows Stovel to run through a number of theories of the comic—Henri Bergson, Elder Olson, George Santayana—without loss of laughter. The essay is joyful and funny, like its subject. It has one function of good criticism that is all too often absent in many a more pretentious treatment: it makes you want to go back to reread the novel itself. With that result alone, even if his rich critical studies did nothing further, I know Bruce Stovel would be more than content.

 Tom Jones and the *Odyssey*

FIELDING STRESSES throughout *Tom Jones* that in it he is "the Founder of a new Province of Writing" (Fielding 77; bk. 2, ch. 1). At one point, in the manner of Polonius, he calls this new literary kind "Prosai-comi-epic Writing" (209; bk. 5, ch. 1). Whether or not Fielding was literally trying to create a novel that would at the same time be a modern epic (as Tolstoy and Joyce would later attempt to do), he certainly wanted to give his innovative comic novel the monumental dignity and mythic universality of the great epic poems. And whenever Fielding refers to serious epic he has in mind primarily three poets: Homer, Virgil, and Milton. For instance, when he is about to start the final section of his novel in book 13, chapter 1, Fielding adopts the epic stance and invokes the muse (better late than never!) in the following words: "Thee, whom *Mæonia* educated, whom *Mantua* charm'd, and who, on that fair Hill which overlooks the proud Metropolis of *Britain*, satst, with thy *Milton*, sweetly tuning the Heroic Lyre" (683). Not only were these three epic poets the ones Fielding knew best and admired most; even more important, like Pope in his mock-epics, he could count on his educated readers to recognize allusions to their poems.

Fielding's allusions to Virgil and Milton in *Tom Jones* are prominent, indeed scarcely avoidable; they give to the novel's action much of its epic, if hardly solemn, universality. Allworthy's estate is called Paradise Hall, and when Tom is expelled from it Fielding comments, "*The World*, as *Milton* phrases it, *lay all before him*; and *Jones*, no more than *Adam*, had any Man to whom he might resort for Comfort or Assistance" (331; bk. 7, ch. 2)—and he thereby hints that Tom is also like Adam in having Providence as a guide. The same lucidity and shaping function characterize Fielding's many allusions to the *Aeneid*; he gradually suggests, aided by Partridge's portentous Virgilian tags, that Tom, like Aeneas, is on an epic journey to his proper home—and with three Didoes, not merely one, to distract him from his task.

The relationship between Homer's epic poem and Fielding's novel is different and more puzzling. As Martin Battestin's footnotes to the Wesleyan edition of the novel reveal, Fielding makes the *Iliad* the main source for his mock-epic battles and his extended heroic similes. But his use of Homer's second great epic, the *Odyssey*, is more enigmatic. The *Odyssey* is not an important source of mock-epic: it contains no heroic combats, and its epic similes are short, pungent, and homely. Furthermore, Fielding's allusions to the *Odyssey* are relatively casual and incidental—and they inevitably seem so because the situations of Odysseus and Tom Jones are so obviously different. Odysseus is a king of about fifty years of age, a legendary hero known for his cunning; Tom Jones is an orphan about twenty years old, a manifestly fictitious, private person notable mainly for his ingenuousness. This difference between the two heroes is so great that W. B. Stanford, in his authoritative study of the Ulysses figure in European literature, *The Ulysses Theme: A Study in the Adaptability of a Traditional Hero*, does not even mention *Tom Jones*. Similarly, though critics frequently note the Miltonic and Virgilian dimensions of *Tom Jones*,[1] the relationship between the *Odyssey* and Fielding's novel has been relatively ignored. This neglect is all the more strange when we consider that Fielding draws upon the *Odyssey* for his epigraph, "Mores hominum multorum vidit" ("He saw the customs of many men"), using Horace's paraphrase in *The Art of Poetry* of the *Odyssey*'s opening. Is the *Odyssey* relevant to *Tom Jones* or not?

Some critics answer no. Ian Watt, for instance, who devotes a chapter in *The Rise of the Novel* to "Fielding and the Epic Theory of the Novel," concludes that "The remarkable coherence of the plot of *Tom Jones* surely owes little to the actual example of Homer or Virgil...; it is very palpably the product of Fielding's experience as a practising dramatist" (257–58).[2] A second group of critics, among them Frederick W. Hilles and Henry Knight Miller, admit in passing that Fielding had the *Odyssey* in mind when he wrote his novel, but do not pursue the point (Hilles 99–100; Miller 101). A third, smaller group of critics have discussed at some length the relationship between the two works. J. Paul Hunter has argued that Fielding drew upon the *Odyssey* to create a modern epic; Hunter, however, considers the story of Odysseus's son Telemachus the essential point of contact, and, in fact, proposes that Fénelon's *Télémaque* (1699), the French prose reworking of the story of Telemachus, was Fielding's model for *Tom Jones* (*Occasional* 130–35). Similarly, Thomas E. Maresca argues that Fielding recreates epic in *Tom Jones* by creating a hero who "emulates literally and allegorically both Aeneas and Odysseus" (203)—but Maresca says very little about the connections between the *Odyssey* and *Tom Jones*, concentrating instead on the relationship between the *Aeneid* and Fielding's novel.[3] In fact, the most detailed and helpful treatment of this subject occurs, not in the vast body of Fielding criticism, but in Robert Torrance's discussion of *Tom Jones* in his *The Comic Hero*, a study of representative comic heroes from Homer's Odysseus to Joseph Heller's Yossarian and Ken Kesey's R. P. McMurphy (187–96).

I would like to argue here that there are striking resemblances of three kinds—in plot and theme, in structure, and in narrative perspective—between Homer's prototypical epic poem and Fielding's pioneering epic novel. My underlying assumption is that the *Odyssey* is not only, as Miller claims, the "great *Urquell* of the romance tradition" (101), but also the great progenitor of comedy. The view that the *Odyssey* is the prototypical comedy goes back at least as far as Aristotle, who argues that the *Odyssey* provides the pleasure proper to comedy, since it has a double plot and an opposite outcome for good and bad characters;[4] in our century, this view underlies both Joyce's *Ulysses* and several suggestive scholarly accounts of comedy.[5] My point is not that *Tom Jones* is modelled directly on the *Odyssey* in the way that *Joseph Andrews* is professedly modelled on *Don Quixote* or *Amelia* on the *Aeneid*; rather, it is that the *Odyssey* was one of several precursors—in addition to comic romances, romances, stage comedies, personal essays, and much else—that Fielding drew upon when he created the comic novel as a literary form. The presence of the *Odyssey* within *Tom Jones* is thus a specific instance of the process Mikhail Bakhtin has called "novelization": the eighteenth-century novel's incorporation of traditional genres within its own new and more various discourse" (6, and *passim*).

⁕ Fielding's epigraph from Horace's *Art of Poetry* draws attention to the plot of both his own novel and Homer's epic. Horace is advising the poet that when he begins his work he should get right to the point: follow the example, Horace says, of the man "qui nil molitur inepte" ("who builds with complete fitness"; Horativs Flaccvs 140)—and he begins with the words "'dic mihi, Musa, virum, captae post tempora Troiae / qui mores hominum multorum vidit et urbis'" ("Tell me, Muse, of the man who, after the times of captured Troy, saw the customs of many men, and their cities"; 141–42).[6] By paraphrasing the exordium of the *Odyssey*, Horace points to the perfect construction, the unity of action, of Homer's epic, and it is the plot of his own novel that Fielding draws to our attention in his epigraph. James Beattie grasped Fielding's intention when in his *Dissertation Moral and Critical* (1783) he said of *Tom Jones*, "'Since the days of Homer, the world has not seen a more artful Epick fable'" (qtd. in Swedenberg 112). It may be helpful to specify four ways in which these two artful fables resemble each other: in their comprehensiveness, in their heroes, and in their unifying themes of love and justice.

As for comprehensiveness, the epic sweep of *Tom Jones* is the one obvious characteristic that it shares with the *Odyssey*. As the epigraph suggests, each hero is exposed to the whole range of the known world—both to its diverse social orders and to the murderous ogres, seductive nymphs, and traitors that make up its moral realm. The first chapter of *Tom Jones*, Fielding's "Introduction to the Work, or Bill of Fare to the Feast," tells us that the "prodigious Variety" of "HUMAN NATURE" will be his subject (31, 32). This comprehensiveness is the one link between the two works regularly noticed by critics of the novel: Watt, for instance, says that the action of the novel "presents a sweeping panorama of a whole society" (251); Sheridan Baker, in his Norton Critical Edition of the novel, says of the epigraph in a note, "Fielding, perhaps with a touch of irony, thus casts Tom Jones as something of a young and modern Odysseus, discovering the ways of the world as he wanders to find his proper home" (4). The attitude to variety, however, is just as important in each work as the variety itself; like other works that are comic in outlook—*The Canterbury Tales*, *Don Quixote*, *The Pickwick Papers*, *Ulysses*—*Tom Jones* delights in and celebrates the variety it contains. In his first chapter Fielding invites us, not to a lecture, but to a feast; and Tom Jones, like Odysseus, welcomes the diverse and unexpected vicissitudes he encounters: no less than Odysseus, Tom must hear the sirens' song for himself.[7]

Our two eponymous heroes are in fact much more alike than it might appear. Each is an everyman. Odysseus appears in a great many roles and guises; he is as truly a beggar when he arrives in his own kingdom as he is later its king. As Joyce pointed out, Odysseus encompasses the experience of all men: he is son and father, husband and lover, warrior and diplomat, voyager and homebody.[8] Similarly, Tom's universality is suggested, not just by his character, but by his simple, generic name and his status as a natural son of unknown parents. Odysseus's disguises emphasize his comprehensive identity: his most famous deception is his claim to Polyphemus to be Οὖτις, Nobody, and someone who is nobody can also be everybody. Tom is also in disguise throughout the novel, since his true social identity and moral nature are not known. The novel culminates, as does the *Odyssey*, in the removal of disguises and the restoration of the hero to his rightful place in society. Granted Tom, a foundling like many a romance hero,[9] does not choose his disguises; even when he appears in costume at the masquerade, Lady Bellaston gives him his role. Still, like Odysseus, Tom is a man of many roles (scapegrace, lover, soldier, knight-errant, gallant, reformer, man of honour, etc.) but one single desire: to return to his home. That Tom is a returner rather than simply a wanderer is stressed by Partridge's recurrent scheme to persuade Tom to go back home; Fielding remarks that Partridge hopes that in doing so he will himself be restored to his native country, "a Restoration which *Ulysses* himself never wished more heartily than poor *Partridge*" (427; bk. 8, ch. 7). In their wanderings, both Odysseus and Tom depend upon the kindness of strangers: what hospitality is in the world of the *Odyssey*, charity is in the less ritualized and more secular world of *Tom Jones*.

Furthermore, the comprehensive, outward-looking hero of each work has also, necessarily, a simple and undivided character: both Odysseus and Tom Jones have no inner conflict, unlike Homer's

Achilles, Virgil's Aeneas, and Milton's Adam. Odysseus may have moments when his nerve fails, but he is always impelled by the desire to return. Tom Jones may hold rhetorical debates with himself as to his course of action, but he is never in real doubt, and so never in real pain, because he has an inward monitor, his own good heart, which always tells him what he should do—even if, as is often the case, that monitor opposes the orthodox code of his society (so, for instance, Tom does not hesitate to lie to Mr. Allworthy in order to protect Black George). This is why both Tom and Odysseus, literally tourists, *see* the customs of many men: both the Homer of the *Odyssey* and Fielding present what Maynard Mack, contrasting the comic outlook of *Tom Jones* with the tragic vision in Richardson's *Clarissa*, calls "life apprehended in the form of spectacle rather than in the form of experience" (xv). In both the *Odyssey* and *Tom Jones*, extension is gained at the cost of intensity. And where there is no inner conflict, the heroes cannot change in character; their social status and allegiances change dramatically, but such changes are rewards for their persistence in being what they have always been—great in all the important ways.[10]

Further, both Tom and Odysseus are heroes of experience, marked and known by their scars. They can wander so widely and see so much because both pass through life under the special protection of the heavens: Odysseus is the favourite of Athena, goddess of wisdom, and Tom is equally a favourite of Fortune. Since both are heroes of experience, both are heroes of wisdom. After lapses into imprudence, both triumph through the exertion of practical wisdom. Odysseus foolishly yields to his impulses at times, most notably in his parting boast to Polyphemus, which allows Poseidon to find out his identity and persecute him. In general, however, Odysseus triumphs through his wiliness: telling Polyphemus that he is Nobody turns out to be not an expression of self-pity but a brilliant stratagem. Tom's wisdom is more paradoxical: he begins the book as a kind of Noble Savage and must learn prudence. But he does learn from his experience. "Wisdom...teaches us...a simple Maxim," Fielding remarks in book 6, chapter 3, "And this is not to buy at too dear a Price" (283). Tom shows that he has learned this lesson when, in a dazzling display of sexual self-control, he turns down the advances of the wealthy Mrs. Hunt, the forward Mrs. Fitzpatrick, and the fond Mrs. Waters in books 15, 16, and 17 of the novel, with the result that he can be rewarded with the hand of his Sophia in book 18. This reward he earns by his ingenuity in making Sophia see that her image in the mirror is the pledge and guarantee of his love. Tom's character may not have changed, but he has become much more adroit at managing it.

The novel ends with the phrase "the Day when Mr. *Jones* was married to his *Sophia*" (982; bk. 18, ch. 8). The words not only signify Tom's acquisition of wisdom; they also point to another connection between the *Odyssey* and *Tom Jones*. Both tales are love stories and have at their centre heroines who are wise, passionate, and constant. Each heroine is the perfect mate for the hero, the ideal he seeks throughout and earns at the conclusion. Sophia's name, of course, means wisdom, just as the formulaic adjectives attached to Penelope describe her as wise, and both possess a wisdom of the heart. Everyone, even her family and eventually her son, wants Penelope to admit that Odysseus will not return and to choose a second husband, but her intuition, based in her love, tells her otherwise: in fact, Homer suggests that when Odysseus does return disguised as a beggar, Penelope recognizes him at a subconscious and intuitive level long before their formal reunion.[11] Similarly, Sophia's wisdom lies largely in her ability to see and love the true Tom Jones and to be constant to that love when everyone, even Mr. Allworthy, tries to persuade her that Tom is what he seems, base. Both heroines must fend off unworthy but powerful suitors who attempt to displace the hero; Sophia only has two men who want to marry her, Blifil and Lord Fellamar, while Penelope has 108, but in both cases the suitors prove their unworthiness by their inability to love the heroine; instead, they want to despoil her property and possess her status. If Penelope shows her wisdom in her delaying tactics, never actually giving an answer to her suitors but always promising that an answer will be forthcoming, while Sophia displays hers by escaping from her father's house and following Tom, each heroine's form of action suits her hero. And the action of each work culminates with a recognition and reunion scene orchestrated by the heroine. After a great deal of preparation by author and characters in both cases, the hero and heroine finally confront one another again; the heroine, surprisingly, stands off and forces the hero to declare his true identity. It is only when each heroine has satisfied the claims of prudent self-distrust that she gives way to her feelings and accepts the hero. What immediately follows in *Tom Jones* is a wedding and its consummation. The ending of the *Odyssey* is not so very different; just before Odysseus and Penelope are reunited in book 23, Odysseus orders the minstrel to play merry dances so that outsiders will believe a wedding feast is under way inside the royal palace.

It may seem that Lavinia, the princess Aeneas marries at the end of the *Aeneid*, is the epic precursor of Sophia (Maresca 216; Ehrenpreis 63). In fact, however, Sophia "is to Tom as Penelope was to Odysseus, both counterpart and consummation" (Torrance 194). The parallel with Lavinia is largely nominal: she appears only in the final books of the *Aeneid*, she does nothing and says little in the poem, and the hero's feelings towards her are simply dynastic. In contrast, the analogies between Penelope and Sophia are very strong. Take, for instance, the hero's sexual prodigality. When we first meet Odysseus, he has lived for seven years as the love-slave of Calypso, and Homer, describing his longing for home, says pointedly, "the Nymph had long since ceased to please" (Homer 91; bk. 5); similarly, Odysseus shares Circe's bed for a year until his men remind him that it is time to leave for home. Yet these escapades hardly undermine Odysseus's fidelity to Penelope and home; if anything, they make his love for Penelope fuller and more human. Something of the same aura attaches to Tom's three sexual liaisons, and, in fact, Tom's roadside nymph, suitably named Mrs. Waters, is a latter-day Circe: in the chapter in which Fielding remarks that "*Ulysses*...seems to have had the best Stomach of all the Heroes in that eating Poem of the Odyssey" (509; bk. 9, ch. 5), she seduces Tom over a table of food.[12] Furthermore, Tom has not really been unfaithful to Sophia, since, as he explains to her in their reconciliation scene, his amours occurred while he had no hope of ever being allowed to love her—while he was, so to speak, imprisoned in another world.

Both Homer and Fielding stress the sexual bond between their lovers by making a bed the central object in their plots. No reader of the *Odyssey* can forget the living and rooted marriage bed that Penelope makes the test of Odysseus's identity; in fact, the renewal of the marriage in that bed in the middle of book 23 has seemed to many readers, from antiquity to the present, the real end of the poem; in this view, the rest of the poem is a spurious later addition.[13] A bed is also the central prop in Fielding's novel. It begins with Tom's being found in a bed; at its exact midpoint between books 9 and 10, he is in the wrong bed, though Sophia places her muff, as a rebuke, a challenge, a reminder, and an invitation, in Tom's bed (see M. Johnson); and the action of *Tom Jones*, unlike that of Homer's poem, concludes in bed. After mentioning "that happy Hour which had surrendered the charming *Sophia* to the eager Arms of her enraptured *Jones*," Fielding adds:

> Thus, Reader, we have at length brought our History to a Conclusion, in which, to our great Pleasure, tho' contrary perhaps to thy

Expectation, Mr. Jones appears to be the happiest of all human Kind: For what Happiness this World affords equal to the Possession of such a Woman as *Sophia*, I sincerely own I have never yet discovered. (979; bk. 18, ch. 13)[14]

There is hardly a sentence in all of Fielding less likely to contain a literary allusion, but the sentiments are those expressed by Odysseus in his benediction, both diplomatic and deeply felt, to Nausicaa:

And in return may the gods grant you your heart's desire; may they give you a husband and a home, and the harmony that is so much to be desired, since there is nothing nobler or more admirable than when two people who see eye to eye keep house as man and wife, confounding their enemies and delighting their friends, as they themselves know better than anyone. (Homer 107; bk. 6)

If love is a main theme in each work, the other great theme of each is justice. In gaining what they deserve as individuals, both heroes restore justice to their societies. Both works end, in fact, not merely with a picture of the lovers reunited, but with a picture of a just and lasting social order centred upon and created by that reunion. Homer devotes the last section of book 23 and all of book 24 to showing Odysseus reinstated as his father's son and his people's monarch, while *Tom Jones* ends with the sentence, "And such is their Condescension, their Indulgence, and their Beneficence to those below them, that there is not a Neighbour, a Tenant, or a Servant who doth not most gratefully bless the Day when Mr. *Jones* was married to his *Sophia*" (982; bk. 18, ch. 13). This restoration of justice is stressed from the outset in each work. In the very first speech in the *Odyssey*, Zeus tells the assembled gods that men blame the gods for their troubles, when in fact their own wickedness is the source of their sufferings. Zeus mentions Aegisthus, the adulterous murderer of Agamemnon, as a case in point, but we soon realize that the poem will present Penelope's suitors as an even more prominent instance of this principle. In fact, Homer, the council of the gods (who are for once unanimous), and Odysseus himself all see the slaughter of the suitors as a necessary judicial execution, not an act of military prowess. Similarly, there is ultimately no conflict of values in *Tom Jones*: prudence, far from being circumspect selfishness, is, as Mr. Allworthy explains to Tom at the novel's end, "the Duty which we owe to ourselves" (960; bk. 18, ch. 10). Thus, after Tom discovers Sophia's muff in his bed at Upton, Fielding comments that "his past Offences...as is the Nature of Vice, brought sufficient Punishment upon him themselves" (618; bk. 11, ch. 10).

It is their depiction of a just and harmonious world that makes us think of the *Odyssey* and *Tom Jones* as comedies—and the absence of such a depiction that makes the *Iliad* and the *Aeneid* more like tragedy. "'Homer...*manifestly composed the Iliad as a likeness for tragedy, the Odyssey as an image for comedy*,'" said the late-Roman commentator Donatus (qtd. in Torrance 280), and Fielding has some such large orientation in mind, I think, when he describes himself and his work as "a Writer whose Province is Comedy" (743; bk. 14, ch. 1) or as "a Comic Writer" and not "of the Tragic Complexion"; in the latter passage he says that the comic writer's task is completed once he "hath made his principal Characters as happy as he can" (875; bk. 17, ch. 1). By contrast, *Amelia*, explicitly modelled on the *Aeneid*, is a much more sombre work, tragic in tone and implication, if not in outcome.[15]

⁂ Fielding's epigraph to *Tom Jones* provides a clue to the novel's disposition of its action into books, as well as to the nature of that action. By citing Horace's *Art of Poetry* and not the *Odyssey* itself, Fielding suggests what Homer's epic has offered to subsequent writers: a model of lucid form. One striking aspect of the *Odyssey*'s structure is its clear and symmetrical disposition into books. Homer allots twelve books to Odysseus as a wanderer; in the thirteenth book Odysseus arrives in Ithaca, and the second twelve books occur there. The first twelve books fall into three equal parts: four books describe the search of Telemachus for news of his father; books 5 to 8 take Odysseus from Calypso's wild island to the pacific island of the civilized Phaeacians; in books 9 to 12 he recounts his wanderings to the Phaeacians. There are similar four-book units in the second twelve books. Within these large units Homer organizes his story with equal symmetry. For instance, as reflective readers of the epic notice, the adventures of books 9 to 12 fall into a pattern in which two adventures are summarized briefly and then a third is told much more fully: book 9 presents the Cicones and Lotos Eaters briefly and the Cyclops more fully; book 10 presents Aeolus and the Laestrygonians in summary form and then Circe at length; book 11 contains only Odysseus's journey to Hades, but then the pattern resumes in book 12 with the Sirens and Scylla-and-Charybdis episodes presented briefly and the Oxen of the Sun episode recounted at greater length. The design within individual books or episodes is often equally emphatic: in book 8, for instance, scenes in which Odysseus is welcomed by the curious Phaeacians alternate with and frame three separate songs by Demodocus, the Phaeacian bard; the first and third of these songs recount different exploits of Odysseus at Troy, and his reactions to these songs lead to his disclosure that he is Odysseus and to his own song of his adventures since leaving Troy.[16] These structural symmetries enforce upon us an awareness that the story is organized *ab extra*, that it is self-consciously artificial, that it conveys life apprehended as spectacle rather than as experience.

Fielding's novel is famous for exactly the same kind of structure: eighteen books divided into three groups of six books each, one devoted to the country, one to the road, and one to the town. Within these triads, there are six units of three books each (the novel was originally issued in 1749 in six three-book volumes). At the same time, like the *Odyssey*, the novel falls neatly into two matching halves, with the two books at Upton, books 9 and 10, serving as hinges. Within this architectonic patterning there are many intricately worked symmetries. For instance, on the final page of book 1, Doctor Blifil dies of a broken heart, betrayed by his brother and partner in duplicity, Captain Blifil, and then at the end of book 2, "just at the very Instant when [Captain Blifil's] Heart was exulting in Meditations on the Happiness which would accrue to him by Mr. *Allworthy*'s Death, he himself—died of an Apoplexy" (109; bk. 2, ch. 8). The titles Fielding provides for each book and chapter often underline such symmetries.

It seems quite possible that Fielding's model in creating the famous design of *Tom Jones* was the work whose even more famous design is pointed to in the novel's epigraph. Certainly, there is no obvious and agreed-upon source for the novel's architectonic structure—a surprising fact when that structure is so apparent and so important. There is nothing similar in previous English novels, or in the continental comic romances that Fielding knew so well. And, as its title page acknowledges, his one earlier comic novel, *Joseph Andrews*, owes its main debt to Cervantes's *Don Quixote*, and its four-book structure is, like its model's, episodic and sprawling, without the elaborate clarity of organization found in *Tom Jones*.[17] A more obvious candidate is the one Watt points to, Fielding's own plays, but the five-act structure that Fielding favoured in his stage comedies is not very congruent with the eighteen books of *Tom Jones*.[18] The *Odyssey*, however, might well have offered a usable form. Homer had given both his epics twenty-four books, and Virgil and Milton had each used twelve, so that eighteen books would be about the right number of units and also a happy mean.[19] Even more important was the symmetrical, clearly segmented disposition of the narrative; in fact, just as Homer uses four books as his basic structural unit, so Fielding, working at a ratio of three books to every four of Homer's, uses three books as his. Clearly, the two stories are far from identical in structure. Homer uses retrospective narration, while Fielding, telling his story in the manner of romance rather than epic, does exactly what Horace, in the lines immediately following those that form the epigraph to *Tom Jones*, says the poet should not do. He begins, if not *ab ovo*, shortly after his hero's conception and proceeds chronologically. There are, all the same, some striking similarities in structure. The introduction of each hero is delayed to build interest and to show how much his society needs his arrival. Both works have what Aristotle defines as a double plot, a split focus on the hero's and the heroine's separated worlds. Both works accelerate dramatically as the climax approaches, an acceleration accompanied by rapid shifts back and forth from one character or group of characters to another. In any case, each author has cast his narrative into the same kind of symmetrical, clearly segmented structure. This structure, of course, helps create our contemplative detachment from the events presented. Fielding describes an important truth about comedy, and is not simply being facetious, when he tells us in *Joseph Andrews* that one of the "Mysteries or Secrets… of *Authoring*" is "dividing our Works into Books and Chapters": "those vacant Pages which are placed between our Books…are to be regarded as those Stages, where, in long Journeys, the Traveller stays some time to repose himself, and consider of what he hath seen in the Parts he hath already past through" (89–90; bk. 2, ch. 1).

∞ This similarity in narrative perspective provides a final point of resemblance between the two works. Nothing could seem further from Fielding's fictional world than Homer's pantheon—and yet it is just here that a striking connection exists. If Homer's gods guide events to their happy outcome, so does Fielding's Providence, and in each case the divine force does not simply control human events so much as co-operate with them. Even more important, both the epic and the novel invite us to see events from a double perspective, both that of the human agents and that of the divine overseer. Homer begins his epic, after allowing us a glimpse of Odysseus languishing in Calypso's power, with a scene in which the gods in council decree that it is time Odysseus should be allowed to escape and set out for home. And at the start of book 5, the book in which we finally meet the poem's hero, Zeus reminds a second assembly on Olympus that they have agreed to Athena's plan to have Odysseus return to Ithaca, settle accounts with the suitors, and be reunited with his family. A third council of the gods is presented right after Odysseus arrives in Ithaca in book 13, the point at which the second half of the poem begins. Our awareness that a predestined plan is working itself out is further heightened by Athena's appearances to Odysseus and Telemachus throughout the poem, by the omens that punctuate the action, and by the poet's own comments (for example, his remark in book 18 that Odysseus's grave warning to Amphinomus, the one humane suitor, was in vain, since Athena had already marked out Amphinomus to be slain by Telemachus—an event that duly occurs four books later). We thus see all the events in the poem in two simultaneous perspectives: as uncertain and subject to accident, which is the way the human agents experience them, and also as predestined and divinely ordained, which is the Olympian view that the poet allows us to share. In fact, we are more curious about just how the poet will resolve his plot than about what its outcome will be. The poem's narration is thus inherently ironic, since it continually presents us with two levels of meaning, one superficial and one hidden. Of course, all epics display narrative irony, since the author is telling a story already well known to his audience—indeed, a story of central significance for his culture. Only in the *Odyssey*, however, is the story presented throughout from a divine perspective; in *Paradise Lost*, which might seem similar, the poem begins by presenting Satan's point of view, and we later enter Paradise with him in books 4 and 9, so that the statements of God in book 3 and of Michael in books 11 and 12, if theologically correct, offer, in terms of narrative perspective, a second, competing vision.

Fielding creates the same double perspective in *Tom Jones*. We find events surprising and puzzling, on the one hand, and yet we sense that they are part of a fixed, coherent plan, on the other. Unlike Homer, Fielding tells a new story—a novel—whose outcome is apparently unknown; he cannot, like Homer (or Milton, for that matter), present his divine agency in the form of characters who speak and act. His own narrating voice, however, serves roughly the same function as Homer's presiding deities. That voice gives us secret assurances throughout that all will be well; so the reader accepts the author's promise of a happy outcome and rejects the opinion expressed by the characters that Tom is born to be hanged. The real prophecy lies beneath the false prediction. Similarly, when Fielding introduces Blifil to us as "sober, discreet, and pious beyond his Age" (118; bk. 3, ch. 2), his words of praise are both misleading and definitive. The narrator invites us to see, as the characters cannot, the workings of a fixed and predestined plan in what seems to be mere chance—in the death of Captain Blifil, for instance, or in Tom's discovery of Square squatting in Molly Seagrim's bedroom. The turbulent goings-on of the action are always described *de haut en bas*, so that we can enjoy both their manifest confusion and their hidden lucidity. The conventional reading that attributes Olympian irony to Fielding is thus perfectly right. If he cannot bring on the gods, he can speak with godlike authority himself. Fielding conceives of his novel as a coherent universe, "a great Creation of our own" (525; bk. 10, ch.

1), and he invites his readers to share his grasp of "our main Design" (524)—unless we prefer to be little reptile critics. It is thus doubly ironic when Fielding tells us at the start of book 17 that, unlike the ancient poets, whose deities were always at hand to deliver their heroes from danger, he is "a poor circumscribed Modern" (876) and will have great trouble delivering Tom Jones from prison:

> If he doth not therefore find some natural Means of fairly extricating himself from all his Distresses, we will do no Violence to the Truth and Dignity of History for his Sake; for we had rather relate that he was hanged at *Tyburn* (which may very probably be the Case) than forfeit our Integrity, or shock the Faith of our Reader. (876)

∞ My concern has been to outline the large epic resonances that connect *Tom Jones* and the *Odyssey*, rather than to identify the sources, or even the equivalents, in Homer for particular scenes in Fielding's novel (though I might note that Tom's reunion in the final book with Mr. Allworthy, whose first name he bears and whose estate he will inherit, corresponds to Odysseus's reunion with his father Laertes, and that Lady Bellaston, who first meets Tom in the guise of Queen of the Fairies and whose service soon becomes very tiresome, serves as Tom's Calypso). One of the most searching books on Fielding of recent years, C. J. Rawson's *Henry Fielding and the Augustan Ideal under Stress*, devotes a chapter to discussing Fielding's uneasy relationship to epic, and concludes, "the 'comic epic' experiments of *Joseph Andrews* and *Tom Jones* did not really involve any large-scale or structural epic resonance, as distinct from mock-heroic as one of several devices of distancing and stylization" (164–65).[20] It is just such large-scale and structural resonances of the *Odyssey* within *Tom Jones* that I have tried to demonstrate. Their existence should not surprise us. After all, Fielding describes the author of the *Odyssey* as "him, who, of all others, saw farthest into human Nature" (202; bk. 4, ch. 13)—and does so while he is dishing up for our entertainment that very human nature.

NOTES

1. See, for example, Battestin 181 (for Milton); Ehrenpreis 63 (for Virgil).
2. Sheridan Baker, arguing the same position, says that the novel's epigraph has a very simple explanation: "[Fielding] certainly adds this after writing the book, to give it a handy classical seal of approval, and not necessarily to point to the *Odyssey* as model, which the book hardly resembles in either contents or form" ("Fielding's Comic Epic-in-Prose Romances Again" 64).
3. Ira Konigsberg has some helpful remarks on the relationship of Fielding's novel to classical epic, though he also emphasizes the influence of the *Aeneid* and not the *Odyssey* (112–14).
4. See Aristotle's *Poetics*, ch. 13. Torrance has an appendix summarizing the classical and Renaissance tradition that the *Odyssey* provides a model for comedy (279–82).
5. Two examples are Albert Cook's *The Dark Voyage and the Golden Mean: A Philosophy of Comedy* and Northrop Frye's *A Natural Perspective: The Development of Shakespearean Comedy and Romance*.
6. Translations are my own.
7. Richard Keller Simon argues that *Tom Jones* is comprehensive in another, less obvious way: it constitutes an encyclopaedia of the kinds of comic writing (53–77).
8. Joyce's description of Odysseus as the "'complete all-round character'" is quoted by Frank Budgen (15).
9. This point is developed by Miller, and in several other articles by Sheridan Baker, notably "Henry Fielding's Comic Romances" (411–19).
10. Konigsberg remarks, "We do not have here a reflection of the journeys of such comic-romance figures as Don Quixote or Gil Blas, for Tom is closer in character to the epic heroes, and his adventures take on a corresponding significance. He is a great warrior, a passionate lover, and fundamentally he represents the best qualities of his time" (113).
11. This interpretation, which goes back at least as far as Seneca's *Epistles*, is developed persuasively by Anne Amory (100–21).
12. Miller points to the connections between Mrs. Waters and Circe (51).

13. Stanford reviews this debate in *The Ulysses Theme* (55–65).
14. Hilles, Ehrenpreis, and Robert Alter (*Fielding* 117–20) all develop the notion that Fielding sets up parallel scenes at opposite ends of the novel to underline his symmetrical plot and his moral themes—though none of the three cites the three crucial beds as an instance. Douglas Brooks makes a thoroughgoing attempt to define such structural symmetries in his discussion of *Tom Jones* in his *Number and Pattern in the Eighteenth-Century Novel: Defoe, Fielding, Smollett and Sterne*.
15. Fielding described the *Aeneid* as the "noble model" for *Amelia* in the *Covent-Garden Journal*, no. 8, on 28 January 1752 (Fielding, *Covent Garden* 186). Alter's discussion of the relationship of the two works and of the epic and the novel forms is especially illuminating (*Fielding* 141–46).
16. The preceding two sentences are indebted to Cedric H. Whitman's account of the "Geometric design" (287) of the *Odyssey* in his *Homer and the Heroic Tradition* (286–89).
17. Two essays that explore *Joseph Andrews*'s debt to the *Odyssey* are Leon Gottfried's "The Odyssean Form" (19–43) and Douglas Brooks's "Abraham Adams" (794–801).
18. Baker argues that the novel's structure is, in fact, greatly influenced by the five-act form Fielding used in most of his plays; see Baker, "Fielding and the Irony of Form" 138–54.
19. Ehrenpreis describes eighteen books as "a figure which stands midway between the twenty-four books of Homer's epic and the twelve of Virgil's, so that the very number suggests a new genre derived from the heroic tradition" (16). Hunter's claim (133–35) that *Télémaque* is the primary model, since it consisted in its first edition of eighteen books, is rendered questionable by the fact that the English translations of Fénelon's works—and Fielding owned and referred to the English version—all had twenty-four books; see Baker, "Fielding's Comic Epic-in-Prose Romances Again" 69–72. It would seem that Fénelon and Fielding decided independently that an eighteen-book structure would be suitable for a modern reworking of Homeric material.
20. Similarly, Simon Varey says, "*Tom Jones* imitates classical epic in only the most casual and incidental ways" (79).

 *Tristram Shandy* and the Art of Gossip

AFTER THREE TANTALIZING CHAPTERS that allude to an unparalleled interruption, lament the terrible vulnerability of the HOMUNCULUS, and describe the way in which knowledge of this interruption has been handed down, the narrator of *Tristram Shandy* promises in the fourth chapter that we will finally be "let into the whole secret from first to last." First, though, he warns readers who are not "curious and inquisitive" to skip over the remaining part of the chapter (4; vol. 1, ch. 4). Having thus ensured our continued attention, he then makes a distinctive gesture and, like the wife of King Midas, whispers the secret knowledge:

> —Shut the door.—I was begot in the night, betwixt the first *Sunday* and the first *Monday* in the month of *March*, in the year of our Lord one thousand seven hundred and eighteen. I am positive I was.—But how I came to be so very particular in my account of a thing which happened before I was born, is owing to another small anecdote known only in our own family, but now made public, for the better clearing up this point. (6; vol. 1, ch. 4)

Tristram, it seems clear, is adopting the stance and tone of a gossip—the sort of person Samuel Johnson characterized in his dictionary as "one who runs about tattling like women at a lying-in." This essay will argue that Laurence Sterne, who began *Tristram Shandy* four years after the appearance of Johnson's *Dictionary*, recreated in his novel the satisfactions found in the familiar, everyday activity of gossiping. Sterne must have been struck by the fact that the realistic novel, as it had been developed by Defoe, Richardson, and Fielding, possessed some striking similarities in material and treatment to gossip.[1] In *Tristram Shandy*, he seems to have decided to exploit the forms and conventions of gossip, partly in order to show the strange ways in which daily life and sophisticated art interpenetrate each other.

Interpretation consists of placing a text within a context; if we consider *Tristram Shandy* within the context of gossip, we can see that both text and context have the same subject, substance, purpose, structure, narrative situation, style, and tone. I would like to develop each one of these resemblances in turn; in doing so, a more precise sense of what gossip is, as well as what its usefulness as an interpretive tool might be, will emerge.

For my purposes, gossip is informal and casual talk between two or more people about the private lives of other people known to them.[2] The subject of gossip—my first resemblance—is thus the racy, the naughty, the veiled: things like Walter Shandy's misconception of his son, or Toby Shandy's disillusioning discovery about the opposite sex, or Tristram's unplanned circumcision, or how Uncle Toby acquired his modesty, or how Trim and Bridget managed between them to break the bridge to pieces. As these instances suggest, gossip deals most often with sexual incidents, with the kind of "small anecdote" that women would discuss at a lying-in. This is because the most concealed part of our lives is that for which we reserve the term *private parts*. Even when its material is not sexual, gossip consists of domestic facts about other people that those people would not willingly discuss publicly. Gossip exists at second or third hand because self-analysis is too rigorous, confession too intense, for its relaxed and impulsive mood. Gossip is small talk, idle chit-chat. Tristram thus tells us about his family and not himself; even when he recounts his own experience, he almost always makes it plain that he is not recounting his own experience first-hand, but, as in the opening, reporting what his Uncle Toby has told him that his father said, or, later in volume 1 (ch. 16), what Uncle Toby has repeated of Tristram's mother's complaints. The nature of gossip dictates, then, that *The Life and Opinions of Tristram Shandy* will be almost all opinions and almost no life, since Tristram's own life is present as merely another occasion for gossip.

To turn from subject to substance: there is a related reason why the novel will consist almost entirely of opinions. If gossip claims as its subject what Tristram calls "the whole secret," or what we might call the bare facts, the facts are only a starting-point for detached speculation, hypothetical connections, possible explanations. The novel's epigraph from Epictetus is especially true of gossip: "It is not actions, but opinions concerning actions, which disturb men." Gossip is by its very nature inconclusive, since it can no longer exist if all the facts to be explored are public knowledge. The subject, or topics, that characterize gossip are thus less important than its substance, or object. The object of speculation is knowledge of the true characters of other people, an object that can never be fully and finally attained (in real life, anyway), since, as Tristram points out, we have no window into the souls of others: "our minds shine not through the body, but are wrapt up here in a dark covering of uncrystalized flesh and blood; so that if we would come to the specifick characters of them, we must go some other way to work" (83; vol. 1, ch. 23). Going to work that other way, gossip makes its necessary limitation its source of delight. How much the imagination can do with a few suggestive facts! With, for instance, an unaccountable obliquity in the way a boy sets up his top (4; vol. 1, ch. 3). If Tristram chooses to present a rare glimpse of his adult experience, all is conveyed by one fact: we see him "as I stood with my garters in my hand, reflecting upon what had *not* pass'd" (624; vol. 7, ch. 29). This substance of gossip, the play of conjecture, is present in the novel at two levels. It exists within the anecdotes that Tristram reports to us, as when we see Yorick's parishioners busy speculating upon his riding habits, his help to the midwife, and the relationship between the two, or when we see the Strasburgers of volume 4 speculating on just what the long nose of the stranger might mean. Such speculation is also a very important part of our relationship as fellow gossipers with Tristram; in this relationship, which might be called the novel's frame-tale, Tristram again and again teases us into speculation by putting before us intriguing facts: the precise nature of Uncle Toby's wound, for instance, or just what Toby was looking at when he declared that he did not know the right end of a woman (118; vol. 2, ch. 7), or exactly where and how Toby laid down his pipe when Trim told him the naked truth about the Widow Wadman (vol. 9, ch. 31).

We can now consider the purpose of gossip. It has none, at least no ostensible purpose. Performed for its own sake, for sheer pleasure, gossip lacks concrete purpose or explicit justification; it is a play time for the mind and has the same relation to serious discourse as play does to work. Gossip, in fact, is so enjoyable that almost all of us spend a great deal of our waking lives doing it; this pleasure is so unadulterated by usefulness that we almost all feel guilt about the time we spend gossiping ourselves, and regard the sight of other people doing so with an uneasy mixture of contempt and fear. Johnson's dictionary definition captures precisely this scorn—and yet we remember that it comes from a man who loved to gossip and did so with unforgettable flair. Of course, considered philosophically, every work of literature is play in its relation to real life. Yet some works magnify and celebrate their status as play, while others minimize it in order to concentrate upon other satisfactions; *Tom Jones* and *Clarissa* serve as opposites in this respect, as in so many others. Sterne's novel is clearly at Fielding's end of this spectrum. Tristram puts his readers into the playful, pleasure-seeking attitude that characterizes gossip; we find ourselves in the same frame of mind as Walter Shandy, who suggests that, "as we have nothing better to do, at least till *Obadiah* gets back," we might as well extract some pleasure from what is at hand—in this case, a sermon on conscience (139; vol. 2, ch. 15). Again and again, in fact, Tristram presents within the novel something that was originally a serious communication, but is now transformed into a vehicle for gossip; the sermon, which Sterne himself had preached, is the outstanding example. Other instances include the judgement of the Sorbonne theologians about infant baptism (vol. 1, ch. 20), the curse of Ernulphus (vol. 3, ch. 11), and even, amusingly, a witty passage from Rabelais describing intellectual gymnasts, which is inserted verbatim and thus made one degree more playful (vol. 5, ch. 29). As Sterne says in the epigraph to volumes 3 and 4, "it has always been my purpose to pass from the gay to the serious and from the serious to the gay." The effect of this shiftiness is to intensify the novel's gaiety and undermine its seriousness; as Elizabeth Drew remarks, Sterne "was unique in his own day and unlike any other major novelist since in making no pretensions to be doing anything but enjoy himself and entertain his readers" (75).[3] On the very first page of the novel we see—or, more precisely, hear—Tristram converting serious facts into the playful, pleasurable stuff of gossip:

>—you have all, I dare say, heard of the animal spirits, as how they are transfused from father to son, &c. &c.—and a great deal to that purpose:—Well, you may take my word, that nine parts in ten of a man's sense or his nonsense, his successes and miscarriages in this world depend upon their motions and activity, and the different tracks and

trains you put them into; so that when they are once set a-going, whether right or wrong, 'tis not a halfpenny matter,—away they go cluttering like hey-go-mad; and by treading the same steps over and over again, they presently make a road of it, as plain and as smooth as a garden-walk, which, when they are once used to, the Devil himself sometimes shall not be able to drive them off it. (1–2; vol. 1, ch. 1)

In structure, a bout of gossip is unsystematic, casual, and impulsive: ostensibly formless. Organized exposition belongs to the work world, not the world of play; the demand for pleasure requires that gossip must move in rapid and unpredictable leaps, circling constantly about certain fascinating and never fully understood facts. Gossip concentrates upon character and disregards formal plot. All of this, of course, is strikingly applicable to *Tristram Shandy*. Tristram, for instance, explains, at the end of volume 1:

> What these perplexities of my uncle *Toby* were,—'tis impossible for you to guess;—if you could,—I should blush; not as a relation,—not as a man,—nor even as a woman,—but I should blush as an author; inasmuch as I set no small store by myself upon this very account, that my reader has never yet been able to guess at any thing. And in this, Sir, I am of so nice and singular a humour, that if I thought you was able to form the least judgment or probable conjecture to yourself, of what was to come in the next page,—I would tear it out of my book. (89; vol. 1, ch. 25)

The novel, thus, has an even more wayward structure than the narrator's squiggly lines at the end of volume 6 would suggest. Two further implications of gossip's formless form can be related to *Tristram Shandy*. Any given interchange of gossipers is never completed in the way that works of art are: rather, the exchange swells and shrinks to fit the time available, and, in most cases, just as Tristram does with his uncle Toby's amours, the choicest morsel is saved for the last contribution. *Tristram Shandy* is thus finished, not completed, by its final volume. A second implication is that interruption is, paradoxically, the one clear principle of connection in gossip, since gossip rejects logical coherence in favour of idle, whimsical mental association. The book opens and closes with an interruption, and Tristram advances his story through every imaginable kind of interruption; he is so ingenious in doing so that, at one point in the novel, one of his own characters interrupts *him* when he is expatiating upon the nature of love:

> It is a great pity—but 'tis certain from every day's observation of man, that he may be set on fire like a candle, at either end—provided there is a sufficient wick standing out; if there is not—there's an end of the affair; and if there is—by lighting it at the bottom, as the flame in that case has the misfortune generally to put out itself—there's an end of the affair again.
>
> For my part, could I always have the ordering of it which way I would be burnt myself—for I cannot bear the thoughts of being burnt like a beast—I would oblige a housewife constantly to light me at the top; for then I should burn down decently to the socket; that is, from my head to my heart, from my heart to my liver, from my liver to my bowels, and so on by the meseraick veins and arteries, through all the turns and lateral insertions of the intestines and their tunicles, to the blind gut—
>
> —I beseech you, doctor Slop, quoth my uncle Toby, interrupting him as he mentioned the *blind gut*, in a discourse with my father the night my mother was brought to bed of me—I beseech you, quoth my uncle Toby, to tell me which is the blind gut; for, old as I am, I vow I do not know to this day where it lies. (674; vol. 8, ch. 15)

Tristram's novel begins with (in a punning sense, at least) *coitus interruptus* and proceeds by *discursus interruptus*.[4]

If gossip consists mostly of narrative, both factual and conjectural, then the situation in which this fitful narrative is created is worth examining. Gossip is indulged in by people who know each other and, in fact, get to know each other better through the act of gossiping, since, in doing so, they are pooling their knowledge, exposing their values and assumptions, and moving tentatively toward a common viewpoint. This coming to know each other on the part of the gossipers is, I suspect, the real purpose of gossip, the real social function that it serves. Gossip is thus only apparently aimless. Certainly Tristram himself holds forth the promise of just such mutual knowledge; he tells us at the start of the novel:

> I have undertaken, you see, to write not only my life, but my opinions also; hoping and expecting that your knowledge of my character, and of what kind of mortal I am, by the one, would give you a better relish for the other: As you proceed further with me, the slight acquaintance which is now beginning betwixt us, will grow into familiarity; and that, unless one of us is in fault, will terminate in friendship.—*O diem præclarum!*—then nothing which has touched me will be thought trifling in its nature, or tedious in its telling. (9; vol. 1, ch. 6)

Gossip not only requires a spoken voice, that is, physical exchange, but it also creates a special kind of intimacy: it not only conjectures about what takes place behind closed doors, but itself takes place when the door is shut against those outside. Tristram himself, of course, enters into just such an intimate friendship with us.[5] Furthermore, we cannot help contrasting our playful relationship with Tristram, in which there is just such a slow and steady growth into mutual understanding, with the relationships within the novel, all of which are marked by an attempt at serious exchange and by almost total frustration in that attempt; the fluid ease with which we and Tristram develop a common understanding in the frame-tale is highlighted by the misunderstandings that exist within that frame.

Gossip also has its own distinctive style. As we have seen, that style is spoken; even when gossip occurs in letters and not in person, the letters reproduce the patterns of spontaneous speech, not those of formal prose. Furthermore, gossip employs a distinctive kind of spoken style: allusive, full of veiled reference and innuendo, of nuance and *double entendre*. It is somehow very pleasant to convey the most charged facts without ever having been indiscreet enough to name them outright. Tristram, for instance, in the chapter of explanation with which I began, employs just this knowing sort of suggestiveness when he describes the cause of his mother's inopportune question:

> My father…had made it a rule for many years of his life,—on the first *Sunday night* of every month throughout the whole year,—as certain as ever the *Sunday night* came,—to wind up a large house-clock which we had standing upon the backstairs head, with his own hands:—And being somewhere between fifty and sixty years of age, at the time I have been speaking of,—he had likewise gradually brought some other little family concernments to the same period, in order, as he would often say to my uncle *Toby*, to get them all out of the way at one time, and be no more plagued and pester'd with them the rest of the month….
>
>   [M]y poor mother could never hear the said clock wound up,—but the thoughts of some other things unavoidably popp'd into her head,—& *vice versa*:…. (6–7; vol. 1, ch. 4)

This allusive shorthand allows for a shared play between those gossiping; the reader's imagination must be ready to give ordinary words a richer texture and fuller meaning. Tristram describes the style of his novel, and its origin in the nature of gossip, in just these terms:

> Writing, when properly managed, (as you may be sure I think mine is) is but a different name for conversation: As no one, who knows what he is about in good company, would venture to talk all;—so no author, who understands the just boundaries of decorum and good breeding, would presume to think all: The truest respect which you can pay to the reader's understanding, is to halve this matter amicably, and leave him something to imagine, in his turn, as well as yourself. (125; vol. 2, ch. 11)

My final point is that gossip has a distinctive tone or mood, one that, as I have suggested, is intimate, secretive, relaxed, detached, playful, impulsive, zestful. Each one of these adjectives describes both the characteristic mood of gossip and the special atmosphere, indeed the special appeal, of *Tristram Shandy*. This mood creates, or at least intensifies, friendships by its atmosphere of shared delight; Tristram holds before us the prospect that, as friends, we will eventually not only understand each other, but also have a better relish for each other. This mood of shared delight in speculative contemplation magnifies the importance of the gossipers at the expense of those who are being gossiped about. For the talkers to grow, those discussed must become smaller (whence, by the way, the vague fear that we feel when we see friends talking idly on a street corner). We can note that, beginning with the HOMUNCULUS, every character in *Tristram Shandy* is belittled: Walter Shandy, his wife, Uncle Toby, the Widow Wadman, even Yorick, even Tristram. It is hard to imagine how any character could be presented within the novel and not be comically diminished by becoming a source of gossipy anecdote and speculation.[6]

To recapitulate, I believe that *Tristram Shandy* transforms into art the real-life experience of gossip, and that the novel's distinctive subject, substance, purpose, structure, narrative situation, style, and mood recreate that experience. When we recall the puritanical reaction that almost all of us have at the sight of other people tattling together like women at a lying-in, we can see why F. R. Leavis dismissed Sterne in a footnote to the opening pages of *The Great Tradition* as a nasty and irresponsible trifler (11n3).

If this perception of the importance of gossip to *Tristram Shandy* is valid, it helps explain a number of puzzling facts about this most puzzling of novels; I would like to examine one of these puzzles by way of a conclusion, or perhaps I should say, finish. Not many readers in recent years have found *Tristram Shandy* lacking in moral seriousness, as Leavis does, but an increasing number have found the novel very serious in another way, as a presentation of a philosophy of art. In the most persuasive and searching of these accounts, Robert Alter constructs a great tradition of his own, a counter-version of the novel's development (*Partial Magic passim*). Alter is interested in the novel that concentrates its imaginative energy upon depicting its own complex relationship with the real world; Sterne forms an important link in this tradition, which begins with Cervantes, and moves through to Nabokov, Barth, and Fowles in our day. But Alter, and those who approach *Tristram Shandy* as he does, omit to mention one striking fact: Sterne never suggests, as Cervantes, Nabokov, et al. do so pervasively, that all of the events and characters of *his* books are made up. Fielding, for instance, Sterne's great predecessor in the English comic novel, repeatedly reminds us that we are enjoying the sophisticated pleasures of imaginary events, not a straightforward transcription of real experience; the very first words of *Tom Jones* force this awareness upon us—"In that Part of the western Division of this Kingdom, which is commonly called *Somersetshire*, there lately lived (and perhaps lives still) a Gentleman whose Name was Allworthy" (34; bk. 1, ch. 2)—and we all recall the slyness of book 17, chapter 1 of *Tom Jones*, in which the narrator laments his hero's apparently inevitable doom, and hopes that Tom can be extricated from his calamities by natural and credible means. Tristram, however, never allows such reflections to arise, and a glance at Nabokov will assure us that Sterne's choice of first-person narration is not a sufficient explanation for this lack of Cervantesque irony. How could a man with Sterne's subtle and playful mind, a man who knew and admired *Don Quixote*, fail to recreate such an important element in Cervantes's appeal? Fielding, we note, seizes upon and elaborates just this element. The answer, I suspect, resides in the paradoxical nature of gossip; while its substance is largely hypothesis, as I have argued, those hypotheses are meant to account for real events and real causes in our own experience. This is precisely why gossip is so disreputable, while fiction, so similar in many ways, is comparatively respectable.[7] The hypotheses of gossip are provisional; what they try to explain is real. After all, why shut the door and whisper the whole secret if you, and your secret, are admittedly imaginary?

NOTES

1. Several critics have noticed this resemblance. In "The Fact in Fiction," Mary McCarthy argues that "Even when it is most serious, the novel's characteristic tone is one of gossip and tittletattle" (264–65). Homer O. Brown speculates that the realistic novel shares the formal properties of two opposed forms of communication in everyday life, gossip and letters: the first is spontaneous, communal, evanescent; the latter deliberate, individual, and permanent (573–99).

2. My generalizations throughout this essay are indebted to two essays by Patricia Meyer Spacks: "In Praise of Gossip" and "Gossip: How It Works."

3. This view of the novel is also developed in Richard A. Lanham's *Tristram Shandy: The Games of Pleasure*.
4. For a provocative exploration of this notion, see J. Paul Hunter, "Response as Reformation: *Tristram Shandy* and the Art of Interruption."
5. "A feature of Sterne's peculiar genius is the relationship he establishes with his readers. This is far closer to friendship, in the normal sense of that term, than any other novelist ever comes" (Dyson 36).
6. Gossip has always been thought of as detraction, originating in malice. In *The Canterbury Tales*, Chaucer's "The Parson's Tale" considers that back-biting originates in envy; Chaucer identifies five forms it commonly takes in everyday conversation (lines 490–98). Modern social science, in very different language, takes the same position: "gossip is a surreptitious aggression," according to Samuel Heilman, a contemporary sociologist (qtd. in Spacks, "Gossip" 562).
7. Spacks makes this point: "If the story has nothing to do with anyone we know, better, if it has nothing to do with anyone real—under such circumstances, we can enjoy it with no culpability" ("In Praise" 38).

 "Female Difficulties"

Charlotte Lennox's The Female Quixote
and Frances Burney's Camilla

"TOWARDS THE END OF THE EIGHTEENTH CENTURY," Virginia Woolf says in *A Room of One's Own*, "a change came about which, if I were rewriting history, I should describe more fully and think of greater importance than the Crusades or the Wars of the Roses. The middleclass woman began to write" (62–63). Women had, in fact, been writing novels since the time of Defoe and even earlier, but, just as the novel form reached a brilliant first maturity with the publication of *Clarissa* in 1747–1748 and *Tom Jones* in 1749, so women novelists came into their own after 1750. In fact, by 1771 Smollett's travellers in *The Expedition of Humphry Clinker* discover that "that branch of business is now engrossed by female authors," forcing some male hack-writers to publish novels under female pseudonyms or to try other genres (128). Furthermore, novelists of the age assumed a largely female readership. No wonder, then, that many later-eighteenth-century novels by women dramatize the heroine's confrontation with "female difficulties"—a phrase that Frances Burney, the most respected woman novelist of the period, used as the subtitle of her last novel, *The Wanderer* (1814). In this essay, I will argue that two of the best novels by women of this period, novels very different from each other in many obvious ways, both have as their central theme the difficulties women face in a male-dominated society.[1]

Midway through Burney's third novel, *Camilla* (1796), the worldly but perceptive Mrs. Arlbery refers to the novel's heroine as "my fair female Quixote" (417). This allusion points to some striking similarities between Charlotte Lennox's novel *The Female Quixote* (1752) and *Camilla*. Both present stories of love and courtship in which the hero and heroine love each other from the outset, but are separated by psychological barriers; both novels have the conventional comic outcome of a marriage in which the wayward heroine has been restored to a mentor-hero and to social and psychological stability. Most striking of all, however, is the ambivalence of each novelist about her plot: while in each case the heroine deeply loves the hero and finds her happiness dependent upon their mutual love, she at the same time feels she can only be happy if she enjoys much more power and independence than the social framework (embodied in and endorsed by the hero) allows her. Lennox's Arabella creates, by transposing romance for reality, an alternate society in which she has life-and-death power over all men; Camilla is desperately anxious to win the approval of her sober guardian-figure, Edgar Mandlebert, but that very subjection to his judgement also puts her into a continual state of half-conscious rebellion against the propriety and submission that he expects of her.

As a result of this ambivalence on the author's part, each novel is muted and tragicomic in vision and tone. Both novels bear much the same relation to Burney's earlier *Evelina* (1778) or Austen's *Pride and Prejudice* and *Emma* as Shakespeare's problem-plays do to his comedies: the plot outcomes do not resolve the issues that have been raised. For one thing, neither Arabella nor Camilla is cured, as Austen's heroines are, *by* their love. Mr. Glanville's love for Arabella is powerless before her Quixoticism, Arabella ingeniously refuses to choose between her love and her delusions, and when she is finally persuaded that her fantasy-world is false and must be renounced, she is left a nonentity. Similarly, a rescue operation in the final page of *Camilla* restores the heroine to complete submission and self-suppression.

These ideas seem to me starkly evident in Charlotte Lennox's *The Female Quixote, or The Adventures of Arabella*, which is far shorter, lighter, and simpler than Burney's *Camilla*. *The Female Quixote* is a witty and very funny novel. It is usually seen as that and no more. Margaret Dalziel, the novel's editor in the Oxford English Novels series, believes that "Mrs. Lennox's purpose, unlike that of Cervantes, is wholly comic" and that, as a result of the heroine's disillusionment and self-knowledge, that comic purpose is achieved "without too much emphasis on the suffering inevitable to such growth" (xiv).[2] On the one hand, if we take "purpose" to refer to conscious intent, Dalziel is arguably correct: the omniscient narrator's occasional hints of an attitude and the Fieldingesque chapter titles suggest that Arabella is simply to be a figure of fun, a misguided miss. After all, in 1752 English readers were only beginning to see the ambivalence within *Don Quixote* itself (see Tave, *Amiable* 151–63). On the other hand, an author's conscious intent may not adequately account for his or her achieved "purpose." Charlotte Lennox's novel is, I would argue, another instance of a pattern described by Patricia Meyer Spacks in her chapter on minor women writers of the period in *Imagining a Self: Autobiography and Novel in Eighteenth-Century England*: "female novelists, upholding the established system, find images and action to express profound ambivalence" (63). In short, Lennox makes us sympathize with her heroine and her romantic delusions, rather than simply presenting them as laughable.

Arabella is sympathetic because, unlike Emma Woodhouse, for instance, her delusions are less wilful than inevitable. Her father, the Marquis of _____, has fallen from power at court and brings up his only child, Arabella, in complete seclusion in a remote part of the kingdom. Arabella's mother died giving birth to her; as a result she, like Scott's Edward Waverley half a century later, has found her education—and indeed her whole mental life—in the romances that she finds in her father's library. In this case, however, the romances are distinctly female: a "great Store of Romances" translated from the French, which "The deceased Marchioness had purchased...to soften a Solitude which she found very disagreeable" (Lennox 7). From the start, Arabella's world of romance is a female refuge from, and substitute for, a reality in which women are impoverished and powerless.

In fact, Arabella's romance-world is an exact inversion of the social world around her. In the fantasy world, Arabella has an endless series of adventures, as the novel's subtitle suggests: attempted abductions, narrow escapes from ravishers, duels fought in her honour. In reality, Arabella has virtually no freedom to act for herself: ironically, even in her fantasy-world her role is entirely passive. Even the crucial—and virtually the only—choice of her life is imposed on her by her father, who has arranged for her to marry her cousin, Mr. Glanville, a man whom she has not seen since she was eight years old; he invites Mr. Glanville down to his estate, telling him, "I will allow you...but a few Weeks to court her" (31). In fantasy, Arabella expects to roam the known world, saying, for instance, at one point, "And may I not be carried into *Macedonia* by a Similitude of Destiny with that of a great many beautiful Princesses...?" (261). In reality, Arabella is brought up in virtually complete isolation: her father *sometimes* allows her to attend the church service at the nearby village (8); "the only Diversion she was allowed, or ever experienced" (19) is a ride out into the countryside attended by servants. In fantasy, Arabella has extraordinary power as the result of her regal beauty: at her command, humble lovers recover on their deathbed, and insolent lovers are banished from the kingdom. In reality, Arabella has no power to initiate action; as a woman, her role is to re-act to men's acts—in other words to suffer action. The acts that Arabella performs spontaneously, under the influence of her delusions, all have to be apologized for and undone. The novel begins with her written banishment from her house of Mr. Glanville as "*the most presumptuous Man in the World*" for the "Affront" of confessing his love for her before she has given him permission to love her (33); however, her father hears of it and makes her write and ask him back again (40). In fantasy, Arabella is caught up in the fate of kingdoms, the destinies of heroes; in reality, all the women Arabella meets are preoccupied, as is her cousin and foil, Miss Glanville, with clothes, cards, gossip, and the like. When she visits Bath, she exclaims, "What room, I pray you, does a Lady give for high and noble Adventures, who consumes her Days in Dressing, Dancing, listening to Songs, and ranging the Walks with People as thoughtless as herself?" (279).

Furthermore, in fantasy, Arabella is sexually alive and alluring, someone who knows all about erotic impulses, since she is perpetually forced to fight off the ravishers drawn to her; in reality, she is expected to be chaste, innocent, and ignorant. When asked for her adventures, Miss Glanville explains to Arabella that no decent young lady has any adventures to confess (88); the Countess of _____, the novel's model woman, tells Arabella, "The Word Adventures carries in it so free and licentious a Sound in the Apprehensions of People at this Period of Time, that it can hardly with Propriety be apply'd to those few and natural Incidents which compose the History of a Woman of Honour" (327); and the one young lady whose adventures Arabella does manage to hear recounted is Miss Groves, who proves to be the cast-off mistress of a young nobleman and mother of two bastards. In fantasy, Arabella seeks fame for her exploits; as she explains, "the good Reputation of a Lady...depends intirely upon... the Noise and Bustle she makes in the World" (128). In reality, far from occupying centre-stage, the good woman is one of whom nothing can be said. The Countess explains to Arabella:

> And when I tell you,...that I was born and christen'd, had a useful and proper Education, receiv'd the Addresses of my Lord ____, through the Recommendation of my Parents, and marry'd him with their Consents and my own Inclination, and that since we have liv'd in great Harmony together, I have told you all the material Passages of my Life, which upon Enquiry you will find differ very little from those of other Women of the same Rank, who have a moderate Share of Sense, Prudence and Virtue. (327)

When Arabella is forced to admit at the novel's end that she has confused two worlds, the fantasy world and the real one, she adds, "I am afraid...that the Difference is not in Favour of the present World" (380).

All of this explains the deadlock in the novel's central relationship, that between Arabella and her faithful suitor, Mr. Glanville. Glanville's devotion, sympathy, and handsome charm clearly win Arabella's heart very quickly; the narrator explains in the final chapter of book 1 (of the novel's nine books) that Arabella is so deeply hurt by his inability to read his way through the romances she has given him because "she was beginning to imagine, by the Alteration in his Behaviour, that he would prove such a Lover as she wished; for Mr. *Glanville*'s Person and Qualifications had attracted her particular Notice: And, to speak in the Language of Romance, she did not hate him" (53). When he suddenly becomes very ill, she "discovered a Grief for Mr. *Glanville*'s Illness, little different from that she had felt for her Father's" (134). Arabella only acknowledges her own love for Glanville, however, in the novel's final scenes. She encounters a woman in Richmond Park who claims to be an exiled princess (but is actually an actress hired for the occasion by Glanville's rival, Sir George Bellmour); the "princess" tells how she was seduced and abandoned by a false lover and then points to Glanville as the villain (349). Exactly like Emma Woodhouse listening to Harriet Smith,

> Our charming Heroine, ignorant till now of the true State of her Heart, was surpriz'd to find it assaulted at once by all the Passions which attend disappointed Love. Grief, Rage, Jealousy, and Despair made so cruel a War in her gentle Bosom, that unable either to express or to conceal the strong Emotions with which she was agitated, she gave Way to a violent Burst of Tears. (349)

Why can Arabella not admit her love for most of the novel? It seems clear that, again just like Emma Woodhouse, to admit her own love would mean accepting Mr. Glanville's hand in marriage, and that would put an end to her independence and power. Early in the novel Arabella decides that Glanville is "a Lover, whose Aim was to take away her Liberty, either by obliging her to marry him, or by making her a Prisoner" (35), and in the final sentences of book 3 of the novel, having visited Glanville's sickbed and given him explicit permission to love her, she contemplates their joint future: "when…his Constancy [is] put to a few Years more Trial; when he has killed all his Rivals, and rescued her from a thousand Dangers; she at last condescends to reward him with her Hand; and all her Adventures are at an End for the Future" (138). For now, however, adventures suffice.

For his part, Glanville loves Arabella from the start, and not so much despite her follies as because of the vitality and wit they allow her to express. Glanville loves Arabella as she is, but can only marry her if she changes. Early in the novel, the narrator says,

"As he feared it was impossible to help loving her, his Happiness depended upon curing her of her romantic Notions; and, though he knew not how to effect such a Change in her as was necessary to complete it, yet he would not despair, but comforted himself with Hopes of what he had not Courage to attempt" (117). Ironically, in fact, Glanville has no power to change Arabella. He is cast as a mentor-lover: he makes an admirable lover, but is completely ineffectual as a mentor. Even after Arabella realizes her love for Glanville in the novel's final book, she commits one of her most quixotic acts: she flees from approaching horsemen that she suspects to be ravishers and "plung[es] into the *Thames*, intending to swim over it, as *Clelia* did the *Tyber*" (363). Glanville, however, changes dramatically as a result of Arabella's influence: at the end of book 2 he saves her from an unknown gentleman who has said that Arabella is "fit for a Mad-house" (157); in the final scenes, when she accuses him of being false, he falls to his knees before her and presses her hand to his lips; in the novel's climax, he is infuriated with what he takes to be his rival's attempted seduction of Arabella and almost kills him in a sword fight. Glanville's courtship has hardly been the quiet few weeks of winning Arabella over that her father and her suitor expected.

If Glanville's love cannot of itself cure Arabella, what can? Mr. Glanville and the other characters continually discuss this problem, but no one can find an answer. The novel's narrator introduces the Countess of _____ in such a way as to suggest that she holds the solution: a whole chapter entitled "In which is introduc'd a very singular Character" (322) is devoted to describing her when she appears late in the novel. Although the Countess is entirely respectable and rational, she sympathizes greatly with Arabella because "she herself had when very young, been deep read in Romances; and but for an early Acquaintance with the World, and being directed to other Studies, was likely to have been as much a Heroine as Lady *Bella*" (323). The Countess befriends Arabella and wins her trust; she then begins tactfully undermining Arabella's total faith in romances. Glanville is delighted; he believes, and the novel's readers must, too, that the Countess will be Arabella's miracle-worker. However, the Countess is abruptly called away to care for her dying mother and disappears from the novel nine pages after she entered it. Charlotte Lennox obviously changed her mind in the course of writing the novel; some recently discovered letters between Lennox and Samuel Richardson, written while Lennox was writing the final section of the novel, show that she originally intended the novel to have three volumes, and that during the third volume Arabella would be cured when the Countess led her to read Richardson's *Clarissa*—presumably to discover that fiction can reveal the truth about everyday experience and not simply be an alternative to it (Isles 418–26). Dissuaded from this plan by Richardson himself, Lennox cut her novel back to two volumes. Arabella is abruptly cured, but not by her lover, nor by the maternal Countess. Instead, a *deus ex machina* appears in the novel's final pages: a "good Divine" identified only as "the Doctor," a man who thinks and sounds so much like Samuel Johnson that many readers, including the novel's editor Margaret Dalziel (414–15), believe that Johnson, Lennox's friend and literary mentor, actually wrote the conversion scene, a long chapter entitled "Being, in the Author's Opinion, the best Chapter in this History" (Lennox 368). In any case, as Arabella is recovering from pneumonia caused by her attempted swim of the Thames, the Doctor is called in to counsel her, and after Glanville has explained to him "the Disorders Romances had occasion'd in her Imagination" (367), he takes on and performs the Johnsonian task of reasoning the lunatic out of her lunacy. In fifteen pages of careful abstract reasoning that might well be an episode from *Rasselas*, the Doctor leads Arabella, who now sounds more like the Princess Nekayah than the lively, infatuated sixteen-year-old we have come to know, to see that her absorption in romance is immoral: it has allowed her to become presumptuous and arrogant; it has destroyed her humility and compassion (380–81). Arabella abjures romance, and the novel ends in the next chapter, a perfunctory finale less than two pages long, during which the Doctor introduces the new Arabella to Mr. Glanville; she expresses her penitence; she agrees to marry him; the two marry and live in harmony. All this is a far cry from Emma Woodhouse changing in order to regain Mr. Knightley's regard. Arabella has attained rational dignity through her conversion, but at the cost of denying and even extirpating her emotional and imaginative self. The end of the novel is not really all that unlike the end of *Don Quixote*: when the Don is forced to give up his illusions, he dies; when the "adventures of Arabella" are at an end, Arabella as a distinct character also dies.

Camilla is obviously a very different kind of novel from *The Female Quixote*. It is more than twice as long, being originally published in five volumes rather than two. It was written more than forty years later, at a time when England's political, social, and literary orders were under attack. Its heroine, unlike Arabella, Edward Waverley, Emma Woodhouse, and a host of novel protagonists, is not a virtual or de facto orphan; she has been given the most thorough and careful upbringing by her devout and devoted parents. Though Camilla is, like Arabella, young and innocent (she is seventeen, and the book is subtitled *A Picture of Youth*), she is hardly in open rebellion against social conventions—in fact, her great preoccupation is not to offend against decorum. Camilla is perceptive and self-aware, not grossly deluded; for most of the novel she is far too anxious to share Arabella's insouciance. Her story is much more sombre than Arabella's: in the novel's climactic scenes she believes herself condemned by God, society, her former fiancé, and her own parents, and she wishes only for her own death. Nevertheless, there are some striking similarities between the two novels. Mrs. Arlbery is quite right to describe Camilla as a female Quixote, since, as Mrs. Arlbery points out again and again, Camilla regularly replaces what is actually before her with a beautiful and idealized imaginative projection of her own. "The reigning and radical defect of her character," the narrator comments early in the novel, is "an imagination that submitted to no control" (Burney, *Camilla* 84). The irony is that Camilla's quixoticism consists of her conformity to decorum, not her rebellion against it: she is determined to be completely proper, to act in complete accord with the conventional code for young ladies. Nevertheless, her story is like Arabella's: she runs up against "female difficulties," and by the novel's end she has won a Pyrrhic victory, a victory that feels like defeat.

The conflict at the heart of *Camilla* is essentially the same as that in *The Female Quixote*: the central pair, Camilla and Edgar Mandlebert, are in love with each other from the novel's start; the match is expected and welcomed by all about them, but the lovers are separated by psychological barriers. The barriers here are much more perverse and deeply rooted than those in *The Female Quixote*. There, Glanville knows that he loves Arabella and offers her his love; she does not know that she loves and only offers him her love on the novel's final page. Here, each lover knows that he or she loves, but neither can express that love. The inhibitions exist on both sides; if Camilla were wooed by a Mr. Glanville, the 913-page novel (in the Oxford edition) would be over within the first 100 pages.

Both Edgar and Camilla are strenuously virtuous, and each is kept from a confession of love by allegiance to an extreme version of conventional propriety. Edgar adheres to a travesty of deliberation and prudence. He is an orphan, the only son of parents who have left him a wealthy estate. Camilla's father is his guardian, but the person who has educated and moulded him is his tutor, Dr. Marchmont, a neighbouring clergyman. Dr. Marchmont persuades Edgar that he must be deliberate, cautious, prudent, and rational in his choice of a wife; though he loves Camilla and believes she loves him, he must be certain that she loves him genuinely and for himself. She might, Dr. Marchmont points out, love him simply because of his situation in life; her apparent love might only be the result of flattered vanity at his evident feeling for her; her feelings for him might turn out to be only temporary; she might seem in Edgar's prejudiced eyes to be more than she really is. For many reasons, then, Dr. Marchmont says that Edgar must observe her impartially and judge deliberately: in his first scene in the novel, he tells Edgar, "you must study her, from this moment, with new eyes, new ears, and new thoughts.... you must view as if you had never seen her before.... you must become positively distrustful" (159–60). This counsel, which brings to mind both Iago and some of the more eerie characters of Hawthorne, at first repels Edgar: "I would sooner renounce every prospect of felicity, than act a part so ungenerous" (160). But the Doctor soon learns that, like Iago, he can control his victim by playing on his pathetic lack of self-confidence: "You cannot be happy if not exclusively loved; for you cannot excite, you cannot bestow happiness" (178), he tells Edgar in a devastating letter that sums up his arguments. In short, Edgar believes he must conceal his love and study Camilla for evidence of "independent, unsolicited, involuntary possession" of her heart (160); only then will his choice of her be justified.

Dr. Marchmont's caution is indeed ungenerous, but it is possible only because of an injustice built into the courtship code. Here, as in general, men are to act, and women are to react; but in this case the action required is a formal profession of love and offer of marriage, and before that point the man has freedom to approach, to examine, to befriend, and then deliberate, while all the while the woman under investigation is powerless. The man can woo forever, as long as he does not woo in words. An immense and cruel power thus lies with the man if he chooses to exercise it—whether intentionally, like Lovelace in *Clarissa*, or unintentionally, like Edgar. As the Doctor puts it in his letter to Edgar, "Remember, you can always advance; you can never, in honour, go back" (179). The author reveals three-quarters of the way through the novel that Dr. Marchmont's position has a psychological explanation: he hates women as a result of the humiliating betrayals he suffered during his two ill-advised marriages, which he describes in aggrieved terms to Edgar (642–45). Ironically, by the time Edgar hears this, he is so infected with Dr. Marchmont's poison that he believes the Doctor's hidden past proves, rather than disproves, all that Dr. Marchmont has told him. We can see, however, that, again like Iago, the Doctor must see the lovers defeated so that he can be vindicated.

Camilla is a victim of the same set of rules, but as they apply to women. The code governing Camilla is spelled out to her by *her* clergyman-advisor, her father, the Reverend Augustus Tyrold, in an eight-page letter that was so impressive to first readers of the novel that one reviewer in 1796 cited the whole of this letter in his review of the novel (Epstein 204); in 1809, the letter was reprinted as part of a conduct-book, together with John Gregory's *A Father's Legacy to His Daughters* (Doody, *Frances Burney* 414). Mr. Tyrold's letter, the counterpart of Dr. Marchmont's letter to Edgar, is prompted by his fear that Camilla will be unable to conceal her love for Edgar from him and explains why such concealment is necessary. It outlines in full and painful detail the situation of women. They are "doubly appendant" creatures, as children dependent upon parents and as adults upon a husband; because the eventual husband is unknown till adulthood, "the proper education of a female, either for use or for happiness, is still to seek, still a problem beyond human solution" (Burney, *Camilla* 357). He admits that nature, theory, and even common sense dictate that men and women fall in love freely, and not according to rule; if in theory men and women are thus equals in some abstract sense, "Meanwhile, it is enough for every modest and reasonable young woman to consider, that where there are two parties, choice can only belong to one of them: and then let her call upon all her feelings of delicacy, all her notions of propriety, to decide: Since Man must choose Woman, or Woman Man, which should come forward to make the choice? Which should retire to be chosen?" The question is rhetorical. If Camilla finds that she loves Edgar before he has professed love for her, "Struggle then against yourself as you would struggle against an enemy.... where allowed only a negative choice, it is your own best interest to combat against a positive wish" (358-59). She must not only try to overcome her love, but she must also conceal all signs of it: "Carefully, then, beyond all other care, shut up every avenue by which a secret which should die untold can further escape you" (360). The echoes of Dr. Marchmont become especially precise here: Mr. Tyrold tells his daughter that the woman who lets a man discover her "undisguised prepossession" is doomed to be cruelly deceived: "It is not that she has failed to awaken tenderness; but it has been tenderness without respect;...it has been a flattery to raise himself, not its exciter in his esteem" (360). Just as Dr. Marchmont had, Camilla's father points out that "the most rigid circumspection" is called for in her relationship with Edgar: "The person in question is not merely amiable: he is also rich" (361). The implication emerges that the code imposed upon Camilla by her clergyman-counsellor is just as perverse as the code imposed upon Edgar by Dr. Marchmont. Furthermore, both Camilla and Edgar internalize the demands their counsellors make upon them. Edgar makes Dr. Marchmont part of himself: eventually he takes Dr. Marchmont everywhere with him and rushes off to consult him after every conversation with Camilla. In the same way, Camilla takes her father's letter to heart: "with reverence she pressed [it] to her lips, [and] offered up the most solemn vows of a strict and entire observance of every injunction which the letter contained" (363).

Given protagonists with these motives, the action of the novel has a grim, farcical circularity: Edgar and Camilla relentlessly watch each other for signs of love—the very thing that each has vowed not to reveal. Far from being a comic mating-dance of the sort we find in *Evelina* (or, indeed, in Shakespeare or Congreve or Austen), events here seem closer to the world of Lewis Carroll or Franz Kafka or Joseph Heller. Jane Spencer notes that Burney's anxious heroine "rarely shows the vivacity that is supposed to be her charm and her danger" (163). The stage equivalent to *Evelina* is *Love for Love*; when the characters in Burney's first novel attend a performance of Congreve's comedy, their reactions make us realize that they are re-enacting what they watch (*Evelina* 78–82). The characters go to see a play together in *Camilla*—but they see an unintentional travesty of *Othello* put on by "actors…of the lowest strolling kind" (318). This performance, more in the vein of Monty Python than of David Garrick, comes to an abrupt end: Othello enters Desdemona's bed-chamber carrying a candle, and, "while Othello leant over the bed to say—'Vhen I've pluck'd the rose / I cannot give it wital growth again, / It needs must vither'— his black locks caught fire" (322). Rather than comic lovers, Edgar and Camilla find themselves enacting a ludicrous tragedy: he is a noble dupe, she utterly virtuous and trusting, but obtuse. The novel presents, in Margaret Doody's words, "*Othello as performed by extremely poor actors*" (*Frances Burney* 224). The novel's action consists mainly of misunderstandings between the two lovers: he formally volunteers to serve as her "monitor": "to offer you, from time to time, a hint, a little counsel, a few brief words of occasional advice" (Burney, *Camilla* 267–68). Edgar is, thus, not a mentor-lover, but a monitor-lover, which turns out to be a very different thing. Camilla, however, welcomes his assumption of this chivalric role. Edgar is four years older than Camilla, he is a man, and he is impeccably proper: his advice thus always proves to be correct.

The problem is that Camilla regularly finds herself disobeying his precepts—partly because, like Evelina, she is naive, easily flustered, and uncertain when non-conformity is justified, but even more because she senses that there is something degrading in Edgar's treatment of her. His shock when she acts against his precepts and his delight when she obeys are equally demeaning. When he tells her, quite justifiably as it turns out, that it would be unwise to visit Southampton for some weeks in the company of the romantic quasi-widow Mrs. Berlinton, she decides to go: "his dislike to that acquaintance rather urged than impeded her plan, for her wounded spirit panted to prove its independence and dignity" (582). Acting at the suggestion of Mrs. Arlbery (and of her own heart), she flirts with other men, assuming that a little jealousy will make Edgar appreciate her. Camilla's rebellion is not really deliberate, all the same; in her eyes, "a cruel perversity of events seemed to cast her every action into an apparent defiance of his wishes" (793). Edgar finally does propose to Camilla late in the novel and is accepted—but the vicious circle of his reserve and suspicion, accompanied by her reserve and unconscious rebellion, continues, and soon afterwards Camilla calls off the wretched engagement, telling Edgar, "'I am lessened in your esteem'…; struck and afflicted by the truth she had pronounced, he could not controvert it" (640–41).

Edgar and Camilla do come together in the end, but only after Edgar has renounced her and gone off on a tour of Europe (accompanied as far as the Isle of Wight by Dr. Marchmont) and after Camilla has almost died. The scene in which they are reunited has some suggestive symbolism. Camilla has a temporary room at a squalid roadside inn identified only as "the halfway house"; believing that she has been abandoned by Edgar and her family, she lies in a comatose fever. Edgar has returned to England, having met Camilla's scapegrace brother on the continent and heard that she is much less to blame than he had thought, and stops at the inn.

There he agrees to impersonate a clergyman and read the prayers for the dying from the *Book of Common Prayer* to the anonymous lady who, lying in a delirium, has begged to hear them. The suggestion that accepting Edgar means a kind of death is reinforced by the fact that, before Edgar appears, Camilla, believing herself to be on her deathbed, writes a final note: "O Edgar! in this last farewell be all displeasure forgotten!—from the first to the final moment of my short life, dear and sole possessor of my heart!" She writes his name on the cover and adds the direction, "*Not to be delivered till I am dead*" (870). The landlady, however, gives the note to Edgar as soon as she discovers that Edgar and Camilla know each other, and it is only by this note that "every doubt was wholly, and even miraculously removed, by his learning thus the true feelings of her heart" (898). The equivalent sentence in Austen's *Pride and Prejudice* is a measure of how far from the comic vision we are in *Camilla*: there, Darcy tells Elizabeth, "Lady Catherine's unjustifiable endeavours to separate us, were the means of removing all my doubts" (381).

In short, Camilla's story has dramatized the injustices that she has by good fortune survived (McMaster, "Silent" 236). Still, the end of the novel is formally comic: Camilla marries Edgar, and all conflicts are over. Edgar renounces his distrust, Camilla "voluntarily promised...to repose the future choice of her connections, where she could never be happy without their approvance" (Burney, *Camilla* 903), all around them give their blessing, and Dr. Marchmont acknowledges the injustice, the narrowness, and the arrogance of "the hypothesis which he had formed from individual experience" (913). But the comic ending is hardly felt to be a genuinely happy one. One of the first readers of this novel was Jane Austen, then twenty years old; she was one of the 600 prepublication subscribers to *Camilla* and championed it in her letters and in the pages of *Northanger Abbey*. Still, at the end of the last volume of her own copy of the novel, Austen wrote the following sentence: "Since this work went to the press a circumstance of some assistance to the happiness of Camilla has taken place, namely that Dr. Marchmont has at last died" (Doody, *Frances Burney* 272).

We might note, by way of conclusion, that both female novelists were themselves dependent upon the approval of male sponsors. Samuel Richardson, as we have seen, told Charlotte Lennox how to end her novel, and Lennox's allegiances are evident in her text: Mr. Glanville heatedly defends Young, Richardson, and Johnson to Sir George Bellmour, and says that the language and ethics of the *Rambler* "[reach] to Perfection" (253). The Johnsonian Doctor who converts Arabella tells her:

> Truth is not always injured by Fiction. An admirable Writer of our own Time [identified in an author's footnote as "Richardson"], has found the Way to convey the most solid Instructions, the noblest Sentiments, and the most exalted Piety, in the pleasing Dress of a Novel ["*Clarissa*," a footnote says], and, to use the Words of the greatest Genius in the present Age ["The Author of the Rambler," a footnote says], "Has taught the Passions to move at the Command of Virtue." (377)

Henry Fielding devoted an issue of his *Covent-Garden Journal* to a review of *The Female Quixote*, in which he argues that in some respects it surpasses *Don Quixote* itself (281–82). Similarly, once Frances Burney was known to be the author of *Evelina*, she became the protégée of the greatest literary figures of the age—not only Johnson himself, but Edmund Burke, Richard Brinsley Sheridan, Sir Joshua Reynolds, and others. The greatest influence upon her life, without any doubt, was her father, Dr. Charles Burney, who hovered over *Camilla* during its composition, choosing the heroine's name, for instance, and arranging for it to be favourably reviewed (Doody, *Frances Burney* 207–16). In short, both women had men as their literary mentors and monitors. It is hardly surprising, then, that both novelists are inconclusive and divided on the question of "female difficulties": ambivalent proto-feminists rather than outright feminists as thinkers, and shrewdly realistic rather than programmatic as artists. As Deborah Ross says of Charlotte Lennox, "Johnson wanted novels to present a model moral universe. The women novelists of his time persisted in presenting the real universe, showing its unfairness without advocating rebellion" (470).

NOTES

1. In speaking of "Frances" Burney, I follow Margaret Anne Doody, being convinced by her argument that "'Fanny' is a patronizing diminutive. It makes the author sound the harmless, childish, priggish girl-woman that many critics want her to be—as if the heroine of *Mansfield Park* had set up as novelist" (*Frances Burney* 6). Doody's nomenclature has been followed by several subsequent writers on the novelist, including Julia Epstein and Juliet McMaster. The new terminology has at least the advantage of drawing the reader's attention to the issue under debate.
2. It should be noted that the Dalziel edition of 1970 was republished in 1989 by Oxford University Press in the Oxford World's Classics series, with a new introduction by Margaret Doody and a revised bibliography.

 # *Waverley* and the *Aeneid*
Scott's Art of Allusion

LATE IN SCOTT'S *Waverley*, the Baron of Bradwardine, in flight for his life after the failure of the Jacobite rebellion of 1745, pauses to sum up his situation before climbing back into the cave that is his hiding place:

> "I did what I thought my duty," said the good old man, "and doubtless they are doing what they think theirs. It grieves me sometimes to look upon these blackened walls of the house of my ancestors; but doubtless officers cannot always keep the soldiers' hand from depredation and spuilzie;...To be sure we may say with Virgilius Maro, *Fuimus Troes*—and there's the end of an auld sang. But houses and families and men have a' stood lang enough when they have stood till they fall wi' honour; and now I hae gotten a house that is not unlike a *domus ultima*." (303; ch. 65)[1]

The Baron has been a largely comical figure up to this point in the novel: more pedantic than heroic, more tedious than eloquent. His unexpected dignity here has impressed readers of the novel; Francis Jeffrey described the speech as "a happy mixture of the ludicrous and interesting" when he reviewed the novel in 1814 (238), and several of Scott's best modern critics offer analytical comments. Donald Davie suggests that the tag from Virgil associates the Scottish culture destroyed in 1745 with Augustan Rome (33); D. D. Devlin notes that the Baron's colloquial paraphrase of Virgil, "there's the end of an auld sang," epitomizes the action of the whole novel (69). The most helpful insight, however, seems to me that of A. O. J. Cockshut, who considers the context in Virgil central to the Baron's speech—and, by implication, to Scott's novel as a whole:

> This is the moment when the Baron's Latin studies are suddenly made to tell, in a way we could not have guessed when we were first introduced to them. Instead of appearing merely bookish, he now has a right to his quotation. Like the Trojans in the midst of the burning of their city he has devoted all his strength to try to save a civilization which is now ending. Perhaps Scott, who, after all, was not Jacobite himself, had it in mind here that as the Trojans would become Romans, so the Jacobites would become a true part of Britain. But if he did, he was no doubt right not to make the point explicit, because at the moment of the failure of all one's hopes, all distant, slow consolations must seem impossible or irrelevant. (116)

In this essay, I would like to take up Cockshut's point and examine more closely the connection between Virgil's military epic and Scott's military novel. I will do so by looking first at Scott's allusions to the *Aeneid* in *Waverley*, and then by suggesting how these allusions, if given their full force, emphasize the novel's themes and intensify its mood. The result, we will find, is that Virgil allows us one more means of understanding just how epic is Scott's view of historical process.

Before entering into detailed analysis, however, I would like to point out that Scott's use of Virgil illustrates a general characteristic of his art: he uses allusions subtly and powerfully. As with the *Fuimus Troes* tag, the full significance of his allusions is often implicit. *Waverley*, in fact, contains many more allusions to Shakespeare's plays than to the *Aeneid*; the novel's epigraph, for instance—"Under which King, Bezonian? speak, or die!"—comes from *Henry IV, Part II*. Yet the allusions to Shakespeare, even the extended discussion by the characters of *Romeo and Juliet* in chapter 54, consist mainly of witty, indeed often facetious, applications of a familiar text to unexpected circumstances. We can find similarly playful uses of the *Aeneid* scattered throughout Scott's *Journal*. For instance, one favourite method there of describing his rheumatism is to consider himself nailed to his chair, like Theseus in book 6 of the *Aeneid*. However, his allusions to the *Aeneid* in *Waverley* are almost all charged with meaning, and they form a consistent pattern. Not that they are the only significant literary allusions: Scott uses images from Spenser and other poets of romance to characterize Waverley's romantic cast of mind; similarly, there are interesting connections between Scott's novel and the *Henry IV* plays—both present rebels waging a civil war in the name of an obsolete code of feudal honour. Whatever their source, then, and whether meant seriously or as cultivated play, Scott's allusions give his novels range and complexity. His contemporary, Jane Austen, boasted of being "the most unlearned, & uninformed Female who ever dared to be an Authoress" (*Jane Austen's Letters* 306).[2] We need not take her words literally to see that Austen and Scott represent opposite poles in their use of learned allusion, just as Defoe and Fielding did before them, and as Dickens and Thackeray, or Emily Brontë and George Eliot, or D. H. Lawrence and James Joyce, did after them. In fact, as Alexander Welsh has remarked, one cause for the decline in Scott's reputation in our century is that the power of allusion in his novels has been lost as knowledge has become more specialized (362).

We have some hope of reward, then, if we examine the allusions to the *Aeneid* in *Waverley*. The epic does not appear in the novel until the Baron himself does. The action of *Waverley* begins when young Edward Waverley visits the Baron's estate in Perthshire, but before this occurs there are some fifty pages of leisurely preparation. The first six chapters provide a general sketch of the upbringing of Waverley: virtually abandoned by his turncoat father, a Whig placeman in London, Edward is raised by his uncle, Sir Everard Waverley, the present Baronet, on the ancestral estate, Waverley-Honour, in rural England. Since Sir Everard is unmarried, Edward will be his heir. Sir Everard, a Tory and sentimental Jacobite, and his spinster sister immerse the young Waverley in legends of family heroism and allow him unsupervised use of the family library. There, Edward naturally prefers tales of chivalry to study of the classics: "'I can read and understand a Latin author,' said young Edward, with the self-confidence and rash reasoning of fifteen, 'and Scaliger or Bentley could not do much more'" (12; ch. 3). Waverley's education really begins when his family obtains a commission for him as a cavalry captain in the Hanoverian army. In chapter 7, he joins his regiment in Scotland; in chapter 8, he visits the manor-house of the Baron of Bradwardine, a Jacobite friend of his uncle. From this point on, Scott shows Waverley being lured, like Kurtz going up the Congo River, further and further into the primitive and irrational realm of Jacobitism—first as a tourist, then as an unwitting and unwilling partisan, and finally as a sworn officer in the Pretender's army.

The Baron, who is to provide the final resting-place as well as the first stop on Waverley's journey, enters the novel with the following words: "Upon the honour of a gentleman...but it makes me young again to see you here, Mr Waverley! A worthy scion of the old stock of Waverley-Honour—*spes altera*, as Maro hath it" (42; ch. 10). The tag alludes to the passage in book 12 of the *Aeneid* in which Ascanius, the son of Aeneas, marches into battle next to his father: "et iuxta Ascanius, magnae spes altera Romae" ("and beside him Ascanius, second hope of mighty Rome"; Virgil 12: line 168). The Baron's allusion suggests much more than he intends. It identifies Waverley with future triumph by succession, since Ascanius is to establish the Latin dynasty that will eventually lead to mighty Rome: Virgil frequently reminds us that Aeneas himself is fated to die soon after the devastating war with Turnus. The father-and-son motif is essential to the *Aeneid*, which is a poem about succession: Aeneas flees Troy carrying his father on his shoulders and leading his son by the hand (his wife gets lost in the shuffle). Similarly, in *Waverley*, the hero's final marriage with Rose Bradwardine is presented as his choice of a new father, the Baron, and, at the same time, a means of ensuring that the Baron's line will inherit his estate. Waverley, in fact, sells his own father's estate, after that luckless opportunist dies unmourned, in order to buy back the Baron's patrimony. The Baron's one moment of great emotion in the novel occurs when Waverley asks permission to marry his daughter; the Baron "gave way to the feelings of nature, threw his arms around Waverley's neck, and sobbed out,—'My son, my son! if I had been to search the world, I would have made my choice here'" (316; ch. 67). Just as the dispossessed Aeneas is to triumph through Ascanius, then, the dispossessed Baron will prevail through his adopted son, Waverley.

This allusion also identifies the Baron, for the first and not the last time, with the Virgilian perspective, with the sense of fate, stoical dignity, and tragic sacrifice that pervades Virgil's epic of history. Thus the Baron, in the subsequent chapter, describes the origin of his family's crest during the Crusades by means of a punning citation of lines describing the night-battle of Greeks and Trojans in book 2 of the *Aeneid* (see Scott 45; ch. 11; and Virgil 2: 389–90; the pun connects "a gigantic Dane" with Virgil's "Danaum"). The quotation, if fanciful, shows the Baron deriving his feudal heritage from the primitive conflict that Aeneas must leave behind him.

Throughout the novel, Scott uses the Baron to give a Virgilian resonance to events. For instance, the chapter presenting the ball on the night before the battle of Prestonpans ends with the Chevalier's gallant farewell to his followers: "Good night, and joy be with you!—Good night, fair ladies, who have so highly honoured a proscribed and banished Prince.—Good night, my brave friends; may the happiness we have this evening experienced be an omen of our return to these our paternal halls, speedily and in triumph, and of many and many future meetings of mirth and pleasure in the palace of Holy-Rood!" (210; ch. 43). The chapter then closes with Scott's remark, "When the Baron of Bradwardine afterwards mentioned this adieu of the Chevalier, he never failed to repeat, in a melancholy tone, 'Audiit, et voti Phœbus succedere partem / Mente dedit; partem volucres dispersit in auras'" ("Phoebus heard, and in his heart vouchsafed that half the prayer should prosper; half he scattered to the flying breezes"; Scott 211; ch. 43; Virgil 11: 794–95). Here, again, the Baron suffuses historical fact with Virgilian inevitability.

Waverley, having gone from rural England to rural Scotland, next advances from the Baron's Lowland estate into the wild Highlands. His visit is prompted by a sudden act of theft: one Donald Bean Lean and his men have driven off the Baron's milk cows. Donald Bean Lean, however, is merely the agent in this of Fergus Mac-Ivor, the neighbouring Highland chief, who has ordered the theft to force the Baron to resume paying him protection-money. Evan Dhu Maccombich, Fergus's lieutenant and emissary to the Baron, invites Waverley to return with him to the Highlands; Waverley is fascinated by the chance to see primitive life at first hand, and visits Donald Bean Lean in his cave, and then moves on to Glennaquoich, the feudal stronghold of the Mac-Ivor clan.

A series of allusions connects Donald Bean Lean with Cacus, the fire-breathing monster in book 8 of the *Aeneid*. In Virgil, Aeneas visits Evander, king of the Arcadians, and finds the Arcadians celebrating a sacred triumph: Evander explains how Cacus, the giant son of the fire god Vulcan and a human mother, slaughtered and ate men and animals in his underground cave, and how Hercules strangled Cacus:

> hic Cacum in tenebris incendia vana vomentem
> corripit in nodum complexus, et angit inhaerens
> elisos oculos et siccum sanguine guttur. (Virgil 8: 259–61)

> Here, as Cacus in the darkness vomits forth unavailing fires, he seizes him in a knot-like embrace and, close entwined, throttles him till the eyes burst forth and the throat is drained of blood.

The Baron quotes this last line in calling down upon the Highland robbers "the fate of their predecessor Cacus" (Scott 70; ch. 15); in the next chapter, Scott says that Waverley "[felt] his curiosity considerably excited by the idea of visiting the den of a Highland Cacus" (75), and we subsequently see the robber in his own cave, surrounded by the hanging corpses of animals he has stolen and butchered. In Virgil, Hercules's defeat of Cacus is an inset emblem of the eventual triumph of Aeneas; Cacus represents those fiery primitive forces, embodied in Turnus in the plot, which must be extirpated if the social and moral order is to prevail. The connection with Scott's Highlanders is clear: not only is Donald himself hanged after the rebellion ends, but Fergus, the Turnus to Waverley's Aeneas, is hanged, drawn, and quartered. We can conclude that Scott is being ironic, and not merely facetious, when he says that the founder of the Mac-Ivor dynasty behaved "like a second Æneas" when he and his followers moved into the Perthshire Highlands in search of plunder some three centuries earlier (91; ch. 19).

Once Waverley enters the Highlands and is slowly drawn into the Jacobite cause, the Baron disappears from view and does not enter the novel again until after Waverley has sworn allegiance to the Pretender, Charles Edward. During this central section of the novel, specific allusions to the *Aeneid* are replaced by a consistent set of words and images alluding, implicitly, to Virgil's *furor*. *Furor*, or frenzy, is the great enemy of Aeneas's rational dedication to the public good; it is, socially, the primitive code of honour, based upon courage in physical combat; psychologically, it is being ruled by raging emotion. The two main opponents of Aeneas's mission destroy themselves by giving themselves over to *furor*—Dido kills herself on her own funeral pyre, and Turnus's assertion of his heroic pride against all the signs of inevitable defeat is a disguised version of the same impulse and leads to the same outcome. Cacus is, in fact, an emblem of *furor*. Virgil asserts the *furor* theme in the opening sequence of the epic: Neptune's silencing of Juno's angry storm is likened to a great leader quieting a mob whose *furor* has led it to take up arms (1: 148–53), and this is followed by Jupiter's prophecy to Venus, Aeneas's mother, that from her son will spring the Romans who will rule all the known world (a prophecy that Augustus had fulfilled in Virgil's time by closing the temple of Janus for the first time in two centuries):

> aspera tum positis mitescent saecula bellis;
> cana Fides et Vesta, Remo cum fratre Quirinus
> iura dabunt; dirae ferro et compagibus artis
> claudentur Belli portae; Furor impius intus
> saeva sedens super arma et centum vinctus aënis
> post tergum nodis fremet horridus ore cruento. (1: 291–96)

Then shall wars cease, and the rough ages soften; hoary Faith and Vesta, Quirinus [i.e., Romulus] with his brother Remus, shall give laws. The gates of war, grim with iron and close-fitting bars, shall be closed; within, impious Rage, sitting on savage arms, his hands fast bound behind with a hundred brazen knots, shall roar in the ghastliness of blood-stained lips.

In *Waverley*, the Highlanders are shown again and again to be driven by *furor*, just as Waverley is increasingly forced to see that his true allegiance is to reason and its social codification, law. In the first scene at Glennaquoich, the Highland banquet, the ardour of MacMurrough, Fergus's bard, communicates itself to his audience: "Their wild and sun-burned countenances assumed a fiercer and more animated expression; all bent forwards towards the reciter, many sprung up and waved their arms in ecstacy, and some laid their hands on their swords" (Scott 98; ch. 20). Fergus's sister Flora translates the bard's song for Waverley; the last stanza contains the couplet, "Be the brand of each chieftain like Fin's in his ire! / May the blood through his veins flow like currents of fire!" (109; ch. 22). It is little wonder that Flora's words stir a "wild feeling of romantic delight" in Waverley that "amounted almost to a sense of pain" (107). Flora is singing her translation on a wild mountaintop; to approach her, Waverley has had to pass the junction of two streams and, avoiding the placid one, pursue uphill the course of a smaller, but more violent, current: "the motions of the lesser brook were rapid and furious, issuing from between the precipices like a maniac from his confinement, all foam and uproar" (104–05). As critics have noted, this landscape is symbolic: the larger, level stream represents Hanoverian Britain; the smaller current bursting forth from the heights represents the Jacobite rebellion (Devlin 64–65; D. Brown 26). I would add that Scott's image of the rebellion as a maniac escaped from confinement seems based upon Virgil's conception of *furor*, in the passage above, as a madman kept securely bound only by the greatest of efforts.

When Waverley decides to leave the Highlands, having told Fergus that rebellion against the established government is "mere frenzy" (Scott 132; ch. 27), he runs straight into *furor* unleashed by Jacobitism. The blacksmith's wife at Cairnvreckan, a neighbouring Lowland village, is drunk with revolution:

> a strong large-boned hard-featured woman, about forty, dressed as if her clothes had been flung on with a pitchfork, her cheeks flushed with a scarlet red where they were not smutted with soot and lamp-black, jostled through the crowd, and brandishing high a child of two years old, which she danced in her arms, without regard to its screams of terror, sang forth, with all her might,—
> "Charlie is my darling, my darling, my darling,
> Charlie is my darling,
> The young Chevalier."
> "D'ye hear what's come ower ye now, ye whingeing whig carles? D'ye hear wha's coming to cow yere cracks?"...
> "And that's a' your whiggery," re-echoed the virago; "that's a' your whiggery, and your presbytery, ye cut-lugged graning carles. What d'ye think the lads wi' the kilts will care for yere synods and yere presbyteries, and yere buttock-mail, and yere stool o' repentance? Vengeance on the black face o't! mony an honester woman's been set upon it than streeks doon beside ony whig in the country." (151–52; ch. 30)

"This exulting Bacchanal" (151), as Scott calls her, defies all law, even the marital authority of her husband, and the result is a bizarre brawl in which the townspeople, led by the blacksmith, who is "eager to discharge upon some more worthy object the fury which his helpmate had provoked" (153), attack Waverley as a Jacobite. He defends himself by firing his pistol at them, and only the appearance of the local clergyman "put a curb upon their fury" (153).

That *furor* is the psychological engine and social bond of the rebellion becomes even clearer as battle, the primitive counterpart of legal trial and judgement, approaches. As the Highland troops advance to combat at Prestonpans,

> Waverley felt his heart at that moment throb as it would have burst from his bosom. It was not fear, it was not ardour,—it was a compound of both, a new and deeply energetic impulse, that with its first emotion chilled and astounded, then fevered and maddened his mind. The sounds around him combined to exalt his enthusiasm; the pipes played, and the clans rushed forward, each in its own dark column. As they advanced they mended their pace, and the muttering sounds of the men to each other began to swell into a wild cry. (225; ch. 47)

It is hardly surprising that, on the field of battle, Waverley suddenly feels caught in a nightmare, "a dream, strange, horrible, and unnatural" (221; ch. 46). Far from trying to kill others himself, he saves an English officer whose head is about to be split by the battle-axe of Dugald Mahony (225–26; ch. 47), and he watches in horror as his former commanding officer, Colonel Gardiner, is "brought from his horse by the blow of a scythe" and hacked to pieces before his eyes (226). No wonder Rose Bradwardine thinks Waverley has nothing in common with "all the gunpowder Highlanders…the fierce, hot, furious spirits, of whose brawls we see much and hear more" (249; ch. 52). Flora's reply to Rose is hardly a defence of primitive heroism:

> For mere fighting…I believe all men (that is, who deserve the name) are pretty much alike: there is generally more courage required to run away. They have besides, when confronted with each other, a certain instinct for strife, as we see in other male animals, such as dogs, bulls, and so forth. (249–50)

The rebellion slowly collapses after its initial success; as it does so, Waverley sees more and more clearly that Fergus is driven by *furor*. He notes that Fergus has the "look...of a demoniac" when his prince turns down his request for an earldom; Scott ends this episode by observing of Fergus that "[his] fury had now subsided into a deep and strong desire of vengeance" (251, 254; ch. 53). Later, when Waverley rejects the alliance with Flora that Fergus has promoted, and insists on his own right to marry Rose Bradwardine, Fergus's pride is wounded and, infuriated, he draws his sword on Waverley, who calls Fergus's rage "absolute madness" (270; ch. 58). Fittingly, Fergus's final defeat in the darkness at Clifton is caused by his frenzied pride: after the English cavalrymen have been beaten back, "[u]nsatisfied with the advantage thus gained, Fergus, to whose ardent spirit the approach of danger seemed to restore all its elasticity," draws his sword and leads his men into an exposed position. The Highlanders, "disordered by their own success," are surrounded and routed (278; ch. 59). As in Virgil, *furor* defeats itself in the end.

After the battle at Clifton, the novel does not follow the Jacobite army on to its decisive defeat at Culloden; instead, the remaining chapters survey its results for the characters caught up in it. Waverley, who escaped from the rout at Clifton and has subsequently become thoroughly disillusioned with his part in it, wins a royal pardon through the intercession of Colonel Talbot, the English officer whose life he had saved at Prestonpans. The Baron of Bradwardine is pardoned; Fergus Mac-Ivor is tried and executed as a traitor. During these concluding chapters, Scott returns to explicit allusions to the *Aeneid*; through them, he characterizes the historical change that occurred when the power of the Highland clans was eradicated. The execution of Fergus, for instance, is presented as being, like Aeneas's killing of Turnus, an extinction that is gruesome, even sickening, but necessary. Fergus, in his final interview with Waverley, considers the British law of high treason barbarous:

But I suppose one day or other—when there are no longer any wild Highlanders to benefit by its tender mercies—they will blot it from their records, as levelling them with a nation of cannibals. The mummery, too, of exposing the senseless head—they have not the wit to grace mine with a paper coronet; there would be some satire in that, Edward. I hope they will set it on the Scotch gate though, that I may look, even after death, to the blue hills of my own country, which I love so dearly. The Baron would have added,

"Moritur, et moriens dulces reminiscitur Argos." (326; ch. 69)

The line, adapted from Virgil—"caelumque / aspicit et dulcis moriens reminiscitur Argos" ("He...gazes on the sky and, dying, dreams of his sweet Argos"; 10: 781–82)—identifies Fergus with Antores, a comrade of Hercules in the old, heroic days. Fergus's attribution of the quotation to the Baron again links that old warrior with the cause of lost glory.[3] Scott, however, may not share Fergus's view of his own punishment. Scott allows Colonel Talbot to justify the execution forcefully: "this young gentleman has studied and fully understood the desperate game which he has played. He threw for life or death, a coronet or a coffin; and he cannot now be permitted, with justice to the country, to draw stakes, because the dice have gone against him" (318–19; ch. 67). Scott's own position is probably close to Waverley's own—having tried unsuccessfully to obtain a pardon for Fergus, Waverley stands by him to the end, saddened but not indignant.

After the execution, Waverley seeks out Fergus's Catholic priest and pays for masses to be said in his memory. For the first time, Waverley himself can see the relevance of Virgil: "'*Fungarque inani munere,*' he repeated as the ecclesiastic retired. 'Yet why not class these acts of remembrance with other honours, with which affection, in all sects, pursues the memory of the dead?'" (329; ch. 69). The allusion is to a famous scene in the *Aeneid*. Aeneas has gone to the underworld to meet his father, Anchises, who shows him the magnificent future of their descendants. But the pageant of Roman glory concludes with the view of Marcellus, the adopted son of Augustus who died in his youth; Anchises says of him

> heu! miserande puer, si qua fata aspera rumpas,
> tu Marcellus eris! manibus date lilia plenis,
> purpureos spargam flores animamque nepotis
> his saltem accumulem donis et fungar inani
> munere. (Virgil 6: 882–86)

> Ah! child of pity, if haply thou couldst burst the harsh bonds of fate, thou shalt be Marcellus! Give me lilies with full hand: let me scatter purple flowers; let me heap o'er my offspring's shade at least these gifts and fulfil an unavailing service.

Waverley sees that Fergus can no more escape the harsh bonds of fate and live on as Fergus than could Marcellus; he also sees that this fate is incapable of being palliated by formal mourning. Waverley has now joined Fergus, the Baron, and Scott himself in seeing Fergus's destruction as a Virgilian necessity. His literary sensibility seems to have matured along with his moral awareness: we may doubt that he would now dismiss Latin authors as self-evident.

We can now see even more point in the novel's richest allusion to the *Aeneid*, the Baron's *Fuimus Troes* with which we began this essay. In book 2 of Virgil's epic, Aeneas awakes from sleep to find the Greeks sacking Troy. His first impulse is to fight:

> arma amens capio; nec sat rationis in armis,
>   sed glomerare manum bello et concurrere in arcem

cum sociis ardent animi; furor iraque mentem
praecipitant, pulchrumque mori succurrit in armis. (2: 313-17)

Frantic I seize arms; yet little purpose is there in arms, but my heart burns to muster a force for battle and hasten with my comrades to the citadel. Rage and wrath drive my soul headlong and I think how glorious it is to die in arms!

He then encounters Panthus, the priest of Apollo, who counsels flight:

venit summa dies et ineluctabile tempus
Dardaniae. fuimus Troes, fuit Ilium et ingens
gloria Teucrorum; ferus omnia Iuppiter Argos
transtulit; incensa Danai dominantur in urbe. (2: 324-27)

It is come—the last day and inevitable hour for Troy. We Trojans are not, Ilium is not, and the great glory of the Teucrians; in wrath Jupiter has taken all away to Argos; our city is aflame, and in it the Greeks are lords.

The Baron's allusion underlines several important parallels of novel and epic: Waverley is the Baron's Aeneas, the man who survives by flight and not *furor*; Troy represents the heroic way of life, the rule of honour maintained by combat, that the Baron now gives up as lost. There is a further point, though: the Baron himself, unlike Panthus, will survive as an important part of the new order, though neither he nor Waverley realizes this at the moment. The Baron is a Lowlander, a representative of the meeting-ground between Highlander and Englishman, and Waverley is going to absorb the best aspects of the Baron's feudal heritage, the dignified and disinterested loyalty embodied in his stance in this scene, when Waverley redeems the Baron's estate and settles on it. Fergus dies, the last of his race; the Baron's line lives on in the union of Waverley and his daughter.

These, then, are Scott's specific allusions to the *Aeneid* in *Waverley*. What larger bearing do they have upon the novel? For one thing, they emphasize certain themes and attitudes. Just as, for example, Virgil opposes the rule of *furor* with that of law, so the idea of law plays an important role in *Waverley*. Waverley is himself an unthinking proponent of the individual's right to legal redress from the time he enters Scotland. Furthermore, Scott cleverly arranges that Waverley's first actual awareness that the Jacobite rebellion has begun, even though he has been living in the middle of it, occurs when he is formally examined in a court of law on a charge of treason; this legal examination follows immediately upon the outbreak of mob violence at Cairnvreckan. Similarly, as David R. Brown has pointed out, at the end of the novel Waverley reinstates the Baron in his own estate by legal purchase of it: the Baron no longer holds his property by ancient feudal right, but by force of modern British law (24).

Virgil is also used to underline Scott's attitude toward war. The Latin war of the last half of the *Aeneid*, the struggle between the forces of Aeneas and Turnus, is presented as a civil war, an especially self-destructive and unnecessary battle between men belonging to the same society. Scott, too, sees the 1745 uprising as such a war. Even before joining the conflict, Waverley "felt inexpressible repugnance at the idea of being accessary to the plague of civil war" (140; ch. 28); after he has escaped from the nightmare of battle, he "devoutly…[hoped]…that it might never again be his lot to draw his sword in civil conflict" (283; ch. 60). Civil war, in fact, becomes in both authors a metaphor for the irrational savagery of war itself.

The analogy with Virgil's epic also helps us to understand the central importance of historical process in Scott. All of the allusions from the *Aeneid* convey a brooding sense of history as fated and tragically destructive. At the novel's end, Flora Mac-Ivor blames herself for her brother's death: she feels she incited him to concentrate all his energy and ambition upon the Jacobite rebellion. She explains to Waverley, "I do not regret his attempt, because it was wrong: O no; on that point I am armed; but because it was impossible it could end otherwise than thus" (323; ch. 68). Fergus's rebellion, then, like Turnus's war against Aeneas, is wrong *because* it was impossible: Fergus was fighting against what Virgil calls *ineluctabile tempus*: the ineluctable hour. At the same time, the hero in both works has the task of making a better and more civilized future out of a dead past; this task, in itself, gives a moral order to experience. Society—more precisely, the idea of society—is the real protagonist of Scott's novel; here, too, Virgil is his precursor. Aeneas transcends the heroic code by sacrificing his home, his family, his emotional life, even his very individuality, to his duty to found the Roman idea.

Scott also uses the *Aeneid* to intensify the mood of his novel. Almost all of the allusions to Virgil deal with suffering, loss, and defeat. Both *Waverley* and the *Aeneid* contain much more sadness than a summary of their plots or an outline of their themes would lead a reader to expect. In each case, this is largely because of the author's sympathy for the losers, for those, like Dido and Turnus, or Fergus and the Baron, whose cause is not so much wrong as impossible. In each case, this sympathy is based upon a grasp of what historical development costs: the rejection of some impulses and loyalties in favour of other, more civilized values. Thus, the hero in each work is, like his author, radically split: Aeneas throughout must conquer his own impulses, even, finally, the impulse to spare the defeated Turnus; Waverley similarly wavers between the two sides in the Jacobite conflict, able to see more than those who belong only to one side or the other, to either the placid or the furious stream alone. Waverley is perhaps less manly than Colonel Talbot or Fergus, but he is more fully human than either.[4] It is this inclusiveness of vision that makes both works sombre and saddening, even if each ends officially in triumph.

Finally, Scott's use of the *Aeneid* in *Waverley* allows us to see more clearly two important things about his achievement as a novelist: how epic is his vision of history, and how important allusion is to his art. As for the first, Georg Lukács has observed that Scott created the historical novel as a literary form in *Waverley* by one striking innovation: he gives his leading characters strengths and weaknesses that concentrate the strengths and weaknesses of conflicting historical forces (40, *passim*). This means that heroes like Waverley embody a union of the forces that, for Scott, make up British society. We should note, though, that the heroes of epics are figures who embody the elemental, distinguishing truths of a whole nation or culture. Achilles, Odysseus, Aeneas, Milton's Adam and Eve, even Tom Jones, even Leopold Bloom—all are far from being simply individuals: they live out the ethos on which their whole civilization rests. This is what makes them heroes, and their stories epics. In other words, Scott's presentation of British history has a precedent in traditional epic practice: like the *Aeneid*, *Waverley* depicts a hero whose story embodies the whole history and nature of the society he founds. If Waverley is a hero who forswears traditional kinds of heroism, so, in his way, is Aeneas. In this novel, then, Scott is attempting to appropriate something of the conflicts and scope of classical epic for the new form of realistic prose fiction; his attempt is serious, unlike Fielding's parallel, but comic, use of mock-epic description and playful allusion some seventy years earlier. A measure of that seriousness is that, unlike Fielding's practice, Scott's allusions to Virgil originate from his characters, and not from his narrator.

This essay also suggests something important about Scott's use of allusion. Unlike Jane Austen, he makes no pretence of being unlearned and uninformed: we read his novels in Scott's own scholarly editions, bracketed by prefaces, appendices, and scores of footnotes; his narrative seems cluttered with scholarly allusions and antiquarian explanations; many of his own favourite characters are pedants like the Baron, bristling with fragments of obscure knowledge. I hope I have suggested, however, by examining one set of literary allusions, that Scott does not scatter his learning through his pages for its own sake; instead, like Fielding or George Eliot or Joyce, he uses allusion as an artistic device, one capable of adding subtlety, range, and coherence to the work of art.[5]

NOTES

1. In her Clarendon edition of the text, Claire Lamont identifies most, but not all, of the Virgil allusions treated in this essay; as she notes (418), most of Scott's allusions in *Waverley* had already been traced by two previous editors of the novel, Andrew Lang, in his Border edition of 1892, and Andrew Hook, in his Penguin edition of 1972.
2. In this letter of 11 December 1815, Jane Austen is writing to the Rev. J. S. Clarke, domestic chaplain to the Prince of Wales.
3. The reviewer of *Waverley* in the *British Critic* noted that Scott had slightly misquoted Virgil in both this and the following allusion ("Unsigned Review, *British Critic*" 73). Clearly Scott could assume, as had Fielding, that his readers had an exact knowledge of Virgil's text.
4. Francis R. Hart makes this point in more general terms in his *Scott's Novels: The Plotting of Historical Survival* (29–30). This essay is indebted at several points to Hart's very fine chapter on the novel.
5. A similarly consistent pattern, it might be noted, can be found in Scott's allusions to Shakespeare's *Henry IV* cycle; see Brown 16, Hart 29, and Scott's own oblique association of Fergus with Hotspur at the start of chapter 59.

 # Jane Austen and the Pleasure Principle

MY POINT OF DEPARTURE is the scene near the start of *Emma* in which Mr. Knightley and Mrs. Weston discuss Emma's new intimacy with the orphan Harriet Smith. Mr. Knightley is strongly opposed to this relationship; he fears that Harriet's ignorance, lowly status, and abject dependence on Emma is "doing them both harm" (Austen, *Emma [E]* 39). However, Mrs. Weston points out that opposing Emma's new choice of a companion is futile:

> Pray excuse me; but supposing any little inconvenience may be apprehended from the intimacy, it cannot be expected that Emma, accountable to nobody but her father, who perfectly approves the acquaintance, should put an end to it, so long as it is a source of pleasure to herself. (40)

In other words, Emma is accountable to no one but herself, and she will go on doing what she is doing as long as she enjoys it.

Emma certainly is presented as someone who is extraordinarily devoted to her own pleasure: we are reminded repeatedly that she is unwilling to work at her reading, her music, or her drawing; in Mr. Knightley's words during this same conversation, "She will never submit to any thing requiring industry and patience, and a subjection of the fancy to the understanding" (37). In fact, in the opening pages of the novel, we learn that she considers her governess Miss Taylor (now Mrs. Weston) to have been her friend because she allowed Emma to live pain-free, without inhibitions or guilt: Miss Taylor was "peculiarly interested in herself, in every pleasure, every scheme of her's;—one to whom she could speak every thought as it arose, and who had such an affection for her as could never find fault" (6). The Emma of the novel's opening pages has a mythical dimension; though she is almost twenty-one years old, she has yet to really suffer: "It was Miss Taylor's loss which first brought grief" (6). In fact, the narrator comments, "The real evils indeed of Emma's situation" are her "power of having rather too much her own way" and her "disposition to think a little too well of herself"—but, naturally enough, "The danger...was at present so unperceived, that they [these "real evils"] did not by any means rank as misfortunes with her" (5–6).

We might think, then, that the plot of *Emma* is thus a dramatization of the process by which Emma learns not to live for pleasure, but subdues her will to a more mature awareness of her real social obligations. In Freudian language, she becomes socialized as a responsible adult when she learns to restrain her instinctive drive for pleasure and to acknowledge the reality-principle. Freud has had an immense influence on how we think today; one might substitute Freud in the sentence Edmund uses to describe Shakespeare's universality in Austen's *Mansfield Park*: "we all talk [Freud], use his similes, and describe with his descriptions" (338), and one of the main emphases of Freud is the emotional and imaginative cost to the individual of adhering to the reality beyond oneself.

However, my argument here is that Jane Austen presents a much different—and distinctively eighteenth-century—conception of the relationship between pleasure and obligation. Austen considers that the greatest pleasure lies in following duty and obligation. She believes seriously what the boys in Twain's *Tom Sawyer* are tricked into thinking: that a heavy obligation (in Tom's case, whitewashing a fence) is actually a great pleasure. Emma Woodhouse discovers that her greatest pleasure lies in her love for and marriage to Mr. Knightley, even though he embodies all of those claims of conscience that she has found "very disagreeable,—a waste of time—tiresome" (*E* 155), and even though she considers love and marriage "not my way, or my nature" (84). She also discovers that her domination of Harriet causes her great pain: if it begins pleasurably, it ends by creating in Emma "terror…consternation…humiliation" (405, 407, 411). When Mr. Knightley proposes to Emma, she feels overwhelming joy: "The dread of being awakened from the happiest dream, was perhaps the most prominent feeling" (430). Her renunciation of her relationship with Harriet is a "spontaneous burst of Emma's feelings: 'Oh God! that I had never seen her!'" (411). In short, pleasure as much as moral choice brings Emma to Mr. Knightley's side and away from Harriet; in fact, pleasure and moral choice happily coincide.

In short, harmony, not sacrifice or conflict, prevails in *Emma* and in all of Jane Austen's novels. Her vision is comic. And I would like to suggest that the conception of comedy advanced by the German poet, playwright, and historian Friedrich von Schiller throws some light upon this happy coincidence of pleasure and duty in Austen's novels. Schiller, in his long essay *On the Naive and Sentimental in Literature*, published in 1795 and 1796, while Jane Austen was writing her early novels, argues that comedy is superior to tragedy:

> If tragedy sets out from a more exalted place, it must be allowed, on the other hand, that comedy aims at a more important end; and if this end could be actually attained it would make all tragedy not

only unnecessary, but impossible. The aim that comedy has in view is the same as that of the highest destiny of man, and this consists in liberating himself from the influence of violent passions, and taking a calm and lucid survey of all that surrounds him, and also of his own being, and of seeing everywhere occurrence rather than fate or hazard, and ultimately rather smiling at the absurdities than shedding tears and feeling anger at the sight of the wickedness of man.

The comic poet thus creates in his work the harmony of reality and the ideal, so that what is is seen as what *ought to be*, and vice versa. And what holds true in the realm of philosophy is also true in the moral realm, in that the claims of nature and duty are shown to be one and the same: what the hero wants to do is shown to be also what he *ought to do*. (66–67)

Schiller is best known to the English-speaking world as the author of the "Ode to Joy" set to music by Beethoven in his Ninth Symphony, and Schiller's ideas about comedy allow us to see comic works in general, and Jane Austen's novels in particular, as odes to joy. The reader of Austen's novels, "taking a calm and lucid survey of all that surrounds him [or her]," is invited by Austen to share Emma's response as she surveys Mr. Knightley's house, Donwell Abbey: "It was just what it ought to be, and it looked what it was" (358).

I will develop my argument by discussing the three Austen novels—*Northanger Abbey*, *Pride and Prejudice*, and *Emma*—in which the heroine single-mindedly pursues a childlike pleasure, but finds that this pursuit leads her to the very different, and greater, pleasures of mutual love and self-reform. In the final section of this essay, I look briefly at Jane Austen's other three novels—*Sense and Sensibility*, *Mansfield Park*, and *Persuasion*. I will be arguing that the same pattern underlies one of these novels, *Persuasion*, though with a switch in gender and point of view, and that its absence in the remaining two novels, *Sense and Sensibility* and *Mansfield Park*, helps to account for their somber and unsettling quality. These latter two are Austen's problem-novels, just as Shakespeare's darkest comedies are described as his problem-plays.

The heroine of *Northanger Abbey*, Catherine Morland, is a simple, even generic, seventeen-year-old whose emotions are similarly simple and transparent. She thus provides a clear model of the way that pleasure and obligation coincide in Austen's novels. From the time that Catherine meets Isabella Thorpe in Bath, she gives herself up to the pleasures of reading Gothic novels—but Austen stresses that she has an even greater pleasure in the company of her first dancing-partner at Bath, Henry Tilney. On the one hand, "the luxury of a raised, restless, and frightened imagination over the pages of Udolpho" (51) is deeply appealing; she tells Isabella, "Oh! I am delighted with the book! I should like to spend my whole life in reading it" (40). Henry Tilney, who serves as Catherine's mentor, admits, "The person, be it gentleman or lady, who has not pleasure in a good novel, must be intolerably stupid. I have read all Mrs. Radcliffe's works, and most of them with great pleasure" (106). Jane Austen herself, in her famous defense of novels in *Northanger Abbey*, claims, "our productions have afforded more extensive and unaffected pleasure than those of any other literary corporation in the world" (37).

However, the novel also shows that Catherine's delight in Henry Tilney is even deeper and more powerful than the imaginative pleasures she finds in Gothic fiction. She feels much more regret when she discovers she has apparently rebuffed Henry and his sister in going with the Thorpes to explore Blaize Castle than she does three days later when she walks out with the Tilneys and passes up the Thorpes' outing to Clifton and Blaize castle. Similarly, she passes a sleepless night in pain and humiliation after she is summarily dismissed from Northanger Abbey by Henry's father. At the heart of her suffering is her belief that now "Every hope, every expectation from [Henry is] suspended, at least, and who could say how long?" (226). This sleepless night is contrasted with the night she found herself terrified by the discovery of what seemed to be a Gothic manuscript: "That room, in which her disturbed imagination had tormented her on her first arrival, was again the scene of agitated spirits and unquiet slumbers. Yet how different now the source of her inquietude from what it had been then—how mournfully superior in reality and substance!" (227). An index of this difference is that on her first night at Northanger Abbey Catherine felt repose was out of the question, but she "unknowingly fell fast asleep" (171) at three a.m. and slept until wakened by the housemaid in the morning.

Catherine's whole-hearted absorption in Gothic novels is presented as a natural adolescent enjoyment—but then so is her attraction to Henry Tilney. In fact, the two satisfactions are regularly presented as rivals. Catherine tells Isabella early in the novel, "I do not pretend to say that I was not very much pleased with him [Henry]; but while I have Udolpho to read, I feel as if nobody could make me miserable" (41), and when she sets off in the carriage for Blaize Castle with John Thorpe, since her promised walk with the Tilneys seems to have been rained out, she is "divided between regret for the loss of one great pleasure, and the hope of soon enjoying another, almost its equal in degree, however unlike in kind" (86). As the word "almost" tells us, her devotion to Henry Tilney outweighs her devotion to Gothic fiction. When she is invited to visit Northanger Abbey, the narrator describes Catherine's double delight at the prospect:

> She...was to be for weeks under the same roof with the person whose society she mostly prized—and, in addition to all the rest, this roof was to be the roof of an abbey!—Her passion for ancient

edifices was next in degree to her passion for Henry Tilney—and castles and abbies made usually the charm of those reveries which his image did not fill. (141)

This "passion for Henry Tilney" is what makes his discovery of her fanciful suspicions about his father so much more painful than her earlier discoveries that she has transformed a clothes chest, a laundry list, and an unlocked cabinet into Gothic props:

> Henry's address, short as it had been, had more thoroughly opened her eyes to the extravagance of her late fancies than all their several disappointments had done. Most grievously was she humbled. Most bitterly did she cry. It was not only with herself that she was sunk—but with Henry. Her folly, which now seemed even criminal, was all exposed to him, and he must despise her for ever. (199)

With this motive to think and to change, Catherine makes a series of inner reforms and outer realizations. She also becomes a much more perceptive reader, as she shows soon afterwards when she has no difficulty in seeing through Isabella Thorpe's letter asking Catherine to try to salvage Isabella's marriage hopes. She cries, "She must think me an idiot, or she could not have written so; but perhaps this has served to make her character better known to me than mine is to her" (218). In short, moved by her love for Henry, her strongest desire and her greatest source of pleasure, Catherine becomes self-aware and able to judge and act properly. In Schiller's terms, she now is what she ought to be, and what she wants to do is also what she ought to do.

Catherine Morland's search for pleasure is simple and generic, but Elizabeth Bennet's in *Pride and Prejudice* is much more idiosyncratic and sophisticated. Elizabeth begins the novel as someone who finds her greatest pleasure in dispassionately judging other people. She is "a studier of character," as she admits to Mr. Bingley; she adds, "intricate characters are the *most* amusing" (42). Dancing at Netherfield with Mr. Darcy, a man whose character she finds particularly fascinating, she asks him a series of personal questions. He replies:

> "May I ask to what these questions tend?"
>
> "Merely to the illustration of your character," said she,.... "I am trying to make it out." ...
>
> "I could wish, Miss Bennet, that you were not to sketch my character at the present moment, as there is reason to fear that the performance would reflect no credit on either."
>
> "But if I do not take *your* likeness now, I may never have another opportunity."
>
> "I would by no means suspend any pleasure of yours," he coldly replied. (93–94)

Elizabeth's pleasure in judging presumes that she is apart from and superior to those she judges. In a pointed phrase, the novel's narrator tells us that the indifference of Bingley's two sisters to Jane, when she is sick at Netherfield, "restored Elizabeth to the enjoyment of all her original dislike" (35). She admits, "Follies and nonsense, whims and inconsistencies *do* divert me, I own, and I laugh at them whenever I can" (57). Elizabeth is her father's favourite child, and presumably she has learned the pleasures of Olympian judgement from her father. He calls her "my little Lizzy" in the opening chapter and claims that Elizabeth has more "quickness" than her sisters (4–5), and when he reads aloud to the family Mr. Collins's letter inviting himself to Longbourn, only Lizzy can see that Mr. Collins's prose reveals him to be a fool. "Can he be a sensible man, sir?" she asks, and his reply to her reveals his great delight in the prospect of a new specimen:

"No, my dear; I think not. I have great hopes of finding him quite the reverse. There is a mixture of servility and self-importance in his letter, which promises well. I am impatient to see him" (64). Mr. Bennet has married a noisy, stubborn, and silly woman, but he has not sought comfort "in any of those pleasures which too often console the unfortunate for their folly or their vice. He was fond of the country and of books; and from these tastes had arisen his principal enjoyments. To his wife he was very little otherwise indebted, than as her ignorance and folly had contributed to his amusement" (236). Late in the novel, when Elizabeth finds his philosophic detachment obtuse and painful rather than amusing, he says to her, "For what do we live, but to make sport for our neighbours, and laugh at them in our turn?" (364).

However, Elizabeth's search for pleasure proves to be as foolish as Catherine Morland's. Like Catherine, she ends up feeling "absolutely ashamed" once she reads and carefully considers Darcy's letter. She realizes that she has been "blind, partial, prejudiced, absurd" (208). She also realizes the vain motives that caused her, the self-proclaimed expert on character, to be so mistaken:

> "How despicably have I acted!" she cried.—"I, who have prided myself on my discernment!—I, who have valued myself on my abilities! who have often disdained the generous candour of my sister, and gratified my vanity, in useless or blameable distrust.—How humiliating is this discovery!—Yet, how just a humiliation!—Had I been in love, I could not have been more wretchedly blind. But vanity, not love, has been my folly." (208)

Elizabeth's self-castigation is ringing and thorough—and apparently complete; but we are only just over halfway through the novel at this point, and Elizabeth has yet to discover what a powerful motive love has been and will be in her relationship with

Darcy. Love has been her folly, as well as vanity; she has unconsciously loved Darcy from the start (as her interrogation of him on the dance-floor at Netherfield might indicate). Blake says in *The Marriage of Heaven and Hell*, "If the fool would persist in his folly he would become wise" (line 18), and Elizabeth does persist, and does become wise.

Both Darcy and Elizabeth educate each other and make important changes in character and action as a result of their love for each other. Darcy's love for Elizabeth is obvious: he begins his unexpected proposal by telling her "how ardently I admire and love you" (189), and her powerful impact on him is equally obvious. "By you I was properly humbled," he tells her near the end of the novel, speaking of her scathing rejection of his proposal, and he goes on to say of his changed behaviour when they met at Pemberley:

> My object *then*...was to shew you, by every civility in my power, that I was not so mean as to resent the past; and I hoped to obtain your forgiveness, to lessen your ill opinion, by letting you see that your reproofs had been attended to. How soon any other wishes introduced themselves I can hardly tell, but I believe in about half an hour after I had seen you. (369–70)

In other words, Darcy was determined to show Elizabeth that he has changed and that he has changed for her. His moral reform is also an attempt to win her love. His crucial action in the plot, his secret rescue of Elizabeth's sister Lydia, similarly has two motives: his character, duty, and honour require it of him, on the one hand, and on the other, "[Elizabeth's] heart did whisper, that he had done it for her" (326).

Elizabeth's love for Darcy and his reforming influence upon her are not so obvious, but they mirror exactly Darcy's love for her and its effect upon his character. The story is told from Elizabeth's point of view, and her unawareness of her own growing love for Darcy is perhaps the novel's chief irony. During the first half of the novel, he is to her only "*that* abominable Mr. Darcy" (144). Since "She liked him too little to care for his approbation" (51), she feels free to tease him, taunt him, debate his opinions and question his actions, and point out his character defects; all in all she takes great delight in their verbal combats. No wonder that Darcy believes she is leading him on. We can also note that, despite her vow "*never* to dance with [Mr. Darcy]" (20), she does agree to dance with him at Netherfield, "without knowing what she did" (90), and that, after refusing his proposal at Rosings, "from actual weakness [she] sat down and cried for half an hour" (193)—surprisingly, for someone who dearly loves a laugh. Elizabeth speaks truly when, after returning from the walk in which Darcy proposes to her the second time, she tells her family, "they had wandered about, till she was beyond her own knowledge" (372).

In the same way, Darcy's extraordinary letter teaches Elizabeth to think and to change her attitudes. "She could think only of her letter" (209) in the days after she receives it; and "she was in a fair way of soon knowing [it] by heart" (212). The Elizabeth who had told Jane "one knows exactly what to think" (86) is a very different person from the Elizabeth who is silent and unable to meet Darcy's eyes when he returns to Longbourn with Bingley in the final chapters. Now, instead of assertion to others, Elizabeth relies on questions to herself: "Why is he so altered? From what can it proceed?...Yet why did he come?...Why, if he came only to be silent, grave, and indifferent,...did he come at all?" (255, 336, 339). If Darcy's change in character and the love that inspired it are on display at Pemberley, so are Elizabeth's. When she and her party reach the picture gallery upstairs,

> Elizabeth walked on in quest of the only face whose features would be known to her. At last it arrested her—and she beheld a striking resemblance of Mr. Darcy, with such a smile over the face, as she remembered to have sometimes seen, when he looked at her....
>
> There was certainly at this moment, in Elizabeth's mind, a more gentle sensation towards the original, than she had ever felt in the height of their acquaintance.... Every idea that had been brought forward by the housekeeper was favourable to his character, and as she stood before the canvas, on which he was represented, and fixed his eyes upon herself, she thought of his regard with a deeper sentiment of gratitude than it had ever raised before; she remembered its warmth, and softened its impropriety of expression. (250–51)

The spatial symbolism here is neat: standing before Darcy's portrait, Elizabeth must move until she reaches the exact point at which she can fix *his* eyes upon *her*. The word *regard* contains two meanings: the primary meaning of the word, according to the *Oxford English Dictionary*, is "gaze, steady or significant look," and a figurative meaning is "esteem, kindly feeling or respectful opinion"; when Elizabeth stands before Darcy's portrait and thinks of his "regard," she is responding both to his physical appeal and to the new value that his esteem for her has, now that she has heard his housekeeper's surprisingly warm praise of his character. Elizabeth's deepening love coincides with her new appreciation of Darcy's moral worth. Just as Darcy has two motives, honour and love, for his rescue of Lydia, Elizabeth tells Lady Catherine that the woman who marries Mr. Darcy "must have such extraordinary sources of happiness necessarily attached to her situation" (355) and that, despite Lady Catherine's illogical claims to the contrary, "Neither duty, nor honour, nor gratitude" would be violated by her decision to marry Mr. Darcy (358). "I am only resolved to act in that manner, which will, in my own opinion, constitute my happiness"

(358), she tells Lady Catherine, and this statement, thanks to the novel's ingenious plot, leads directly to Elizabeth's being given the opportunity to choose to find her happiness with Darcy.

Unlike Catherine Morland and Elizabeth Bennet, Emma Woodhouse finds her greatest pleasure in matchmaking: selecting marriage partners, bringing them together, and promoting their union. "It is the greatest amusement in the world!" she proclaims in the novel's opening chapter (Austen, *E* 12), and she befriends Harriet Smith in order to bring about "an excellent match" (34) between Harriet and the man she has chosen as Harriet's mate, the vicar of Highbury, Mr. Elton. Emma considers that love and marriage may be essential for other people, but they are not for her. For one thing, she is perfect as she is: "I cannot really change for the better. If I were to marry, I must expect to repent it" (84), she tells Harriet. For another thing, love threatens her independence and sense of control. She says in the same scene, "never, never could I expect to be so truly beloved and important; so always first and always right in any man's eyes as I am in my father's.... I shall be very well off, with all the children of a sister I love so much, to care about.... it suits my ideas of comfort better than what is warmer and blinder. My nephews and nieces!—I shall often have a niece with me" (84, 86). Imagining for Harriet Mr. Elton's delight in London, showing Harriet's portrait to his relations, Emma says, "it diffuses through the party those pleasantest feelings of our nature, eager curiosity and warm prepossession. How cheerful, how animated, how suspicious, how busy their imaginations all are!" (56).

However, like Elizabeth Bennet, Emma's conscious self is only half the story. Like Elizabeth, she does not understand the depth and power of her feelings of love. From the novel's first scene onward, we can see, if she cannot, the reason for her delight in Mr. Knightley's company, her great concern when they quarrel over Harriet Smith's rejection of Robert Martin and then over

Frank Churchill, her agitation when confronted with the possibility that he might marry Jane Fairfax, her disturbance at the Crown Inn when he stands among the old men who are not going to dance, her great joy when he dances with Harriet, rescuing both Harriet and Emma from being humiliated by the Eltons, and her subsequent inveigling of him to dance with her. Not only does Emma love Mr. Knightley without realizing it, but her love for him changes her character. After her insult to Miss Bates and his stern rebuke, she is deeply wounded:

> Never had she felt so agitated, mortified, grieved, at any circumstance in her life.... She felt it at her heart. How could she have been so brutal, so cruel to Miss Bates!—How could she have exposed herself to such ill opinion in any one she valued! And how suffer him to leave her without saying one word of gratitude, of concurrence, of common kindness! (376)

Of these three exclamations, one concerns her moral offence to Miss Bates, and two deal with her loss of Mr. Knightley's regard and friendship. Just as all three exclamations are parallel in syntax, so the claims of duty and love coincide—and love outweighs duty here in a proportion of two to one. Emma, like Elizabeth after Darcy's proposal, uncharacteristically cries: "Emma felt the tears running down her cheeks almost all the way home, without being at any trouble to check them, extraordinary as they were" (376). When she calls on Miss Bates early the next morning out of penitence, she welcomes the idea that Mr. Knightley might see her on the way or come in during her visit; this does not happen, but when she returns home and finds him there, a charged moment occurs when he learns where she has been:

It seemed as if there were an instantaneous impression in her favour, as if his eyes received the truth from her's, and all that had passed of good in her feelings were at once caught and honoured.—He looked at her with a glow of regard. She was warmly gratified—and in another moment still more so, by a little movement of more than common friendliness on his part.—He took her hand;—whether she had not herself made the first motion, she could not say—she might, perhaps, have rather offered it—but he took her hand, pressed it, and certainly was on the point of carrying it to his lips—when, from some fancy or other, he suddenly let it go.—Why he should feel such a scruple, why he should change his mind when it was all but done, she could not perceive.—He would have judged better, she thought, if he had not stopped. (385–86)

Emma's love for Mr. Knightley is very apparent to us, and almost apparent to her, at this point; she will become aware of that love once she makes two discoveries, one after the other, about the people around her: that Frank Churchill and Jane Fairfax are secretly engaged, and that Harriet secretly hopes to marry Mr. Knightley. Harriet's hopes shock Emma into realizing that she herself has always loved Mr. Knightley: "Till now that she was threatened with its loss, Emma had never known how much of her happiness depended on being *first* with Mr. Knightley, first in interest and affection" (415).

Only when she acknowledges her love for Mr. Knightley does Emma realize how badly she has been acting. In fact, her acknowledgement of her love *causes* her realization that she has been "universally mistaken" (413). After she realizes that she loves Mr. Knightley and that "she had never really cared for Frank Churchill at all!" she sees the truth of her behaviour:

> She was most sorrowfully indignant; ashamed of every sensation but the one revealed to her—her affection for Mr. Knightley.—Every other part of her mind was disgusting.
>
> With insufferable vanity had she believed herself in the secret of everybody's feelings; with unpardonable arrogance proposed to arrange everybody's destiny. (412–13)

Once again, love and moral change have coincided. The new and improved Emma, now capable of love and capable of sacrificing her own comfort in order to counsel another, brings about her own happiness when she unwittingly invites Mr. Knightley to propose marriage to her. Emma now is what she ought to be, as the narrator suggests: "She spoke then, on being so entreated.—What did she say?—Just what she ought, of course. A lady always does" (431).

All three heroines, then, Catherine, Elizabeth, and Emma, pursue pleasure and end up finding happiness: the greater pleasure of love and moral reform. Ironically, the three heroines find happiness in the everyday domestic obligations that they have been trying to escape. But what of Austen's other three novels: *Sense and Sensibility*, *Mansfield Park*, and *Persuasion*? No one would accuse Fanny Price or Anne Elliot of being devoted to pleasure, and the same holds true of Elinor Dashwood, one of the two heroines of *Sense and Sensibility*. Elinor's sister Marianne does pursue pleasure in the form of romantic love, welcoming Willoughby into her life as "the hero of a favourite story" (43), and Marianne does in the end disown her self-centred hedonism—but her moral reform is not the effect of her love for her eventual husband, Colonel Brandon. In fact, even when she marries him she feels "no sentiment superior to strong esteem and lively friendship" (378). Interestingly, the film of *Sense and Sensibility* went to great lengths to create love between Marianne and Colonel Brandon, and to make her change of mind and character in the closing scenes the result of her love for him. The film also increases the reformed Marianne's moral awareness: in the film it is Marianne, and not Elinor, as in the novel, who explains why Willoughby would not have been happy if he had married Marianne instead of the wealthy Miss Grey (350–52).

Both *Mansfield Park* and *Persuasion* have heroines who love the hero from the outset and who do not change morally. In both novels, it is the hero who is deluded and undergoes the bitter shock, the undeception, the self-realization, and the eventual happiness that I have traced in Catherine, Elizabeth, and Emma. However, there is a major difference between *Mansfield Park* and *Persuasion*, and one that makes *Persuasion* much more pertinent to this discussion. Edmund Bertram of *Mansfield Park* is sexually infatuated with Mary Crawford and has little interest in the novel's heroine, Fanny, throughout the novel; it is Mary's own blatant moral failings, and not his own love for Fanny, that brings Edmund to his senses and back to Fanny. Like *Sense and Sensibility*, *Mansfield Park* insists on the schism between pleasure and love, between nature and duty, and this is why I have called these two novels Austen's problem-novels.

However, *Persuasion* tells a much different story. The heroine of this novel plays a much more active role in creating her destiny: while Fanny simply has to wait, suffer, and remain true to her love, Anne Elliot jolts the novel's hero, Captain Wentworth, into awareness at Lyme Regis, and then brings him to her side through a whole series of indirect initiatives at Bath, culminating when she "eagerly" defines in his presence the nature of women's love: "All the privilege I claim for my own sex…is that of loving longest, when existence or when hope is gone" (235). *Persuasion* presents the same kind of love story as *Northanger Abbey*, *Pride and Prejudice*, and *Emma*, but in this case it is the hero who has devoted himself to pleasure—though it is pleasure of a strange and perverse kind—and the hero who is brought by love to understand how wrong he has been and what he ought to do. The Napoleonic Wars are over, and

Captain Wentworth has come ashore, wealthy and distinguished, to court and to be courted. His pursuit of pleasure is indeed strange and perverse, since from the time he enters the novel he is dominated by his keen delight in feeling himself aggrieved and ill-used because Anne Elliot was persuaded to break off their engagement eight years earlier. We glimpse his conscious intentions and his unconscious motives when the narrator leaves Anne's point of view to explain his initial comment upon Anne's appearance—that she is so altered that he would not have recognized her (Austen, *Persuasion* [*P*] 60–61)—and then gives us a conversation between Wentworth and his sister, Mrs. Croft. The narrator says Wentworth is

> ready to fall in love.... He had a heart for either of the Miss Musgroves, if they could catch it; a heart, in short, for any pleasing young woman who came in his way, excepting Anne Elliot. This was his only secret exception, when he said to his sister, in answer to her suppositions,
>
> "Yes, here I am, Sophia, quite ready to make a foolish match. Any body between fifteen and thirty may have me for the asking. A little beauty, and a few smiles, and a few compliments to the navy, and I am a lost man...."
>
> Anne Elliot was not out of his thoughts, when he more seriously described the woman he should wish to meet with. "A strong mind, with sweetness of manner," made the first and the last of the description.
>
> "This is the woman I want," said he. "Something a little inferior I shall of course put up with, but it must not be much. If I am a fool, I shall be a fool indeed, for I have thought on the subject more than most men." (61–62)

That last sentence concludes the chapter and our brief glimpse into Wentworth's heart. The sentence resonates in the reader's mind much as do Mr. Knightley's words in *Emma* at the end of the chapter depicting the Crown Inn ball: "Brother and sister! no, indeed" (331). Wentworth, like Mr. Knightley, is implicitly confessing his love for the heroine—but unlike Mr. Knightley, Wentworth is unaware of his love. By the time of the novel's climactic chapter, Wentworth, in his secret letter to Anne that brings her "overpowering happiness" (*P* 238), confesses that he has loved her all along: "Dare not say that man forgets sooner than woman, that his love has an earlier death. I have loved none but you. Unjust I may have been, weak and resentful I have been, but never inconstant. You alone have brought me to Bath. For you alone I think and plan" (237).

Furthermore, Wentworth's discovery of his love for Anne brings about his self-discovery and moral reform; as he tells Anne in the novel's final pages, he had been shocked out of his courtship of Louisa Musgrove—which he now considers "the attempts of angry pride" (242)—by Louisa's headstrong leap on the Cobb at Lyme and by Anne's composure and courage in the ensuing commotion. He tells Anne that "only at Lyme had he begun to understand himself.... There, he had seen every thing to exalt in his estimation the woman he had lost, and there begun to deplore the pride, the folly, the madness of resentment, which had kept him from trying to regain her when thrown in his way" (242). And, as he tells Anne, he immediately acted upon his new awareness. He had little scope for honourable action, since he regarded himself—and was regarded by everyone around him—as committed to Louisa. Nevertheless, he decided to leave Lyme while Louisa was recovering there:

> He would gladly weaken, by any fair means, whatever feelings or speculations concerning him might exist; and he went, therefore, to his brother's....
>
> He had remained in Shropshire, lamenting the blindness of his own pride, and the blunders of his own calculations, till at once

released from Louisa by the astonishing and felicitous intelligence of her engagement with Benwick. (243)

Nature abhors a vacuum, and Wentworth's strategic absence from Lyme allows both Captain Benwick and Louisa to prove the adage true.

Wentworth, then, undergoes in *Persuasion* the same learning curve as Catherine, Elizabeth, and Emma. In fact, Wentworth's wry final speech in the novel might have been spoken by one of these three heroines at the end of her story: "I must endeavour to subdue my mind to my fortune. I must learn to brook being happier than I deserve" (247).

 # Asking versus Telling

One Aspect of Jane Austen's Idea of Conversation

MY TEXT FOR THIS OCCASION is drawn from *Pride and Prejudice*, volume 1, chapter 1, page 1:

> "My dear Mr. Bennet," said his lady to him one day, "have you heard that Netherfield Park is let at last?"
>
> Mr. Bennet replied that he had not.
>
> "But it is," returned she; "for Mrs. Long has just been here, and she told me all about it."
>
> Mr. Bennet made no answer.
>
> "Do you not want to know who has taken it?" cried his wife impatiently.
>
> "You want to tell me, and I have no objection to hearing it."
>
> (Austen, *Pride and Prejudice [PP]* 3)

Mr. Bennet is here, for the first of many times in the novel, mocking the illogic in his wife's statements. Ostensibly, she *asks* her husband two questions ("have you heard that Netherfield Park is let at last?... Do you not want to know who has taken it?"). In reality, however, as he points out, she is bursting to *tell* him some exciting news that she has just heard. Mrs. Bennet goes on to announce,

"Mrs. Long says that Netherfield is taken by a young man of large fortune from the north of England.... A single man of large fortune; four or five thousand a year. What a fine thing for our girls!" (3–4). Why doesn't she simply tell her husband the news? Because a question is more emphatic, more dramatic, than a statement, and her pseudo-questions are a transparent guise intended to induce Mr. Bennet to ask a genuine question ("Who is the new tenant of Netherfield Park?"). His question, if only he would ask it, would request information that he does not possess, and so would imply that in this matter he is dependent, needy, inferior. But Mr. Bennet, and through him Jane Austen, points out that Mrs. Bennet has tried to collapse the important distinction between asking and telling.

It is much more comfortable and comforting to tell than it is to ask, and for at least three reasons. Asking a real question of another puts one in an inferior, petitioning position: a question needs a reply from another person for its completion, and so, if you ask a question, you can never have the last word. Furthermore, to ask a question is to make an appeal to others to share a subject, a purpose, and a set of assumptions—and this appeal can always lead to a rebuff or a rejection. Mary Crawford's chances of marrying Edmund Bertram dissolve and die as soon as she asks him, "What can equal the folly of our two relations?" (*Mansfield Park* [*MP*] 454). A third reason why questions are uncomfortable for the questioner is one that will be familiar to every classroom teacher: to ask a genuine question means waiting for an answer, and that means suspense and uncertainty until the response is forthcoming. Jane Austen often shows how hard it is to ask a real question. In *Mansfield Park*, Henry Crawford tells Edmund that, while out hunting, he came across Edmund's future home, the parsonage at Thornton Lacey, and adds, "for such it certainly was." Edmund asks, "You inquired then?" and Henry replies, "No, I never inquire. But I *told* a man mending a hedge that it was Thornton Lacey, and he agreed to it" (241). A real man still hates to ask for directions. This is a passing incident, but in one of the greatest of Austen's scenes, in *Pride and Prejudice*, Lady Catherine de Bourgh displays the same determination to tell, even when she has come all the way to Longbourn to ask Elizabeth a question. From the beginning of the scene, Lady Catherine tells rather than asks at every point: "That lady I suppose is your mother.... And *that* I suppose is one of your sisters.... You have a very small park here.... This must be a most inconvenient sitting room for the evening, in summer; the windows are full west" (351–52). More than a page later, Lady Catherine begins to disclose the purpose of her visit, but still finds it next to impossible to ask a question, so she continues to assert: "A report of a most alarming nature, reached me two days ago.... I instantly resolved on setting off for this place, that I might make my sentiments known to you" (353). Finally, many lines later, she is forced to ask the all-important question, "Has he, has my nephew, made you an offer of marriage?" (354).

In short, telling is easy and asking is hard, because telling is a one-way communication, a transmission of opinion and fact, while question-and-answer is a two-way exchange. Question-and-answer is thus the core element in conversation, which is, precisely, an exchange, a mutual creation by two or more people. *Conversation* is defined in *The Concise Oxford Dictionary of Current English* as "the informal exchange of ideas, information, etc. by spoken words." Samuel Johnson's definition of the word *converse* in his *Dictionary of the English Language* of 1755 is remarkably similar: "To convey the thoughts reciprocally in talk." The key notion is *exchange*: Samuel Johnson, Jane Austen's "my dear Dr. Johnson" (*Jane Austen's Letters* [*JAL*] 181), exists in Boswell's *Life of Johnson* as a hero of daily conversation, and Johnson speaks repeatedly about conversation in just these terms. At one point he says to Boswell, "That is the happiest conversation where there is no competition,...but a calm quiet interchange of sentiments" (qtd. in Boswell 623). Johnson frequently distinguishes between *conversation* and *talk*. When Boswell asks him if there was good conversation at a dinner Johnson attended the previous night, Johnson replies, "No, Sir; we had *talk* enough, but no *conversation*; there was nothing *discussed*" (qtd. in 1210).

The narrators of Austen's novels often describe the absence of conversation, of a genuine interchange of ideas. For instance, in *Northanger Abbey* Mrs. Allen and Mrs. Thorpe spend the chief part of every day together at Bath "in what they called conversation, but in which there was scarcely ever any exchange of opinion, and not often any resemblance of subject, for Mrs. Thorpe talked chiefly of her children, and Mrs. Allen of her gowns" (36). Catherine Morland, in the same novel, finds herself wearied by John Thorpe, because "all the rest of his conversation, or rather talk, began and ended with himself and his own concerns. He told her of horses which he had bought for a trifle and sold for incredible sums; of racing matches, in which his judgment had infallibly foretold the winner" (66). The narrator of *Sense and Sensibility* tells us that at Barton Park the characters "could not be supposed to meet for the sake of conversation. Such a thought would never enter either Sir John or Lady Middleton's head, and therefore very little leisure was ever given for general chat, and none at all for particular discourse" (143). In *Emma*, the heroine's "views of improving her little friend's mind, by a great deal of useful reading and conversation, had never yet led to more than a few first chapters, and the intention of going on tomorrow. It was much easier to chat" (69). As Juliet McMaster has remarked, "'Conversation,' unlike mere 'talk,' must go somewhere, must, through a process of verbal exchange and enlargement, refine on a topic and advance it" ("Secret Languages" 120).

Austen clearly thinks that conversation is different from talk or chat, and the distinction between asking and telling is a more particular instance of this difference in speech categories. One interesting point is that in Austen's novels genuine questions are relatively rare and so, correspondingly, very important. Perhaps a precise term for such real questions is that they are *consultative*: one person consults another or others to discover information, or opinion, or a preference. Think of how important it is right at the end of volume 1 of *Persuasion*, when Captain Wentworth, who has, up to this point, spoken to Anne Elliot only in coldly polite terms, asks her:

> I have been considering what we had best do. [Henrietta] must not appear at first. She could not stand it. I have been thinking whether you had better not remain in the carriage with her, while I go in and break it to Mr. and Mrs. Musgrove. Do you think this a good plan? (117)

Similarly, when Darcy meets Elizabeth at Pemberley for the first time after she rejects his proposal and he has written his long letter to her, he asks her a question that is consultative in the extreme: "Will you allow me, or do I ask too much, to introduce my sister to your acquaintance during your stay at Lambton?" (*PP* 256). In much the same way, a major change happens in *Sense and Sensibility* when Marianne Dashwood, after her near-fatal illness, is transformed from a teller into an asker; she begins by asking her sister Elinor what she thinks: "shall we ever talk on that subject [of Willoughby], Elinor?...Or will it be wrong?" (344).

Consultative questions like these are, as I have noted, surprisingly rare in Austen's novels. Most of the questions voiced by the characters resemble Mrs. Bennet's announcement to her husband: they are exclamations—statements disguised as questions, and put in question form to create more energy and intensity than a direct statement. Such a pseudo-question is traditionally known as a *rhetorical question*, which is, according to the *Concise Oxford Dictionary*, "a question asked not for information but to produce an effect." M. H. Abrams, in his *Glossary of Literary Terms*, adds an important point: a speaker generally uses a rhetorical question to persuade his or her audience (271). A sample rhetorical question from everyday life is, "What difference does it make?", which is simply a more emphatic way of asserting, "It makes no difference"—or, to capture the element of persuasion, "Surely we can agree that it makes no difference." Straightforward rhetorical questions are common in Austen's novels: Fanny Dashwood in *Sense and Sensibility*, for instance, convinces her husband that his widowed mother and sisters will be relatively well off through a series of rhetorical questions, including, "Altogether, they will have five hundred a-year amongst them, and what on earth can four women want for more than that?" (12). Lady Catherine believes she has dismissed once and for all Elizabeth Bennet's upstart claims with a resounding rhetorical question: "Are the shades of Pemberley to be thus polluted?" (*PP* 357).

Rhetorical questions come in many forms in the novels. There are Mrs. Bennet's *announcing* questions. There are *leading* questions, which lead the listener, much like a prompter in the theatre, to give a desired answer. This is the kind of question that Emma asks Harriet about Mr. Martin's proposal: "If you prefer Mr. Martin to every other person; if you think him the most agreeable man you have ever been in company with, why should you hesitate? You blush, Harriet.—Does any body else occur to you at this moment under such a definition?" (*Emma [E]* 53). A more altruistic form of the leading question is the *Socratic* question, in which the speaker tries to bring the listener to an awareness of something that the listener already knows, but is not aware of knowing: Henry Tilney, for instance, says to Catherine Morland in *Northanger Abbey*: "And did Isabella never change her mind before?" (133).

Socratic questions easily become *accusing* questions, such as those Elizabeth levels at Darcy during the proposal scene—"Can you deny that you have done it [separated Jane and Bingley]?" (*PP* 191)—or Mr. Knightley's questions to Emma at Box Hill: "How could you be so unfeeling to Miss Bates? How could you be so insolent in your wit to a woman of her character, age, and situation?" (*E* 374). We also find *browbeating* questions like those Sir Thomas asks of Fanny Price: "'Am I to understand...that you mean to *refuse* Mr. Crawford?...Refuse him?...Refuse Mr. Crawford! Upon what plea? For what reason?'" (*MP* 315). At the other extreme are *pleading* questions; Willoughby, for instance, asks of Elinor after he has explained how he came to jilt Marianne: "And now do you pity me, Miss Dashwood?—or have I said all this to no purpose?—Am I— be it only one degree—am I less guilty in your opinion than I was before?" (*Sense and Sensibility [SS]* 329). A more extreme form of the pleading question is the *abject* question, in which the speaker confesses mental incapacity and asks the listener to *tell* him or her what to do. Almost every question that Harriet asks Emma is an abject question, and so are most of the questions that Lady Bertram asks her husband—for instance, "What shall I do, Sir Thomas?— Whist and Speculation; which will amuse me most?" (*MP* 239).

A totally different, and insidious, kind of rhetorical question is the *strategic* question. When Lucy Steele asks Elinor Dashwood, "pray, are you personally acquainted with your sister-in-law's mother, Mrs. Ferrars?... Then perhaps you cannot tell me what sort of a woman she is?" (*SS* 128), she is not *asking* for information, but beginning the process of *telling* Elinor that she has a prior claim to Edward Ferrars. One borderline kind is the *intrusive* question asked by characters such as Mrs. Jennings or Lady Catherine. These questions, often called "attacks" by the narrator, do ask for a response, but, as when Mrs. Jennings indefatigably goes on asking Colonel Brandon why he is suddenly leaving

Devonshire for London (*SS* 64–66) or when Lady Catherine cross-examines Elizabeth Bennet over the way that she and her sisters have been raised (*PP* 164–66), the questioner seems interested primarily not in the content of the answer, but in asserting his or her ingenuity (Mrs. Jennings) or supremacy (Lady Catherine). It is worth noting that intrusive questions do arise out of curiosity, and curiosity is a step towards sympathy—and so a step away from self-absorption. We see in Mrs. Jennings that naked curiosity can coexist with, and grow into, kindness and sympathy.

A rhetorical question precludes a genuine answer because such a question implies that there is only one possible answer. Another common method of preventing a response is the question that does not allow for an answer because the person who asks the question immediately answers it. Mrs. Bennet says, "Well, Lizzy,...what is your opinion *now* of this sad business of Jane's? For my part, I am determined never to speak of it again to anybody" (*PP* 227). Mrs. Bennet is very fond of this way of short-circuiting conversation, as is her favourite daughter, Lydia, who brings about the plot resolution of *Pride and Prejudice* by asking Elizabeth, "Are you not curious to know how [my wedding] was managed?" and resolutely ignoring her negative response (318). This gambit I would identify by the legal term (familiar to anyone who watches *Law and Order* on TV) *asked and answered*. Miss Bingley, again from *Pride and Prejudice*, provides an example. After Elizabeth walks three miles across the muddy countryside to visit Jane, she asks the Netherfield party, "what could she mean by it? It seems to me to shew an abominable sort of conceited independence, a most country town indifference to decorum" (36).

A genuine question, like conversation itself, presupposes the speakers are equals. One of the main signs to the reader that a Jane Austen character is selfish and childishly self-absorbed is that character's use of rhetorical questions and an inability to ask consultative questions. If you can't ask and answer questions, you can't converse. Listen to Isabella Thorpe in *Northanger Abbey* as she ostensibly asks Catherine about Catherine's new friends, Henry and Eleanor Tilney, and at the same time ostensibly asks Catherine's brother James a series of lively questions. Her questions are purely rhetorical; far from waiting for an answer from her listener, she immediately provides her own reply to each question:

> Was not it so, Mr. Morland? But you men are all so immoderately lazy!...But where is her all-conquering brother? Is he in the room? Point him out to me this instant, if he is. I die to see him.... What can it signify to you [James], what we are talking of? Perhaps we are talking about you, therefore I would advise you not to listen, or you may happen to hear something not very agreeable.... How can you be so teasing; only conceive, my dear Catherine, what your brother wants me to do. He wants me to dance with him again.... Nonsense, how can you say so? But when you men have a point to carry, you never stick at any thing. (56–57)

So far is Isabella from conversation that the narrator of *Northanger Abbey* remarks at the end of this scene, "In this common-place chatter, which lasted some time, the original subject [the Tilneys] seemed entirely forgotten" (57).

This distinction between asking and telling sharpens our understanding of two important elements in Austen's novels—the proposal scenes and the eventual achievement of self-knowledge by the heroines. In the remainder of this essay, I will consider each of these elements in turn.

First, the proposal scenes. It is all-important in Jane Austen's novels, as Henry Tilney observes to Catherine in *Northanger Abbey*, that both on the dance floor and in marriage "man has the advantage of choice, woman only the power of refusal" (77). Because the woman's freedom is so severely limited in this arrangement, it is crucial that she exercise it wisely. Again and again in the novels we find a heroine struggling to refuse a marriage proposal *because the question has never actually been asked*. The man is so infatuated with his vision of himself as a suitor, so impressed with the wisdom of his choice, that he *tells* the woman that she is his chosen rather than *ask* her to be so.

The first, and most blissfully obtuse, of these doltish suitors is John Thorpe in *Northanger Abbey*. His idea of asking Catherine to dance is to tell her, "Well, Miss Morland, I suppose you and I are to stand up and jig it together again" (59), or, on another occasion, "Hey-day, Miss Morland!…what is the meaning of this?—I thought you and I were to dance together" (75). He is similarly incapable of asking her to come for a carriage ride or to go out for a walk with him and his sister. So it should be no surprise to the reader that John Thorpe actually succeeds in making what he considers to be a proposal of marriage to Catherine without even coming close to asking the crucial question. Instead, he makes a series of fatuous statements:

> you have more good-nature and all that, than any body living I believe. A monstrous deal of good-nature, and it is not only good-nature, but you have so much, so much of every thing…. But I have a notion, Miss Morland, you and I think pretty much alike on most matters…. My notion of things is simple enough. Let me only have the girl I like, say I, with a comfortable house over my head, and what care I for all the rest? [rhetorical question!] Fortune is nothing. I am sure of a good income of my own; and if she had not a penny, why so much the better. (123–24)

In a significant choice of words, the narrator says that Thorpe comes out of this interview with "the undivided consciousness of his own happy address, and her explicit encouragement" (124).

Unfortunately, and comically, Catherine is, in fact, completely unaware that Thorpe's "address" is meant to be a marriage proposal.

The most egregious of Austen's suitors is Mr. Collins in *Pride and Prejudice*. The chapter in which he attempts to ask Elizabeth to marry him is introduced with, again, a significant choice of words by the novel's narrator: "The next day a new scene opened at Longbourn. Mr. Collins made his declaration in form" (104). As Collins makes his carefully prepared "declaration," the words that he himself uses to describe what he is doing underline the fact that he is *telling* Elizabeth, not *asking* her:

> allow me to assure you that I have your respected mother's permission for this address....Almost as soon as I entered the house I singled you out as the companion of my future life....But the fact is, that being, as I am, to inherit this estate after the death of your honoured father,...I could not satisfy myself without resolving to chuse a wife from among his daughters....I am not now to learn...that it is usual with young ladies to reject the addresses of the man whom they secretly mean to accept....When I do myself the honour of speaking to you next on this subject....You must give me leave to flatter myself, my dear cousin, that your refusal of my addresses is merely words of course. (105–08)

Collins enumerates the reasons that have led him to his decision as if he were an executive reading aloud a favourite memo of his own composition. His concluding assurance, "And now nothing remains for me but to assure you in the most animated language of the violence of my affection" (106), is exorbitantly funny partly because the one thing remaining for him is to ask Elizabeth to marry him. She herself points out this omission, tactfully, when she interrupts him and says, "You are too hasty, Sir.... You forget that I have made no answer" (106).

One of the truly brilliant aspects of *Pride and Prejudice* is the unstated but inescapable parallel between Collins's proposal and the first proposal by Mr. Darcy. A marriage proposal, broken down to its lowest common denominator, consists of seven words, "I love you. Will you marry me?"—three words of telling and four words of asking. Mr. Collins and John Thorpe fail abysmally to convey the required elements. The unreformed Darcy begins his marriage proposal auspiciously: he bursts out with a heartfelt expression of his love: "In vain have I struggled. It will not do. My feelings will not be repressed. You must allow me to tell you how ardently I admire and love you" (189). However, as Elizabeth discovers, he is much better at telling than asking: "He concluded with representing to her the strength of that attachment which, in spite of all his endeavours, he had found impossible to conquer; and with expressing his hope that it would now be rewarded by her acceptance of his hand" (189). The grammar of this sentence sums up the situation: the subject of the sentence is "He," Elizabeth's capacity to choose is buried within the passive voice ("be rewarded") in a subordinate clause, and Darcy's asking Elizabeth to marry him has dwindled to near invisibility in the single, final word, "hand." Darcy, preoccupied with his own internal struggle, assumes Elizabeth will accept, just as Collins had. He, too, is not really asking. He tells Elizabeth at the end of the novel, "I believed you to be wishing, expecting my addresses" (369).

Collins at least makes himself understood, unlike John Thorpe, but he is unable to enter into rational conversation with his intended. Darcy, in contrast, proves that he is capable of such an exchange, both in the proposal scene itself and in the long letter that he writes to Elizabeth (a letter that really amounts to Darcy's Proposal, Part Two). During the proposal scene, Darcy and Elizabeth ask and answer a series of blunt questions: if he asks her why with so little effort at civility she has rejected him (190), she replies, "I might as well enquire...why with so evident a design of offending and insulting me, you chose to tell me that you liked me against your will, against your reason, and even against your character? Was not this some excuse for incivility, if I *was* uncivil?" (190).

Similarly, Mr. Elton proposes to Emma by telling, not asking: "I am sure you have seen and understood me.... Charming Miss Woodhouse! allow me to interpret this interesting silence. It confesses that you have long understood me" (*E* 131). And in *Mansfield Park*, Sir Thomas Bertram, echoing both Mr. Collins in his deliberation and Mr. Darcy in his grammar, relates Henry Crawford's marriage proposal to Fanny in one long, pompous sentence that presents him, Sir Thomas, as the agent and Fanny as a prepositional object:

> "And now, Fanny, having performed one part of my commission, and shewn you every thing placed on a basis the most assured and satisfactory, I may execute the remainder by prevailing on you to accompany me down stairs, where—though I cannot but presume on having been no unacceptable companion myself, I must submit to your finding one still better worth listening to.—Mr. Crawford, as you have perhaps foreseen, is yet in the house." (*MP* 314)

The successful proposals in Austen's novels show the man asking a genuine question—and leaving himself on tenterhooks. Mr. Knightley, ever the model, asks Emma, "Tell me, then, have I no chance of ever succeeding?...My dearest Emma,...tell me at once. Say 'No,' if it is to be said" (*E* 430). The reformed Mr. Darcy says to Elizabeth, "You are too generous to trifle with me. If your feelings are still what they were last April, tell me so at once. *My* affections and wishes are unchanged, but one word from you will silence me on this subject for ever" (*PP* 366). This time, Elizabeth is to do the telling, not Darcy. In *Persuasion*, Captain Wentworth proposes marriage in a letter to Anne that is Jane Austen's most expressive statement of love. The letter certainly contains the seven-word essence of a successful proposal: in it Wentworth tells Anne directly, "I have loved none but you," and "I offer myself to you"; he is, he says, "half agony, half hope," waiting for her reply (237).

Mr. Darcy's second proposal to Elizabeth, just cited, does not contain a question mark; Darcy's speech is in its purport a question but, literally and grammatically, it contains a series of statements. This fact leads me to an interesting point: though none of Austen's heroines overtly proposes to the man of her choice—as Amelia, the character played by Mary Crawford in *Lovers' Vows*, does so shockingly in *Mansfield Park*—several of Austen's heroines do in fact implicitly ask the crucial question. The clearest case is Elizabeth Bennet, who brings on Darcy's proposal with a carefully considered speech:

> Mr. Darcy, I am a very selfish creature; and, for the sake of giving relief to my own feelings, care not how much I may be wounding your's. I can no longer help thanking you for your unexampled kindness to my poor sister. Ever since I have known it, I have been most anxious to acknowledge to you how gratefully I feel it. Were it known to the rest of my family, I should not have merely my own gratitude to express.... Let me thank you again and again, in the name of all my family, for that generous compassion which induced you to take so much trouble, and bear so many mortifications, for the sake of discovering them. (*PP* 365–66)

Literally speaking, Elizabeth asks Darcy no questions, but implicitly she is asking him a question that she has been wondering about ever since she heard of Darcy's rescue of Lydia: has he done it for her (326)? Darcy is given the opening to make the reply she hopes for ("I thought only of *you*"), and his proposal follows immediately (366). When Elizabeth and Darcy, after the fact, talk over the sequence of events that led up to his proposal, Elizabeth admits that she took the initiative: "I wonder how long you *would* have gone on, if you had been left to yourself. I wonder when you *would* have spoken, if I had not asked you! My resolution of thanking you for your kindness to Lydia had certainly great effect" (381). Elizabeth had earlier signalled to Darcy her willingness to be asked the question when she refused Lady Catherine's request to promise that she would never become engaged to Darcy (356). By saying no, Elizabeth is letting Darcy know that she will say yes. As soon as Lady Catherine leaves, Elizabeth reflects, "From what she had said of her resolution to prevent their marriage,...she must meditate an application to her nephew" (360). Darcy tells Elizabeth that he was greatly encouraged as soon as he was told by an outraged Lady Catherine that Elizabeth had refused to make the desired promise:

> It taught me to hope...as I had scarcely ever allowed myself to hope before. I knew enough of your disposition to be certain, that, had you been absolutely, irrevocably decided against me, you would have acknowledged it to Lady Catherine, frankly and openly [and, he implies, taken great delight in doing so]. (367)

Emma Woodhouse is another heroine who, in effect, asks the question that leads to her suitor asking the question. We see this acted out in the scene that leads to their dancing together at the Crown Inn. This scene foreshadows and enacts in dumb show Mr. Knightley's subsequent proposal to Emma. At the Crown Inn, Emma and Mr. Knightley have come closer together than ever before, following his rescue of Harriet (and Emma) from Mr. Elton's snub on the dance floor:

> They were interrupted by the bustle of Mr. Weston calling on every body to begin dancing again.

"Come Miss Woodhouse, Miss Otway, Miss Fairfax, what are you all doing?—Come Emma, set your companions the example. Every body is lazy! Every body is asleep!"

"I am ready," said Emma, "whenever I am wanted."

"Whom are you going to dance with?" asked Mr. Knightley.

She hesitated a moment, and then replied, "With you, if you will ask me."

"Will you?" said he, offering his hand. (*E* 331)

Emma has clearly asked Mr. Knightley to ask, and she does as much in the proposal scene itself. When Emma tells him that she is determined to keep his friendship and to continue to enjoy his conversation, no matter what the cost to her, Mr. Knightley decides that this offer has a double meaning:

"I stopped you ungraciously just now, Mr. Knightley, and, I am afraid, gave you pain.—But if you have any wish to speak openly to me as a friend, or to ask my opinion of any thing you may have in contemplation—as a friend, indeed, you may command me.—I will hear whatever you like. I will tell you exactly what I think."

"As a friend!"—repeated Mr. Knightley.—"Emma, that I fear is a word—No, I have no wish—Stay, yes, why should I hesitate?—I have gone too far already for concealment. Emma, I accept your offer—Extraordinary as it may seem, I accept it, and refer myself to you as a friend.—Tell me, then, have I no chance of ever succeeding?" (429-30)

The proposal scene of Wentworth and Anne in *Persuasion* presents Anne as the initiator of the crucial question. Wentworth's letter is written as a running commentary on a conversation that occurs in a different part of the room between Anne and Wentworth's friend, Captain Harville, a conversation that Anne has good reason to believe that Wentworth can hear, and a conversation in which she states her belief that women's love is deeper and more constant than men's (232–35). Anne's speeches in this debate constitute her implicit answer to an equally implicit question ("Do you still love me?") that Wentworth has been asking her more and more insistently since his return to Bath—a question implied, for instance, when he asks her whether she is disgusted by the memory of their expedition to Lyme (183–84) and also when he asks if she still, after all these years, takes no enjoyment in card-parties (225). Anne's secret answer to Wentworth's secret question is clear: "Yes, I still love you, and as much as ever," and this answer, of course, implicitly asks Wentworth another question: "What are you going to do now?"

I would like to turn now from proposals to the issue of self-knowledge. If only a person who can ask genuine questions—consultative questions—can converse, then we can go one step further and say that only a person who can ask real questions can think and develop. After Mr. Bennet has read aloud Mr. Collins's letter to the Bennets, telling them that he has decided to invite himself to visit them and that he will be arriving Monday, 18 November, at four o'clock, the reactions of the Bennet family are revealing. Mrs. Bennet says, "There is some sense in what he says about the girls,...and if he is disposed to make them any amends, I shall not be the person to discourage him." Jane remarks, "Though it is difficult...to guess in what way he can mean to make us the atonement he thinks our due, the wish is certainly to his credit." Mary adds, "In point of composition,...his letter does not seem defective. The idea of the olive branch perhaps is not wholly new, yet I think it is well expressed" (*PP* 63–64). Kitty and Lydia are too preoccupied with officers to take any interest in the letter or its writer. Only Elizabeth asks questions of her father: "He must be an oddity, I think.... I cannot make him out.—There is something very pompous in his stile.—And what can he mean by apologizing for being next in the entail.—We cannot suppose he would help it, if he could.—Can he be a sensible man, sir?" (64). Elizabeth can think, and that is evident in her ability to ask real questions.

However, for the first half of the novel Elizabeth is determined to tell, not ask, and so she abuses her intelligence and finds herself deluded about the most important events going on around her. When she and Jane are discussing whether or not to believe Wickham's account of Darcy, Jane is unable to decide, but Elizabeth tells her sister, "I beg your pardon;—one knows exactly what to think" (86). If one knows exactly what to think, questions are superfluous. Elizabeth changes once she has read Darcy's letter and admitted that she has been completely wrong in her beliefs about both Darcy and Wickham. She realizes, "As to [Wickham's] real character, had information been in her power, she had never felt a wish of enquiring" (206). Elizabeth means both that she failed to ask others about Wickham's character and that she failed to ask herself about why she was so partial to him. In other words, the question-and-answer method is not only the way that two or more people converse; it is also the way that the individual comes to understand herself or himself.

In the second half of *Pride and Prejudice*, Elizabeth asks herself a series of important questions. For instance, during her painstaking, two-hour consideration of Darcy's letter, after changing her opinion of Wickham, she turns to Darcy's explanation of his behaviour towards Jane and Bingley, and asks herself, "How could she deny that credit to his assertions, in one instance, which she had been obliged to give in the other?" (208). When she is at Pemberley and hears Mrs. Reynolds, the housekeeper, praise his good nature as a child, "Elizabeth almost stared at her.—'Can this be Mr. Darcy!' thought she" (249). When a few minutes later, to the surprise of both, she meets Darcy himself, she asks herself a series of questions, ending with the most important one: "And his behaviour, so strikingly altered,—what could it mean?" (252). She finds Darcy's behaviour even more puzzling when, near the novel's end, he visits the Bennets' home with Bingley, but seems strangely silent and distant. Elizabeth is no longer someone who knows exactly what to think. In fact, she asks herself a series of tough questions:

> Could I expect it to be otherwise!...Yet why did he come?...Why, if he came only to be silent, grave, and indifferent,...did he come at all?...He could be still amiable, still pleasing, to my uncle and aunt, when he was in town; and why not to me? If he fears me, why come hither? If he no longer cares for me, why silent?...A man who has once been refused! How could I ever be foolish enough to expect a renewal of his love? Is there one among the sex, who would not protest against such a weakness as a second proposal to the same woman? (336–41)

Elizabeth, like Austen's other heroines as the plot nears its climax, is as much on tenterhooks as the man whose question she awaits.

The importance of asking oneself hard questions becomes clear if we look at two parallel chapters in *Emma*. In volume 1, chapter 16, Emma has been shocked out of her delusions about Harriet and Mr. Elton when Mr. Elton unexpectedly proposes to her. After castigating herself for her mistakes, she "resolve[s] to do such things no more" (137). As the novel nears its climax, Emma receives a much more complex series of shocks when she discovers that Frank Churchill and Jane Fairfax are secretly engaged; that Harriet, far from caring for Frank, loves Mr. Knightley and believes her love returned; and that she herself loves Mr. Knightley and has done so all along. Once again she realizes that she has been deluded and resolves to reform.

However, in the first self-discovery scene, Emma emphatically tells herself that she has been mistaken:

> The first error and the worst lay at her door. It was foolish, it was wrong, to take so active a part in bringing any two people together. It was adventuring too far, assuming too much, making light of what ought to be serious, a trick of what ought to be simple. She was quite concerned and ashamed, and resolved to do such things no more. (136–37)

The phrase "quite concerned and ashamed" signals that Emma's discoveries have barely made a dent in her complacency, and in fact half a page later she catches herself surmising that the young lawyer William Coxe might be desirable for Harriet. In the five pages devoted to Emma's thoughts in this scene, she does not ask herself a single genuine question. She does begin her attempts at self-analysis with some promising words, "How she could have been so deceived!" (134), but Austen suggests that this is a pseudo-question by having the words followed by an exclamation point, not a question mark, and just ten lines later, after reviewing Elton's ingratiating manners and his charade of a courtship, Emma apparently asks herself a question, "Who could have seen through such thickheaded nonsense?" (134). However, this is a rhetorical question allowing Emma to persuade herself that questions are pointless.

Things are very different in the second self-discovery scene, in which Emma does come to understand her motives and does feel that, apart from her newly understood love for Mr. Knightley, "Every other part of her mind was disgusting" (412). During this second scene, her thoughts progress by means of a barrage of questions:

How long had Mr. Knightley been so dear to her, as every feeling declared him now to be? When had his influence, such influence begun?—When had he succeeded to that place in her affection, which Frank Churchill had once, for a short period, occupied?... Was it a new circumstance for a man of first-rate abilities to be captivated by very inferior powers? Was it new for one, perhaps too busy to seek, to be the prize of a girl who would seek him?—Was it new for any thing in this world to be unequal, inconsistent, incongruous—or for chance and circumstance (as second causes) to direct the human fate?...How Harriet could ever have had the presumption to raise her thoughts to Mr. Knightley!...Alas! was not that her own doing too? Who had been at pains to give Harriet notions of self-consequence but herself?—Who but herself had taught her, that she was to elevate herself if possible, and that her claims were great to a high worldly establishment? (412–14)

These are not rhetorical questions, but consultative questions (for instance, "How long had Mr. Knightley been so dear to her?"). Emma is no longer telling, but asking herself what she thinks.

We can see the same connection between self-questioning and coming to understand oneself near the end of *Sense and Sensibility*. Marianne tells her sister Elinor, "My illness has made me think— It has given me leisure and calmness for serious recollection" (345). Marianne's long "self-reproving" (346) speech that follows shows that, after spending the novel up to this point telling others and herself exactly what she thinks, she has begun to ask herself questions about herself: "Your example was before me: but to what avail?—Was I more considerate of you and your comfort? Did I imitate your forbearance, or lessen your restraints, by taking any part in those offices of general complaisance or particular gratitude which you had hitherto been left to discharge alone?" (304). These may sound like rhetorical questions, and they certainly have allowed Marianne to persuade herself, but it might be more satisfying to see them as an instance of a general truth, if not a truth universally acknowledged, that to ask a question is to be most of the way toward arriving at the answer to it. For instance, when Emma finally reaches the point at which she can ask herself how long Mr. Knightley has been so dear to her, she quickly realizes "there never had been a time" when she did not love him (E 412).

In this essay, I have been in the position of telling my thoughts on asking versus telling, real questions and rhetorical questions, telling and asking in proposal scenes, and learning to ask oneself questions. My reader is in the more taxing position of asking himself or herself what to make of these ideas. And so the conversation goes on.

 # "A Contrariety of Emotion"

Jane Austen's Ambivalent Lovers in Pride and Prejudice

THE OXFORD ENGLISH DICTIONARY defines *ambivalence* as "[t]he coexistence in one person of contradictory emotions or attitudes (as love and hatred) towards a person or thing," and this concept would seem to apply precisely to *Pride and Prejudice*. During the first half of the novel, the central couple, Elizabeth and Darcy, are held together by just such contradictory feelings. Like Beatrice and Benedick in *Much Ado about Nothing*, each is the one the other loves to hate—and hates to love. And, like Beatrice and Benedick, the two lovers are matched in every way, including disdain for the other, and each finds the other a fascinating and inescapable object of attention. That unwilling attraction to the other makes each hate the other as a threat to his or her pride and emotional independence. But one lover's expression of this hatred only increases the other's fascination: the power of the fascination increases the threat, which intensifies the expressions of hatred. This vicious circle can only be broken when the lovers fully accept their love and dismiss their hatred—that is, when their feelings for each other are no longer ambivalent.

Yet *ambivalence* is a word that entered the language only in this century, so it is well to be cautious in applying it to *Pride and*

Prejudice. Not only was Austen's novel composed over 200 years ago, but in it she seems to attack love-as-attraction, a notion presupposed in the idea of emotional ambivalence. We know that the first version of *Pride and Prejudice*, written in 1796–1797, was called "First Impressions"; although Austen dropped the title before her novel was published in 1813 (another novel with that title had been published in 1801),[1] she suggests why she chose the original title late in the novel, after Elizabeth has seen the change in Darcy's manners at Pemberley and feels it can only be due to her influence (Chapman xi):

> If gratitude and esteem are good foundations of affection, Elizabeth's change of sentiment will be neither improbable nor faulty. But if otherwise, if the regard springing from such sources is unreasonable or unnatural, in comparison of what is so often described as arising on a first interview with its object, and even before two words have been exchanged, nothing can be said in her defence, except that she had given somewhat of a trial to the latter method, in her partiality for Wickham, and that its ill-success might perhaps authorise her to seek the other less interesting mode of attachment. (*Pride and Prejudice [PP]* 279)

Like *Sense and Sensibility*, the one novel that precedes it in Austen's career, *Pride and Prejudice* seems designed to discredit romantic love, or love at first sight, and to elevate instead "a less interesting mode of attachment": love grounded in a knowledge of the other's character.

Apart from the question of authorial intention, there is another reason for caution: many of Austen's most persuasive critics see no such ambivalence in the attitudes of Elizabeth and Darcy towards each other. True, many readers have clearly delighted in the lovers' ambivalence, whether or not the term was in existence to describe it. The anonymous reviewer of the novel in *Critical Review* for March 1813, for instance, says of Elizabeth, "She is in fact the *Beatrice* of the tale; and falls in love on much the same principles of contrariety" ("Unsigned review, *Critical Review*" 44). Writing in 1917, Reginald Farrer argued that, as in *Emma*, the heroine of *Pride and Prejudice* is "subconsciously...in love with" the hero from the start—but that in the earlier novel the author failed to make her heroine's real feelings clear ("[Truth]" 344). And several modern critics consider Darcy's and Elizabeth's feelings towards each other as ambivalent, though none, to my knowledge, uses the term; David Monaghan, for example, notes that Elizabeth's acts of rudeness to Darcy "[derive] from an unconscious need to deny that, for all his faults, she finds Darcy attractive" (66). In contrast, however, many acute modern commentators find no such depth of psychology in *Pride and Prejudice*. Susan Morgan, for example, says, "For much of the story, Mr. Darcy cares for Elizabeth in spite of herself, and she does not care for him at all" (82). And Joseph Wiesenfarth says much the same: "Darcy comes to think that Elizabeth loves him whereas she could not care less for him because of the way she feels about his treatment of Jane and of Wickham" (63). Howard S. Babb says of Elizabeth that "the opposition of her whole nature to Darcy" brings about "the chief dramatic effect of the story: overwhelming surprise at his first proposal" (136, 114). And Marilyn Butler, in her convincing account of Austen's moral thinking, *Jane Austen and the War of Ideas*, suggests that Austen meant to ridicule the whole notion of love at first sight by offering hate at first sight: "it is clear that to her love at first sight and hate at first sight are essentially the same. Both are emotional responses, built on insufficient or wrong evidence, and fostered by pride and complacency toward the unreliable subjective consciousness" (213). Thus, she believes, the second half of the novel is necessarily drawn out: "Jane Austen has to allow time...for Elizabeth to change her emotional antipathy for Darcy into a predisposition to love him" (209).

Butler, Babb, Wiesenfarth, and Morgan are all primarily concerned with tracing the moral changes within Austen's protagonists; they analyze moral patterns embedded within Austen's plot, characters, and authorial commentary, and show little interest in psychological analysis. But *Pride and Prejudice* is comic, and comedy has a both/and rather than an either/or vision. The novel invites us to see in its protagonists both a moral pattern and a psychological state, just as its plot shows Elizabeth and Darcy each combining, by the end, the apparent opposites of pride and humility, just as Elizabeth learns to combine her sister's charity with her own judgement, and just as the marriage of Darcy and Elizabeth unites the unalloyed calculation embodied in the hasty and furtive union of Collins and Charlotte with the unalloyed impulse embodied in the equally hasty and furtive union of Wickham and Lydia. This harmonizing, inclusive vision has irony as its technical instrument. What is stated is less important than what is implied. Austen was speaking of *Pride and Prejudice* when, in a letter to her sister, she adapted a couplet from Scott to describe her style: "I do not write for such dull Elves / As have not a great deal of Ingenuity themselves" (*Jane Austen's Letters [JAL]* 202). Thus, any one act or speech in the novel may carry both a moral and a psychological sense, and each sense will then support the other. Elizabeth, for instance, tells Jane at the start of volume 2 that "There are few people whom I really love, and still fewer of whom I think well" (*PP* 135). Morally, Elizabeth is engaged in protecting herself from her own sharp intelligence: she has been humiliated by Charlotte's defection, but rather than asking why she has been so mistaken about Charlotte's character, she considers Charlotte's choice of Collins unaccountable and the world unsatisfactory. At the same time, she reminds us of her psychological predicament: she cannot think well of the people (Darcy included) whom she loves. The moral and psychological implications do not conflict, but illuminate and enrich each other.

Therefore, the question of authorial intention should be approached with this sense of the novel's comic and ironic inclusiveness in mind. Austen may well be presenting in Elizabeth and Darcy's relationship both an ideal form of love, one grounded in a well-tested respect for each other's character, and a more immediate and magnetic attraction. If we think about the passage in which she defends Elizabeth's "less interesting mode of attachment," several counterbalancing implications emerge. For one thing, the novel shows that Bingley and Jane loved each other deeply and truly from their first meeting. "Oh! she is the most beautiful creature I ever beheld," the smitten Bingley says of Jane at the Meryton assembly (11). Furthermore, Elizabeth did not actually give romantic love much of a trial in her partiality for Wickham, since he appeals to Elizabeth, not in himself, but as a weapon she can use in her merry war against Darcy. When we are told, "Elizabeth thought with pleasure of dancing a great deal with Mr. Wickham," the sentence continues, "and of seeing a confirmation of every thing in Mr. Darcy's looks and behaviour" (86). If her response to Wickham shows the unreliability of immediate physical attraction as a basis for love, it also shows the strength of the unacknowledged attraction that binds Elizabeth to Darcy. And if Austen's defence of "the other less interesting mode of attachment" insists that the rational love between her central pair possesses dignity, serenity, and security, that does not preclude their having reached this plateau in volume 3 by a less than smooth and straightforward path during volumes 1 and 2. Their attainment of rational love is even more impressive when we realize the deeply irrational impulses from which it has grown.

In fact, virtually all of Austen's pronouncements on Elizabeth's feelings towards Darcy occur in the second half of the novel: once his letter has been received, Darcy himself is largely absent—but Elizabeth's need to define her attitude towards him is pressing, and so we follow Elizabeth as she reviews "the whole of their acquaintance, so full of contradictions and varieties" (279), and moves from credence to respect to approval to esteem to gratitude to affection and the realization that "he was exactly the man, who, in disposition and talents, would most suit her" (312). But in the first half of the novel, Darcy, with all his dispositions and talents, is before Elizabeth, at least for the most part, and there is no occasion for her to define her feelings about him, since those feelings are of no real interest to her. If she notices during her stay at Netherfield that Mr. Darcy looks at her frequently, she assumes it must be caused by marked disapproval, and decides, "She liked him too little to care for his approbation" (51). Apart from this one ironic summary—ironic because Elizabeth cannot see how much she does like Darcy, how much she does care for his approbation—the novel's hero remains during these scenes, to the heroine, simply "*that* abominable Mr. Darcy!" (144).

In short, despite the novel's original title and the author's comment upon the nature of love, nothing in the novel invalidates, and much encourages, the view that Austen invites us to contemplate a hero and heroine who get to know each other by loving to hate and hating to love. When, halfway through the novel, Elizabeth is forced by Darcy's letter to look back over her thoughts and actions, she castigates herself in very suggestive terms: "How humiliating is this discovery!—Yet, how just a humiliation!—Had I been in love, I could not have been more wretchedly blind. But vanity, not love, has been my folly" (208). Elizabeth, it would seem, even in her great moment of self-recognition, is still protecting herself from full self-knowledge. A further clue to the presence of irony here lies in Elizabeth's self-accusation of vanity, and not pride. In the fifth chapter, Mary Bennet proudly distinguishes between these two apparent synonyms: "Pride relates more to our opinion of ourselves, vanity to what we would have others think of us"

(20); Darcy continues this distinction six chapters later, replying, when Elizabeth obliquely accuses him of vanity and pride: "Yes, vanity is a weakness indeed. But pride—where there is a real superiority of mind, pride will always be under good regulation" (57). In short, Elizabeth should accuse herself of pride in her own superiority of mind, not vanity. Like Darcy, she is proud to be vain—and too proud to admit, at least yet, that she has been so wretchedly blind just because she *has* been in love.[2] Love, not vanity, has been her folly, but this fool will persist in her folly and become wise.

Elizabeth and Darcy, then, neither love nor hate at first sight, but fall quickly into a love-hate relationship that they do not recognize as such. Elizabeth admits something of the sort when Jane asks her at the end of the novel how long she has loved Darcy: "It has been coming on so gradually, that I hardly know when it began" (373). Darcy makes the same confession to Elizabeth: "I was in the middle before I knew that I *had* begun" (380). This ambivalence is highlighted by the symmetrical way in which each lover's feelings mirror the other's during the three main sections of the novel: the episodes leading up to Darcy's proposal; the proposal scene and ensuing letter (which together form the novel's centre); and the whole second half of the novel, which follows from this central episode.

During the first section of the novel, the two lovers seem to be in different predicaments: Darcy is aware that he loves, and he makes conscious advances toward Elizabeth; she is unaware of the love she feels for him, and her advances toward him are unintentional. At the same time, though, the lovers, as lovers, are mirror images of each other: each loves and yet struggles to conquer that love. If Darcy finds, after spending two days in Elizabeth's company at Netherfield, that "She attracted him more than he liked" (59), Elizabeth has exactly the same divided response to him, although she does not realize it. And so she flirts with Darcy: she teases him, taunts him, quarrels with his statements, throws his past words in his face, points out his character defects, criticizes his treatment of his friends and his enemies, takes delight in vexing him—all without realizing that her assumption of easy freedom and intimate concern encourages him to believe that she sees his love and welcomes it. Like Emma with Mr. Elton, Elizabeth must make the humiliating discovery that she had led her suitor on to propose: "I believed you to be wishing, expecting my addresses," Darcy tells her at the novel's end (369). There is ironic accuracy, then, in Darcy's statement to her at Rosings: "I have had the pleasure of your acquaintance long enough to know, that you find great enjoyment in occasionally professing opinions which in fact are not your own" (174). Austen leaves Elizabeth's viewpoint frequently during volume 1 to give us glimpses of Darcy's growing love and of his struggle against that love; these glimpses force us to see Elizabeth's comic ignorance, not only of Darcy's inner conflict, but, by implication, of her own as well.[3]

Darcy's proposal culminates and epitomizes this ambivalent courtship. His offer of marriage is meant to express his love, but unintentionally expresses hatred: he confesses that he proposes against his will, against his reason, and even against his character (189). Elizabeth, in contrast, is vehement in her anger and intends to wound, yet her very vehemence is a sign that she feels more than she realizes. This is part of the point in Austen's careful paralleling of Collins's proposal to Elizabeth with Darcy's. Elizabeth feels no anger towards Collins, no matter how insulting he becomes (and he does tell her that she is unlikely ever to receive another offer of marriage, since her expectations only amount to one thousand pounds in the four per cents). Collins is a fool, and Elizabeth knows that "His regard for her was quite imaginary" (112). However, she realizes that Darcy is more worthy of her and does, in his way, love her, but with a love that undervalues her own, and this is why she is so hurt and vindictive in their great confrontation.

Elizabeth's accusations instigate Darcy to write his long letter to her. It is this letter and not Darcy's proposal that constitutes "the chief dramatic effect of the story" (to use Babb's words, quoted above): Elizabeth may feel overwhelming surprise when Darcy proposes, but we hardly do, since Austen has prepared us for it by the narrative shifts to Darcy's viewpoint during volume 1 and by an increasingly obvious series of hints during the scenes at Rosings (a series something like the signs of Elton's intentions that Emma resolutely ignores). The letter, however, is completely unexpected, and creates a decisive change in the relationship of Elizabeth and Darcy. Like the proposal, the letter epitomizes the ambivalent feelings of both the speaker and his auditor. Darcy begins in bitter hauteur—"Be not alarmed, Madam, on receiving this letter, by the apprehension of its containing any repetition of those sentiments, or renewal of those offers, which were last night so disgusting to you" (196)—and the tone of wounded pride, of vindicating himself at her expense, is clear when he appeals to her justice and refers to the letter as "the explanation...which is due to myself" (197). But, despite appearances, Darcy's letter is really a love letter, as his candour, his scrupulous fairness, his respect for Elizabeth's judgement, the care with which he accounts for his actions, and the confidential revelation about Wickham's attempted seduction of his sister all confess. The letter ends with a sentence—"I will only add, God bless you" (203)—that Elizabeth considers to be "charity itself" (368). If the letter is written out of divided feelings, Elizabeth responds to it with "a contrariety of emotion.... Her feelings as she read were scarcely to be defined" (204). At a first reading, "It was all pride and insolence" (204); she is then indignant, incredulous, ashamed, humiliated in turn. After two hours of wandering in the Hunsford lane, "giving way to every variety of thought," she returns home, fatigued by "a change so sudden and so important" (209). That change is summarized by Elizabeth's reflections after she meets Darcy again at Pemberley some four months later: "she lay awake two whole hours, endeavouring to make [her feelings] out. She certainly did not hate him. No; hatred had vanished long ago, and she had almost as long been ashamed of ever feeling a dislike against him, that could be so called" (265).

These last words suggest the change that occurs within both Elizabeth and Darcy during the second half of the novel: not only does hatred of the other vanish, but its place is taken by shame and humiliation, hatred turned inward. Elizabeth cries, "How despicably have I acted!" (208), about her treatment of Darcy, and he says of his proposal to her, "I cannot think of it without abhorrence" (367). In the first half of the novel, each directed hatred outward in order to protect a love turned inward, a self-love: what Darcy says in the closing pages is equally true of Elizabeth: "I was...allowed, encouraged, almost taught...to think meanly of all the rest of the world, to *wish* at least to think meanly of their sense and worth compared with my own" (369). In the second half, each of them, by a painful act of will caused by the need to love and be loved, reverses this emotional balance, and loves outwardly and hates inwardly. Each finds that mutual love is preferable to self-love enjoyed in isolation. By an elegant homeopathy of the emotions, the expression of hatred has driven out hatred in each case: "How you must have hated me after *that* evening?" Elizabeth asks Darcy at the novel's end, and he replies, "Hate you! I was angry perhaps at first, but my anger soon began to take a proper direction" (369). And Darcy adds that his letter contained "some expressions which might justly make you hate me" (368)—but, of course, Elizabeth learns Darcy's letter by heart, studies every sentence of it, reveals it to no one, and "her anger was turned toward herself" (212). This inner redirection causes a change in behaviour, and each lover moves, tentatively and indirectly, toward the other. Darcy's manners are transformed, and he rescues the Bennet family from disgrace, even becoming best man at Wickham's marriage to Lydia; Elizabeth allows herself to be taken to Pemberley and, after meeting Darcy there, instinctively seeks his sympathy and help by telling him of Lydia's elopement (a confession that parallels and answers his unprovoked confession about *his* sister's relations with Wickham). Amusingly, as love replaces ambivalence in Elizabeth and Darcy, humility and diffidence supplant pride and prejudice, so that their sparkling duels of wit give way to tongue-tied, blushing, floor-scrutinizing encounters that would make Bingley and Jane seem brash and poised by comparison. At the novel's end, the two of them, and all of us, can be grateful, not only to Lady Catherine's attempts to separate them, but to the ambivalence that drew them together.

This psychology of ambivalence is not evident in *Sense and Sensibility*[4] or any of the obvious models for *Pride and Prejudice*, such as Fanny Burney's *Evelina*. Where did Austen discover this new and rich conception? We will never know, of course, but it is interesting to speculate. The idea is consistent with the thinking of Samuel Johnson, Austen's particular authority on moral and religious questions: "Inconsistencies," Imlac points out in chapter 8 of Samuel Johnson's *Rasselas*, "cannot both be right, but, imputed to man, they may both be true" (Johnson, *History* 348). Richardson's self-divided and self-contradictory lovers—particularly Lovelace and Clarissa—may have contributed something to Austen's psychology of love. Perhaps the literary precursors of Elizabeth and Darcy are the wilful heroes and heroines of stage comedy, Shakespeare's Beatrice and Benedick, but also their progeny on the Restoration and eighteenth-century stage, such as Congreve's Mirabell and Millamant. The real source for Elizabeth and Darcy, however, was probably Austen's observation of actual people. Just as many, perhaps most, readers of *Pride and Prejudice* are reminded of real-life counterparts of Mr. Bennet (whose character also lacks a clear literary precedent), so versions of the Elizabeth–Darcy mating dance abound in everyday life. It is a striking fact that the Beatrice–Benedick plot of *Much Ado about Nothing* is the one story in all of Shakespeare's plays that has no known literary source. Similarly, Austen might well have said of Elizabeth Bennet's contrariety of emotion what she says about her heroine at the end of *Northanger Abbey*. After explaining that Henry Tilney came to love Catherine Morland simply because he could see that she loved him, Austen adds, "It is a new circumstance in romance, I acknowledge, and dreadfully derogatory of an heroine's dignity; but if it be as new in common life, the credit of a wild imagination will at least be all my own" (243).

NOTES

1. See Robert Chapman's "Introductory Note" to the Oxford edition of *Pride and Prejudice* (xi–xiii).
2. Andrew H. Wright has noted this irony (113–14).
3. E. M. Halliday makes some important points about the effect of these changes in narrative viewpoint in his article "Narrative Perspective in *Pride and Prejudice*."
4. A first version of *Sense and Sensibility*, entitled *Elinor and Marianne*, was completed before Jane Austen began "First Impressions" in late 1796. See Chapman's introductory note (xi).

 # Once More, with Feeling
The Structure of Mansfield Park

THIS ESSAY ATTEMPTS TO OUTLINE the structure or design of *Mansfield Park*: the large arc that unifies the novel and provides its spine. What might be the equivalent in this novel of alternating between the courtships of two sisters by enigmatic suitors in *Sense and Sensibility*, or the love–hate relationship between Elizabeth and Darcy that unifies *Pride and Prejudice*? My view is that *Mansfield Park*, the first novel of the three that Austen would compose in her final years, develops in its first volume a rising action and climax that are mirrored exactly in the main events of volumes 2 and 3 of the novel. In the theatricals episode that occupies the last six chapters of volume 1, the heroine Fanny Price finds herself isolated and on the defensive, pressured to join the play and accused of ingratitude when she resists the wishes of the entire family, including her one friend and mentor, Edmund. Volume 1 climaxes when Sir Thomas Bertram unexpectedly returns; the play is never acted, and order is restored to the house. In the main events of volumes 2 and 3, Fanny faces a second and much more intense ordeal: she once again opposes the wishes of the household, including Edmund, when she refuses Henry Crawford's marriage proposal, and once again she is pressured and accused of ingratitude.

129

Order is finally restored to Mansfield Park, but only after a terrible sequence of events triggered by Fanny's steadfast resistance to Henry Crawford. This use of volume 1 as a self-contained prologue to the main action is a structure that Austen would elaborate in her next novel, *Emma*, in which volume 1 presents the heroine's fiasco as a matchmaker for Mr. Elton and Harriet, and volumes 2 and 3 a strikingly similar, but much more devious and hard to detect, imaginary courtship created, not by Emma, but by Frank Churchill.

I have to confess that critics and readers of *Mansfield Park* have not seen the structure of the novel in this way—but I have some consolation: as the narrator remarks cheerfully in the final pages of *Northanger Abbey*, "the credit of a wild imagination will at least be all my own" (243).

When the young people at Mansfield Park decide to act out a play in Sir Thomas's absence, Fanny is at first left out of consideration, as befits her status as a dependant, in fact a semi-servant, in the household. However, once the actors have decided on a play, *Lovers' Vows*, and parcelled out the parts, Tom Bertram, master of the house in his father's absence, decides that Fanny must play the part of Cottager's Wife. Fanny politely refuses, saying repeatedly, "I cannot act" (Austen, *Mansfield Park [MP]* 145). The scene escalates as Maria, Henry Crawford, and Mr. Yates join Tom in urging Fanny to act—and Edmund, "kindly observing her, but unwilling to exasperate his brother by interference, gave her only an encouraging smile" (146). At this point, Mrs. Norris angrily says to Fanny, "What a piece of work here is about nothing,—I am quite ashamed of you, Fanny, to make such a difficulty of obliging your cousins in a trifle of this sort,—So kind as they are to you!" Edmund finally speaks up in Fanny's defense: "It is not fair to urge her in this manner.—You see she does not like to act.—Let her choose for herself as well as the rest of us." Mrs. Norris then states, "I am not going to urge her,…but I shall think her a very obstinate, ungrateful girl, if she does not do what her aunt and cousins wish her—very ungrateful indeed, considering who and what she is" (146–47).

Mrs. Norris's words spell out uncomfortably what everyone in the novel thinks of as Fanny's identity: a grateful dependant, lifted out of squalor by the generosity of the Bertram family. Edmund's claim that Fanny is capable of choosing for herself and cannot be called on for obedience by rote underlines an important irony: Fanny disapproves deeply of the whole theatrical project, and so her statement that she cannot act hides a condemnation of her betters that she feels strongly, but also feels unable to state openly. Fanny plans to lay her dilemma before Edmund the next morning in her sitting room, the East room, but is devastated when Edmund appears and tells her that he has decided to join the cast himself in order—he says—to spare Mary Crawford the pain of acting with a stranger (154).

This same sequence of events, but writ much larger, occurs at the start of volume 3 when Sir Thomas, incredulous that Fanny has rejected the match with Henry Crawford that he has been promoting, browbeats Fanny in words that are loftier, but every bit as cruel, as patronizing, and as mistaken as Mrs. Norris's in volume 1:

> I had thought you peculiarly free from willfulness of temper, self-conceit, and every tendency to that independence of spirit, which prevails so much in modern days..., and which in young women is offensive and disgusting beyond all common offence. But you have now shewn me that you can be wilful and perverse, that you can and will decide for yourself, without any consideration or deference for those who have surely some right to guide you—without even asking their advice.... You do not owe me the duty of a child. But, Fanny, if your heart can acquit you of *ingratitude*—... (318–19)

Sir Thomas speaks these words in the East room, one of many ways in which this scene reprises Fanny's ordeal in volume 1. As the ensuing chapters make clear, Sir Thomas speaks for the whole household: even Lady Bertram, even Edmund, urge Fanny to, in Edmund's words, "prove yourself grateful and tender-hearted" and accept Henry Crawford (347). Once again, Fanny is utterly alone, deserted by the one person she has relied on as a guide, Edmund—and, as in the theatricals episode, Fanny simply has to say no and continue saying no.

Another similarity is that in volume 1 Sir Thomas is absent and his authority rests with his scapegrace elder son, Tom, while in volumes 2 and 3 Sir Thomas is physically present, but the control of events lies in the hands of Mr. Crawford—a loss of authority symbolized neatly by Sir Thomas's arrangement to have Fanny meet with Crawford and explain her refusal in his own study. Further, she is once again not free to explain her decision. She cannot tell Sir Thomas the whole truth about her response to Crawford's proposal: she does say to Sir Thomas that it is "quite out of my power to return [Mr. Crawford's] good opinion" (314), but she feels she would be betraying her cousin Maria if she were to tell him what she knows about Crawford's character as a result of observing the flirtation between him and Maria during the theatricals (318). She does tell Sir Thomas that "I cannot like [Mr. Crawford]...well enough to marry him" (315), but she does not tell him that she has the right to marry for love and not to be overwhelmed, as Sir Thomas himself is, by the appeal of Mr. Crawford's wealth and status. And, of course, she does not tell Sir Thomas that her love for Edmund is a primary obstacle.

The narrator's language in each case underlines these similarities. The morning following Tom's pronouncement and Mrs. Norris's attack, alone in the East room, Fanny reflects:

> To be called into notice in such a manner, to hear that it was but the prelude to something so infinitely worse, to be told that she must

do what was so impossible as to act; and then to have the charge of obstinacy and ingratitude follow it, enforced with such a hint at the dependence of her situation, had been too distressing at the time, to make the remembrance when she was alone much less so. (150)

This is a periodic sentence rising in gradations to the climactic words "obstinacy...ingratitude...dependence." Compare Fanny's thoughts right after Sir Thomas's speech: "Her heart was almost broke by such a picture of what she appeared to him; by such accusations, so heavy, so multiplied, so rising in dreadful gradation! Self-willed, obstinate, selfish, and ungrateful" (319).

In both cases, external events unexpectedly end the stalemate between Fanny and the Bertram household: Sir Thomas returns in the very final lines of volume 1 and prevents *Lovers' Vows* from being enacted or even formally rehearsed; Fanny's second ordeal ends abruptly when Maria leaves her husband and runs away with Henry Crawford near the end of the novel. And in both cases Fanny is vindicated. Edmund explains to his father at the start of volume 2: "We have all been more or less to blame,...every one of us, excepting Fanny. Fanny is the only one who has judged rightly throughout, who has been consistent. *Her* feelings have been steadily against it from first to last. She never ceased to think of what was due to you" (187). As soon as Fanny has a chance to reflect on the news of Maria's adulterous elopement with Henry, she realizes, "*She* should be justified. Mr. Crawford would have fully acquitted her conduct in refusing him, but this, though most material to herself, would be poor consolation to Sir Thomas" (452).

In short, the theatricals episode in volume 1 serves as a rehearsal for the main sequence of events in volumes 2 and 3. This similarity draws attention to some striking aspects of the novel—just as in *Emma* the heroine's delusion in volume 1 highlights her more complex misunderstandings and her more complete humiliation in volumes 2 and 3. I would now like to outline five consequences that follow from seeing the structure of the novel in this way.

To start with, we can note an interesting parallel with *Emma*. The first two chapters of volume 2 of *Mansfield Park* depict Sir Thomas's indignant response to the theatricals project: he puts an end to the rehearsals, has the carpenter restore the billiard room to its original function, has the scene painter hired by Tom sent back to London, sees Mr. Yates off the property, and even "burn[s] all [the copies of *Lovers' Vows*] that met his eye" (191). He is entirely concerned with outward behaviour and not the motives for it:

> he…meant to try to lose the disagreeable impression, and forget how much he had been forgotten himself as soon as he could…. He did not enter into any remonstrance with his…children: he was more willing to believe they felt their error, than to run the risk of investigation. The reproof of an immediate conclusion of every thing, the sweep of every preparation would be sufficient. (187)

His attitude seems to me remarkably similar to Emma's speech to herself at the end of the Harriet–Elton fiasco: "The first error and the worst lay at her door. It was foolish, it was wrong, to take so active a part in bringing any two people together. It was adventuring too far, assuming too much, making light of what ought to be serious, a trick of what ought to be simple. She was quite concerned and ashamed, and resolved to do such things no more" (*Emma [E]* 136–37). Emma is, like Sir Thomas, regretting behaviour and not its inner causes; what is lacking in her volume 1 repentance is evident when she castigates herself at the novel's climax: "With insufferable vanity had she believed herself in the secret of everybody's feelings; with unpardonable arrogance proposed to arrange everybody's destiny" (412–13). Since Sir Thomas and Emma ignore the causes of their first humiliation, each is destined to be humiliated again and even more completely.

A second aspect of the novel highlighted by this parallel structure is how different Fanny's position is—in the house and in the novel—in her second dilemma. Fanny is now opposing Sir Thomas himself and not the spiteful but inconsequential Mrs. Norris; her decision to refuse Henry Crawford is not a symbolic moral one, but the central choice of her life; her dilemma lasts not three or four days, but instead four months, most of which is spent in exile in Portsmouth; Fanny is no longer an onlooker in the family, but its central figure. The novel devotes eight chapters to the theatricals project (the final six chapters of volume 1 and the first two of volume 2); by contrast, early in volume 2, Henry Crawford confesses to his sister that he plans to "'mak[e] a small hole in Fanny Price's heart'" (*MP* 229) on the days when he is not hunting, and this courtship continues until the final pages of volume 3. Fanny's second ordeal is much more intense in every way than the first. The novel plays the same melody once more, with feeling.

A third and even more striking difference between the two parallel sequences of events is how much more alone Fanny is the second time. She knows she no longer can rely on Edmund's support. During the theatricals, as we have seen, Edmund defends Fanny's right to refuse; even after he announces to the others his own capitulation, when Tom suggests, "Perhaps...*Fanny* may be more disposed to oblige us now. Perhaps you may persuade *her*" (158), Edmund firmly rejects the idea. However, when Crawford proposes to Fanny, Edmund is away being ordained, and Fanny's response to Sir Thomas's harangue in the East room suggests that Edmund's absence is not simply geographical: "She had no one to take her part, to counsel, or speak for her. Her only friend was absent. He might have softened his father; but all, perhaps all, would think her selfish and ungrateful" (321). When Edmund does return several days later, he is struck by the fact that, strangely, Fanny does not find an opportunity to discuss Crawford's proposal with him, and so he decides to "try what his influence might do for his friend" (345): "Fanny estranged from him, silent and reserved, was an unnatural state of things; a state which he must break through, and which he could easily learn to think she was wanting him to break through" (345). And so they do discuss the proposal, and in this discussion Edmund not only urges Fanny to accept Crawford, as we have seen, but also concludes his appeal to Fanny with a bizarre piece of emotional blackmail; he tells her that his own happiness with Mary Crawford depends on Fanny's accepting her brother: "I confess myself sincerely anxious that you may [accept]. I have no common interest in Crawford's well doing. Next to your happiness, Fanny, his has the first claim on me. You are aware of my having no common interest in Crawford" (351). Edmund's next words, "I was very much pleased by her manner of speaking of it yesterday," make it clear that he is referring to Mary.

A fourth point is that the more alone Fanny is, the stronger she must be. In her first dilemma, Fanny found herself unsure about what she *ought* to do; her very virtues—her humility, her knowledge of her own horror of acting, her capacity for self-doubt, her deep gratitude—make her question her own moral rigour. Just before Edmund enters the East room to announce his decision to join the cast, Fanny thinks,

> Was she *right* in refusing what was so warmly asked, so strongly wished for? what might be so essential to a scheme on which some of those to whom she owed the greatest complaisance, had set their hearts? Was it not ill-nature—selfishness—and a fear of exposing herself? And would Edmund's judgment, would his persuasion

of Sir Thomas's disapprobation of the whole, be enough to justify her in a determined denial in spite of all the rest? (153)

Edmund's defection, however, means she must undergo her first ordeal alone, and by the time she confronts her second dilemma, she no longer doubts her moral allegiance; when Sir Thomas finishes his long speech to her in the East room, she thinks, "Selfish and ungrateful! to have appeared so to him!" (321). The word "appeared" says it all. In the next chapter, her thoughts exhibit, not self-doubt, but condemnation of Sir Thomas's venal "line of conduct": "He who had married a daughter to Mr. Rushworth. Romantic delicacy was certainly not to be expected from him. She must do her duty, and trust that time would make her duty easier than it now was" (331).

A fifth point arises once we grasp the existence of these two parallel sequences. Though I haven't mentioned it so far, Fanny wavers and finally collapses in her first trial, the theatricals, and this raises the possibility that she might again acquiesce in the wishes of all whom she holds dear. Surprisingly, puzzlingly, Fanny actually does succumb to pressure from the family on the night of the first formal rehearsal of *Lovers' Vows*; she agrees to act. Edmund tells his father, in words I have quoted, that Fanny throughout consistently rejected the idea of acting, and readers no doubt expect the very same thing. In fact, one of the best critics of the novel, Joseph Wiesenfarth, says that "no amount of pressure can overcome [Fanny's] resolution not to act" (99). As it happens, Fanny's lapse is largely nominal, since Sir Thomas's return on the same evening prevents the rehearsal from taking place. Still, Fanny's reversal is strange and unexpected. It occurs in the second-last paragraph of volume 1, after Mrs. Grant, who plays the role of Cottager's Wife, is unable to come for that night's rehearsal, and after everyone urges Fanny to take the part: "even Edmund said, 'Do Fanny, if it is not *very* disagreeable to you'" (*MP* 171). Edmund has now become an entreater rather than a protector, and Fanny's response to this switch clearly triggers her acquiescence. In the second-last paragraph of volume 1, we read, "as they all persevered—as Edmund repeated his wish, with a look of even fond dependence on her good nature, she must yield. She would do her best. Every body was satisfied" (172). Fanny collapses out of hopelessness, as is evident in her response to Edmund's own capitulation under Mary Crawford's influence two chapters earlier:

> The doubts and alarms as to her own conduct, which had previously distressed her,...were become of little consequence now. This deeper anxiety swallowed them up. Things should take their course; she cared not how it ended. Her cousins might attack, but could hardly tease her. She was beyond their reach; and if at last obliged to yield—no matter—it was all misery *now*. (156–57)

In Fanny's second trial, with Edmund even more forcefully urging her, and with any hope that he might overcome his infatuation with Mary apparently lost, might not she collapse once again? The novelist has planted this narrative possibility within the course of events, and in fact the novel's narrator does suggest in the novel's final chapter that Fanny might eventually have yielded to Crawford if he had persisted in his pursuit of her—once Edmund had married Mary (467). And, of course, the 1999 film adaptation of the novel, written and directed by Patricia Rozema, presents Fanny reversing herself and accepting Henry—and then reversing herself again the next morning.

So far this essay has developed the parallels between two sequences in the action—and by defining the parallels has highlighted the differences between the two sequences. However, we should remember that these two strands of action are bound together by *causality* as well as by *analogy*. The theatricals episode and Henry Crawford's pursuit of Fanny form the central causal chain in the novel. Fanny will never accept Henry Crawford because she has seen him playing at lovers' vows with Maria in the theatricals episode. She explains this to Edmund in their interview, even if she has felt unable to tell Sir Thomas: "I have not thought well of [Mr. Crawford] from the time of the play. I then saw him behaving…so very improperly and unfeelingly,…paying attentions to my cousin Maria, which—in short, at the time of the play, I received an impression which will never be got over" (349). In the same way, through standing alone during the theatricals against the entire family, without support even from her mainstay Edmund, Fanny develops the moral strength and the confidence in her own judgement that allows her to resist the prolonged assault upon her by all the other characters in the main action of the novel. The theatricals project, then, serves as the novel's pivot, just as Darcy's first proposal, Elizabeth's heated attack upon him in response, and Darcy's long letter of explanation provide the point on which the plot of *Pride and Prejudice* turns.

The ideas I have been outlining seem clear, even self-evident, to me, yet they have not been developed in criticism of the novel, and so one would assume they have also not been apparent to ordinary readers of the novel. This is especially strange when one considers that in *Emma* the same two-phase structure can hardly be missed by critics and ordinary readers. Why would this be? One answer might be that the structure I find in *Mansfield Park* is simply not there. However, I prefer a less radical solution, and I would like to suggest that this design and its resemblance to the structure of *Emma* have been overlooked for two reasons. One lies in *Mansfield Park* itself, and the other in my approach to it.

Looking first at the novel itself: the volume 1 prelude to the main action in *Mansfield Park* is more fragmentary and less clearly separated from volumes 2 and 3 than its counterpart in *Emma*. Volume 1 of *Emma* is a self-contained drama focussed almost entirely upon the three characters in the Emma-Elton-Harriet triangle, and this drama has come to a decisive end before volume 1 ends; volume 2 of *Emma* begins with Emma's visit to Miss Bates—hitherto only a name, but now a fully developed character—and news that Jane Fairfax, previously unmentioned in the novel, is about to come to Highbury, and so we are clearly about to begin a new and much larger sequence of events. By contrast, the *Lovers' Vows* episode takes up the last one-third of volume 1 of *Mansfield Park*—and, as we have seen, spills over into the first two chapters of volume 2. Furthermore, the theatricals episode, far from consisting of a constricted set of characters, includes the entire cast of the novel: even the absent Sir Thomas is mentioned so frequently as to seem present.

However, I would argue that volume 1 of *Mansfield Park* is a more coherent whole than it appears to be. The volume consists mainly of two self-contained episodes: the theatricals and, before that, the expedition to consider improvements to Mr. Rushworth's estate, Sotherton. The Sotherton outing is discussed at length in chapter 6, and then chapters 8, 9, and 10 are devoted to it. However, though the trip to Sotherton and the theatricals are two separate narrative segments, they are very similar in both content and form. In content, the Sotherton outing is a template of the theatricals: the young Bertrams and Crawfords are out exploring while Sir Thomas is away; Henry Crawford drops his attentions to Julia Bertram and pursues Maria, while Maria separates herself from her fiancé, Rushworth, and responds eagerly to Crawford's advances; Julia is sidelined in both cases, and in each Rushworth is tricked into playing a comic and ignominious role;

meanwhile, Mary Crawford lures Edmund away from Fanny's side and into serpentine paths in the wilderness; Fanny is alone, abandoned by Edmund, but observing clearly all that passes.

In form, the two episodes are highly theatrical. This is hardly surprising in the theatricals episode; still, it is worth remembering that the novel shows us characters who are enacting a play within a play in their presentation of *Lovers' Vows:* each character—for instance, Edmund in the role of Anhalt, the idealistic clergyman, or Maria as Agatha, the fallen woman—plays a role that enacts his or her own situation at Mansfield Park. Furthermore, as several critics of the novel have noted, the events at Sotherton are also theatrical.[1] The young people wander through the artificial wilderness in shifting groups of two or three like Shakespearan lovers in the woods. Furthermore, the key moments at Sotherton contain the stark symbolism found in an Elizabethan dumb-show or the play-within-the-play in *Hamlet*. Think of Maria and Henry Crawford finding their way together around the locked iron gates and out into the larger park. An even more striking instance occurs early in the Sotherton episode as the party tours the house's disused chapel:

> Julia called Mr. Crawford's attention to her sister, by saying, "Do look at Mr. Rushworth and Maria, standing side by side, as if the ceremony were going to be performed. Have not they completely the air of it?"
>
> Mr. Crawford smiled his acquiescence, and stepping forward to Maria, said, in a voice which only she could hear, "I do not like to see Miss Bertram so near the altar."
>
> Starting, the lady instinctively moved a step or two, but recovering herself in a moment, affected to laugh, and asked him, in a tone not much louder, "if he would give her away?"
>
> "I'm afraid I should do it very awkwardly," was his reply, with a look of meaning. (*MP* 88)

This little inset drama might well be titled *Lovers' Vows*. Note that Henry Crawford both aggressively steps forward and yet, far from stating a vow, speaks in veiled ambiguities—just as he remains pressing Maria's hand to his heart in an ambiguous tableau as the rehearsal of *Lovers' Vows* comes to a sudden end in the opening lines of volume 2. Thus, we might consider the Sotherton chapters a rehearsal for the theatricals, just as the latter is a rehearsal for the main action of the novel.[2]

A second reason for the general failure to see this design in the novel lies in the approach I have been taking to the novel. This essay has focussed on the moral issues in the novel, as key words in my argument—such as "conduct," "duty," "selfish," "grateful," and "justify"—suggest. I suspect that most readers today grasp these moral issues, and the patterns underlying them, but see them as obvious and dated: what is fascinating is the social context and psychological or political analysis that might explain these issues. By contrast, I have been considering *Mansfield Park* much as one might discuss a Henry James novel, and in fact this novel seems much more like a James novel than any of Austen's other novels. At the very least, Fanny Price's rich moral life can remind us that the protagonists in Austen's other novels share Fanny's complex moral universe.

Mansfield Park is in many ways a strange and puzzling novel; some critics consider it a problem-novel, just as Shakespeare's last formal comedies—such as *Measure for Measure* or *All's Well That Ends Well*—are problem-plays. The novel's strangeness becomes especially apparent if we consider the novel's heroine. Fanny Price is the youngest of Austen's heroines, if we disregard the everygirl, Catherine Morland, who is the protagonist of Northanger *Abbey*, and if we consider Elinor Dashwood, the point-of-view character, to be the heroine of *Sense and Sensibility*. Fanny is much lower on the social scale than the other heroines, and is the only one who lacks "accomplishments": we do not see her drawing or playing or singing. She has no wit at all, unlike the other heroines (and unlike her author); she is also, unlike the other heroines, timid and physically frail. She is the only one whose childhood is presented at any length, and this fact is very important, since Fanny is the heroine of memory and gratitude, and since her love for Edmund is based in his kindness to her, which we glimpse in the novel's opening chapters. Fanny is the only heroine who has to endure seeing the man she loves doting on her rival throughout the novel; and, unlike Elinor vis-à-vis Lucy Steele, or Anne vis-à-vis Louisa and Henrietta Musgrove, Fanny has every reason to believe that the man she loves loves her rival and that this rival will in the end prevail. Edmund finally is undeceived at end of the novel, but we do not see him returning her love or proposing to her. Even more, Fanny is the only heroine who has to endure being the confidante of her beloved; the very prospect is a nightmare for Emma, but one that is no sooner raised than it is revealed to be a grotesque misunderstanding. Fanny is thus the only heroine who has to fight off the ugly emotions of envy and jealousy throughout, from the episode of Edmund's horse early in the novel until his final infatuated letter from London in the novel's final section. Readers do not warm to Fanny as they do to Austen's other heroines. And yet, for these very reasons, Fanny emerges as the strongest and most heroic of Austen's heroines, and I hope to have thrown some light on the design of a novel that, like its heroine, it is all too easy to underestimate.

NOTES

1. David Selwyn remarks, "Quite apart from the use of *Lovers' Vows*, and the readings of Shakespeare, *Mansfield Park* is permeated by a sense of the theatrical, and indeed many of the scenes convey a visual impression that almost suggests the stage: [for instance,] Fanny waiting on the seat in the wilderness at Sotherton

while other characters make exits and entrances in various groupings" (259). See also Armstrong 62–66 and Byrne 178–83.

2. Armstrong sees the Sotherton chapters, the theatricals, and the main plot of the novel in quite similar terms: "The Sotherton episode is a prelude, a curtain raiser, to the 'real' play, *Lovers' Vows*" (62).

Comic Symmetry in Jane Austen's *Emma*

I

"IF ANY WORK BELONGS UNEQUIVOCALLY to any genre," Laurence Lerner remarks, "*Emma* is a comedy" (96). Lerner's insight suggests that it might be profitable to ask what makes the novel seem such a classic comedy. To approach *Emma* as a comedy is to think of it, not in the usual context of nineteenth-century fiction, but rather in conjunction with *Much Ado about Nothing*, *The Way of the World*, and *Tom Jones*. In such comedies, the conflicts and characters are simple and fixed: what interests us is the intricate design, the complex and surprising pattern, into which these elements fall. In fact, the simple constituents are necessary for the intricate design of the whole. Suppose, for instance, that we allow ourselves to doubt Emma's conviction that Mr. Elton's motives in courting her were merely greed and vanity—after all, that conviction is comforting, since it removes any doubt or remorse she might feel about her abrupt dismissal of her first suitor. But the gain in psychological irony, in inner complexity, would slow and blur another set of complex ironies, those emerging from the comic action itself.

Reginald Farrer described the way this comic design works some fifty years ago: "Only when the story has been thoroughly assimilated, can the infinite delights and subtleties of its workmanship begin to be appreciated, as you realise the manifold complexity of the book's web, and find that every sentence, almost every epithet, has its definite reference to equally unemphasized points before and after in the development of the plot" ("Book" 64–65). Farrer's remark suggests that an alert reader of the novel, even an alert first reader, will constantly be thinking backward and forward from the dramatic present as he or she reads: we are kept from immersing ourselves in the moment by becoming aware of the pattern it contains. Farrer also points out that the comic pattern, if precise, is also "unemphasized"—implicit, sly, for us to find.

What is essentially comic in *Emma*, then, lies in its design. But since that design is presented ironically, an accurate account of it can be reached only after a great deal of observation and reflection. In fact, the novel is so subtly symmetrical, so mined with interconnected details, that criticism has, I think, yet to define its structure adequately. An instance of sly patterning that has not been noticed by Jane Austen's critics will illustrate the point.

When we, along with Emma, first meet Harriet Smith in chapter 3, we are told of Harriet, "She was a very pretty girl, and her beauty happened to be of a sort which Emma particularly admired. She was short, plump and fair, with a fine bloom, blue eyes, light hair, regular features, and a look of great sweetness" (Austen, *Emma [E]* 23). This seems innocuous enough, but we learn from Mrs. Weston's praise of Emma in chapter 5 that Emma herself is tall and elegant, with hazel eyes (39). Emma particularly likes Harriet's style of appearance, just as she likes Harriet's style of personality, because it poses no threat to Emma's own—in fact, it forms a perfect foil for Emma's charms. Furthermore, when Emma paints Harriet's portrait in chapter 6, we find that she makes Harriet appear taller and more elegant than she actually is. Emma creates an image of Harriet much more like Emma herself than Harriet really is. The symbolism here not only presents Emma as the artist moulding nature into new and more pleasing shapes, as several critics have pointed out; even more precisely, the portrait also epitomizes what Emma does to Harriet in general: she transforms Harriet's actual self into a monstrous new identity fashioned in the image of Emma herself. In this respect, as in so many others, the outing to Box Hill recapitulates the action of the novel. There, Frank Churchill playfully commissions Emma to produce a wife for him when he returns from abroad: "Find somebody for me. I am in no hurry. Adopt her, educate her." Emma, thinking of Harriet, coquettishly replies, "And make her like myself" (373).[1] And so it is appropriate that, like a comic Frankenstein's monster, Harriet eventually turns unwittingly on her maker, forcing Emma to realize what she has created.

My point is that each of these scenes, beginning with Emma's particular admiration of Harriet's sort of beauty, invites us to see beyond the dramatic moment to the pattern it contains. This pattern, being "unemphasized," is not fixed. We may also note, for instance, that Jane Fairfax is tall and elegant in appearance, like Emma and unlike Harriet. Joseph Wiesenfarth shrewdly juxtaposes Emma's flattering portrait of Harriet with Robert Martin's having taken the exact measure of Harriet's height (129)—a measurement that, but for Emma, would have brought Harriet and the Martins together again.

Much of the most helpful criticism of the novel, in fact, consists of remarking subtle instances of comic symmetry. But, as Farrer suggests, we grasp more than tissues of related words and incidents: through the "manifold complexity" we sense "the book's web," a single comic structure. This deeper, ironic structure is much harder to define. I suggest that Jane Austen's web consists of three main threads, and that all the local symmetries lead to and from these threads in networks that get ever finer as we pursue them. These three lines of action are the hidden love of Emma and Mr. Knightley for each other; the counterpointing of that secret love with the secret engagement of Frank Churchill and Jane Fairfax; and the use of the other characters to embody aspects of Emma herself. This attempt to chart the novel's structure will also, I hope, throw some light on the methods and attitudes of comedy itself.

∞ II

Though every one who likes the novel at all must smile at Emma's unrecognized love for Mr. Knightley, surprisingly little is said about it by critics of the novel. Howard S. Babb, however, has some suggestive remarks; discussing the issue of Emma's snobbishness, he says, "The cause of her compulsive disengagement is her inability to recognize and to admit what she feels for Mr. Knightley.... It is the novel's major irony that an Emma so frequently wrapped up in herself, and one who cultivates detachment, should so radically misconceive her real attachment" (180). We can take Babb's point one step further and say that Emma's unrecognized love is the cause of her foolish mistakes over Harriet Smith and Mr. Elton, over Mr. Dixon and Jane Fairfax, and so on: these mistakings provide a screen of romantic fantasies that disguise her real interest in love from herself. Emma, after all, is preoccupied with affairs of the heart—affairs of other people's hearts, that is; she can see clearly and act decisively when love is not involved.

In Emma's case, then, the course of true love runs in two channels: one, at the visible level, contains Emma's embarrassing errors as an amatory busybody; the other, underground channel, which only surfaces at the novel's climax, contains her real feelings toward Mr. Knightley, which become clearer and clearer to us (if not to her) as the action advances. If the hidden stream is the source of the visible one, the latter provides a chart throughout to the depths concealed within the heroine.

The surface action of the novel falls into two successive and similar patterns of comic nemesis. Volume 1 is a self-enclosed prelude, or image in little, for the main action, which occupies volumes 2 and 3. Though the prelude has a cast of only three and a single broad irony, while the main action is much more varied and convoluted, the pattern is the same in each case: Emma's blunders as the Highbury Cupid become more and more obvious to all but her, until finally circumstances, rebelling against her guiding hand, slap her rudely in the face and wake her up. The comic symmetry is very precise here. Just as in volume 1 she discovers, to her dismay, that she and Mr. Elton have both been using Harriet Smith as a pawn to advance Mr. Elton's charade of a courtship, so in volumes 2 and 3 she finds Frank Churchill and Jane Fairfax have been using her as their "blind" (Austen, *E* 427); like Harriet before, she must learn that another woman has been secretly preferred to her. At the surface level, then, the novel has a two-part, beguiler–beguiled structure: Emma finds herself living out a comic form of the golden rule. So much is worth spelling out, even if almost every reader must enjoy seeing Emma get hers (as we say), because most recent critics have followed Joseph M. Duffy, who argues that the novel falls into three stages: the Emma-Elton-Harriet fiasco; "the Emma-Frank Churchill-Jane Fairfax illusion and masquerade" (chapters 18 through 46 [i.e., through volume 3, chapter 10]); and the relationship between Emma and Mr. Knightley (chapters 47 through 65 [i.e., volume 3, chapters 11 to 19]) (Duffy 51).[2]

We can, though, see the two main comic situations—the two successive romantic triangles—as parallel surface actions, displacements caused by and directing us to the real plot, which lies in Emma's relationship with Mr. Knightley. Unbeknownst to herself,

Emma loves him from the start. After learning that Frank and Jane are secretly engaged, after being shocked by Harriet's hopes into realizing that "Mr. Knightley must marry no one but herself!" (Austen, *E* 408), Emma makes the most surprising discovery of all: "there never had been a time" when she did not love him (412). She would have been able to understand herself at any point, she thinks, if only it had occurred to her "to institute the comparison" between him and the man she thought she loved, Frank Churchill (412). We, however, see a great deal more clearly into Emma's heart than she does herself: the cleverly scattered clues to her real feelings become more and more insistent. This rising curve of ironic disclosure forms the real plot of the novel; certainly, Jane Austen artfully frames the self-enclosed action of volume 1 within three increasingly heated debates between Emma and Mr. Knightley, one at the beginning, one at the middle, and one at the end of the volume. This ironic curve is supported by an echoing, if subordinate, curve of clues about the real nature of Mr. Knightley's concern for Emma.

Why wouldn't Emma admit her love from the start? Why *didn't* it occur to her to institute the comparison? For one thing, like many heroes and heroines of comedy, she does not want to give up her independent selfhood. She tells Harriet in chapter 10, "never could I expect to be so truly beloved and important; so always first and always right in any man's eyes as I am in my father's" (84). Certainly, Mr. Woodhouse is unlikely ever to be outbid in this sort of affection. But, as with, say, Shakespeare's Beatrice and Benedick, events will not so much conquer as correct Emma's selfhood; Emma not only will shed her barren assumptions about love and her own emotional needs, but she will find herself, to her surprise, happy to do so. Emma also fears love because she considers it to be blind. Emma is exquisitely self-contained: the idea of being out of control, of losing her will in the grip of passion, disturbs her. This is why she tells Harriet, in the same scene, that her attachment to her nephews and nieces "suits my ideas of comfort better than what is warmer and blinder" (86). Similarly, after Harriet has confessed her hopes of Mr. Knightley to Emma, Emma thinks that she can have no hopes of her own: "*She* could not. She could not flatter herself with any idea of blindness in his attachment to *her*. She had received a very recent proof of its impartiality" (415). Emma is thinking of his stern rebuke of her treatment of Miss Bates; ironically, of course, that rebuke proves, rather than disproves, his love for her.

The most important aspect of Emma's fear of love—and one she cannot formulate—is her fear of being hurt. Emma is afraid of being undervalued, of being taken as a fluttery, dependent creature, a female, rather than as a person of intelligence and dignity of her own. Listen to her challenging Mr. Knightley in their debate over breathless, brainless Harriet Smith: "'To be sure!' cried she playfully. 'I know *that* is the feeling of you all. I know that such a girl as Harriet is exactly what every man delights in—what at once bewitches his senses and satisfies his judgment. Oh! Harriet may pick and choose. Were you, yourself, ever to marry, she is the very woman for you'" (64). Without realizing it, she is asking Mr. Knightley to declare that he would marry someone like herself, and not a Harriet, but she must content herself with his vigorous generalization, "Men of sense, whatever you may chuse to say, do not want silly wives" (64). In her opinionated confusion, Emma thinks of man and woman as two completely different species, each having its own sphere, its own special kind of knowledge, its own code of action. Like those who make up personality profile tests, Emma assumes men are primarily interested in objects and abstract ideas, while women have expertise in emotional relationships. After her argument with Mr. Knightley about the right man for Harriet, Emma "still thought herself a better judge of such a point of female right and refinement than he could be" (65).

Emma will discover that men and women have much more in common than she thinks, that they can be friends rather than merely symbiotic opposites. In fact, the action of the novel can be seen as Emma's search for, and triumphant discovery of, a true friend. The impulse that sets the action in motion is Emma's loss of Miss Taylor, in Emma's eyes, at least: "they had been living together as friend and friend very mutually attached" (1). Emma tries to fill Miss Taylor's place with Harriet Smith, though Mr. Knightley tells Emma, in words which ring in her mind (137, 402), "You have been no friend to Harriet Smith, Emma" (63). Emma refuses to consider Jane Fairfax for the vacancy, though "Birth, abilities, and education" mark Jane out for it (421), and flirts with the possibility of taking on Frank Churchill as her intimate friend—only to find that her real friend from the start has been Mr. Knightley. It is as a friend that he addresses Emma. He warns her, "as a friend—an anxious friend" (349), that there may be some understanding between Frank Churchill and Jane Fairfax; he ends his stern remarks to her over Miss Bates with the statement, "I will tell you truths while I can, satisfied with proving myself your friend by very faithful counsel" (375). Finally, when he is about to reveal his own feelings to Emma, she at first refuses to hear what she thinks will be a confession of infatuation with Harriet; but, after a moment of sympathy and self-discipline, she determines to hear him out "as a friend" (429). Mr. Knightley at first pauses—"Emma, that I fear is a word—No, I have no wish"—but then decides to give the word a special meaning: "Emma, I accept your offer—Extraordinary as it may seem, I accept it, and refer myself to you as a friend.—Tell me, then, have I no chance of ever succeeding?" (429–30). Emma has shown herself finally worthy of receiving his proposal that he be her friend for life.[3]

The real plot of the novel, then, lies beneath the complicated surface events. This notion helps explain the response of one group of readers. Many in its original audience, like many undergraduates today, found the novel complicated but trivial, lacking in a unified, dramatic, and significant plot. John Henry Newman, for instance, wrote in 1837, "Everything Miss Austen writes is clever, but I desiderate something. There is a want of *body* to the story. The action is frittered away in over-little things" (qtd. in Southam, *Jane Austen* 117). This response, free of canonical, sophisticated sightlines, points to something real in the novel. There *is* a want of body to the story, since the romantic plots that Emma imposes on the world around her lack substance; she is herself in danger of frittering away her life in over-little things. But underneath the over-little things is a single large one, their cause and successor: her response to Mr. Knightley.

∞ III

If Emma is merely an instrument in Frank Churchill's schemes, Jane Austen gives her heroine some recompense by making Frank's plot merely a means of bringing Emma's story to its fruition. As in many traditional comedies, the love story at the work's centre is interwoven with the trials of another pair of lovers, Frank Churchill and Jane Fairfax. The action is neatly contrived, so that the resolution of the Frank–Jane plot brings about, by chain reaction, the resolution of the central plot; further, in the manner of comedy, the two plots are presented in intricate counterpoint to bring out the difference between the two matches, to let each illuminate the other. Both plots turn upon a secret love, but one is secret by conscious deception, the other by unconscious self-deception. One love story, that of Frank and Jane, is resolved wholly by chance, by Mrs. Churchill's completely unexpected and very timely death; the other match is achieved by choice, by change, by mutual self-direction.[4]

This counterpoint reaches a wonderful subtlety in the Box Hill episode. Box Hill is the turning point for both love affairs, the occasion for a quarrel that pulls each pair of lovers apart only to bring them back together all the more intimately and for good. Frank's letter of explanation allows us to understand how crucial Box Hill is for Frank and Jane. Frank, piqued at Jane's unwillingness to walk home with him from Donwell Abbey the day before, flirts with Emma in order to taunt Jane, and then uses the departure of the Eltons as a screen for delivering a private insult: women can't be known at Bath, or any public place, he says, but only when you see them "in their own homes, among their own set" (Austen, *E* 372). Jane, wounded, answers with veiled bitterness: "it can only be weak, irresolute characters, (whose happiness must be always at the mercy of chance,) who will suffer an unfortunate acquaintance to be an inconvenience, an oppression for ever" (373). Frank, highly indignant, leaves Highbury that very afternoon without saying farewell to Jane; that evening, she accepts Mrs. Elton's eagerly offered position with Mrs. Smalridge and writes to Frank breaking off the engagement. Chance, however, intervenes: Frank's aunt dies, and he is not forced to choose between the two ladies who rule his life. Jane's ultimatum, though, does make it advisable that he go directly to his uncle and ask for his permission to marry Jane; now Mrs. Churchill is no more, that permission is quickly granted.

My point is this: we can never be sure Frank Churchill would have been willing to give up his fortune for Jane. He is relieved of the choice. Why, after all, did he insist on keeping their engagement secret? In his letter of explanation, he writes, "But you will be ready to say, what was your hope in doing this?—What did you look forward to?—To any thing, every thing—to time, chance, circumstance, slow effects, sudden bursts, perseverance and weariness, health and sickness" (437). In more simple terms, he was waiting for his aunt to die—or, failing that, to go through some unpredictable alteration. In either case, Frank could marry Jane *and* retain all his aunt's money and status. The force he relies on does reward him in the end: chance allows him to remain a spoiled child, free of painful choices. He closes his letter by saying that Emma had been right in calling him "the child of good fortune" (443).[5]

Emma begins as another Frank, another pampered only child in a rich home. But she has a different, more substantial kind of good fortune: she is allowed to choose, to repudiate, to grow, and to grow up. Emma and Mr. Knightley triumph, not by opportunism, but by stern moral choices. Emma's thoughtless insult to Miss Bates at Box Hill corresponds exactly to Frank's sneer at Jane's domestic circle; Mr. Knightley's rebuke, as difficult for him to make as it is for her to receive, is parallel to Jane's ironic reproof of Frank as weak and irresolute, so wounding to his pride. Mr. Knightley's criticism is open, not veiled, however; unlike Frank, Emma has both the courage and the desire to accept the truth. Emma is so hurt at losing Mr. Knightley's good opinion, and at seeming inadvertently to scorn his advice, that, feeling pain of a sort she has never known before, she genuinely wants to change, and does. As a result, when Mr. Knightley comes calling, Emma brings on his proposal, as she could not have before, by her quiet self-sacrifice. The happy coming together of Emma and Mr. Knightley may lack the dramatic éclat, the spectacular good fortune, of the other couple, but it has the dignity and integrity of something they have made themselves. Mr. Knightley's comment after reading Frank's letter has an uncomplacent precision: "My Emma, does not every thing serve to prove more and more the beauty of truth and sincerity in all our dealings with each other?" (446).

This counterpointing of Frank and Emma becomes explicit in their final meeting. Emma says that she is certain that Frank must have enjoyed deceiving everyone in Highbury, because she knows that she herself would have found great amusement in doing so: "I think there is a little likeness between us," she says drily, to which he bows acknowledgement. Emma adds that, at the least, she and Frank have the same destiny—"the destiny which bids fair to connect us with characters so much superior to our own" (478). But this same scene shows that the likeness only brings out the unlikeness between Emma, who raises herself to her husband's moral level, and Frank, who brings his wife down to his. In this final view of Frank, he ecstatically admires the complexion, hair, and eyes of his bride-to-be, "whispering seriously" to Emma the news that "my uncle means to give her all my aunt's jewels. They are to be new set.... Will not it be beautiful in her dark hair?" (479). Frank ends up with both the aunt's jewels and the beautiful hair, though, as Jane's embarrassed reproach a few minutes later suggests, he does so at the price of remaining the thoughtless boy he has always been. Emma returns home even happier in her happiness with Mr. Knightley for "the animated contemplation of his worth which this comparison produced" (480). She, not Frank, is the lucky one.

∞ IV

The two symmetrical networks I have defined emerge from, and control, the twists and turns of the plot. But our comic detachment also forces on our notice a broader and more static kind of design, that created by character contrasts. Such unchanging patterns are a feature of traditional comedy; throughout *Tom Jones*, for instance, the hero and heroine are poised between Mr. Allworthy's theoretical benevolence and Squire Western's animal vigour. Such broad oppositions chart the perfect happiness toward which the comic action moves, and which it finally attains; that happiness is imaged as a midpoint combining the excellence of one-sided extremes. Emma and Mr. Knightley, for instance, marry out of motives that fall between, and combine, the self-aware calculation of the Eltons and the romantic feeling that unites Frank and Jane.

These comic oppositions have an important consequence: Emma comes to exist, not only in her own self, but as she is reflected and embodied in the characters around her. This extroversion of psychological conflict frequently occurs in sophisticated comedy: when Tom Jones wins his Sophia, when Millamant accepts her Mirabell, inward changes are delicately conveyed. Had these changes been directly presented, we would lose our comic distance, and so our comic perspective; in this sense, my opening assertion that comic characters are simple and fixed should be qualified. In *Emma*, certainly, the heroine has a many-faceted, self-divided personality, since the major characters surrounding her persistently live a double life: they are both themselves and aspects of Emma. Mr. Woodhouse, for instance, embodies one extreme within the unregenerate Emma. He is utterly self-absorbed, so that all events must seem to revolve around his preferences; he resists change or effort of any kind; he is utterly unable to distinguish between his own wishes and what actually is the case.[6]

This notion of alter egos gives a new dimension to the first chapter of the novel. Emma falls into self-pitying loneliness the evening after "poor Miss Taylor" marries Mr. Weston, but she rallies herself to combat the same feelings in her father. When Mr. Knightley calls, though, Emma takes the plaintive pose again, but now her own rational position is uncompromisingly urged upon her by Mr. Knightley: Emma "cannot allow herself to feel so much pain as pleasure. Every friend of Miss Taylor must be glad to have her so happily married" (11).

The chapter suggests that Emma is suspended between a Knightley self and a Woodhouse one. Mr. Knightley, in fact, functions as Emma's deepest or true self throughout the novel. For instance, Emma expresses a stern view of Frank Churchill's procrastinations to Mrs. Weston, but, a few pages later, she perversely claims more sympathy for Frank than she actually feels; she thus finds herself in the ironic position of "making use of Mrs. Weston's arguments against herself," while Mr. Knightley expresses "her real opinion" (145). Jane Austen tells us that Emma can always find excuses to avoid calling on Miss Bates and her mother, though "she had had many a hint from Mr. Knightley and some from her own heart, as to her deficiency" (155). Mr. Knightley embodies, then, Emma's own heart and conscience: this is what makes his rebuke on the subject of Miss Bates so painful.[7] The union of Emma and Mr. Knightley is thus, in part, a psychic one: Emma becomes reunited with a part of herself she had renounced. This is why Mr. Knightley must wait for Emma to educate herself; she can only come to him when she has come to herself.

All this helps to explain the importance of Mr. Knightley's polar opposite within Emma, Mrs. Elton. By leading Mr. Elton on and then rejecting him, Emma has summoned from the depths of Bristol a substitute for herself who embodies, in garish, unmitigated form, all her own complacent, vain, mean, and domineering qualities. The correspondences between Emma and Mrs. Elton are precise and ingenious; many of them have been remarked by the critics, but the function of this pairing in the larger design is much less clear.[8] Mrs. Elton's appearance in Highbury more than halfway through the novel is actually part of Emma's genuine good fortune, a gift to her from comic providence. For now Emma can make a good choice between her good and her bad angels, between her ideal and her selfish selves. The back-to-back excursions to Donwell Abbey and Box Hill, the only occasions in the novel when we leave Highbury, dramatize this opposition: Mr. Knightley refuses Mrs. Elton's offer to organize the first expedition and runs it in his own satisfyingly unpretentious way; the Box Hill trip on the following day is, from the start, Mrs. Elton's party, though

Emma comes home from it under Mr. Knightley's influence, having once and for all repented of her insensitive Mrs. Elton self.

This comic conflict between the Knightley and the Elton in Emma is enacted and defined at the Crown Inn ball. Mrs. Elton, it seems clear, has instigated her husband to spurn Harriet publicly (repeating thereby his earlier spurning of Harriet), but Mr. Knightley ruins her scheme with his quick generosity, just as he will later rescue Harriet from the fate Emma's schemes seem to have made inevitable. After this comic psychodrama, when Emma confesses the reason for the Eltons' spite, Mr. Knightley replies:

> "I shall not scold you. I leave you to your own reflections."
> "Can you trust me with such flatterers?—Does my vain spirit ever tell me I am wrong?"
> "Not your vain spirit, but your serious spirit.—If one leads you wrong, I am sure the other tells you of it." (330)

If Mrs. Elton is Emma's vain spirit, there is good reason for the withering dismissal of her in the final paragraph. We learn there that Mrs. Elton knows of Emma's marriage only "from particulars detailed by her husband"; she is not among "the small band of true friends who witnessed the ceremony" because she embodies a part of Emma that has been exorcised, banished to a realm of white satin and staring Selinas (484).

This extroversion of Emma's conflicts is a familiar device in sophisticated comedy. It is accompanied, however, by a striking innovation: the usual social conflicts of comedy are introverted or internalized. According to theorists such as Suzanne Langer and Northrop Frye, traditional comedy presents the rhythm of life overcoming obstacles and renewing itself; this pattern of upset and regained equilibrium underlies the typical comic plot, in which young lovers overthrow and revitalize a society that obstructs natural energies. In *Emma*, the obstructing society is within Emma herself: it is she who frustrates nature's plans for marriage and erects insuperable barriers between social classes. Any renewal of the novel's society will therefore be the result of a change within Emma herself; Mrs. Weston reminds Mr. Knightley (and us) at the outset that Emma, accountable to nobody but her father, cannot be stopped from indulging any of her projects, "so long as it is a source of pleasure to herself" (40).

But if Emma contains the obstructing society within herself, she also contains the young lover. She is Millamant as well as Lady Wishfort, Good Heavens Gwendolyn as well as Lady Bracknell. Something within Emma makes Mr. Knightley more important to her than anything else. This ability to respond to him, without her knowledge and against her will, is at the heart of the novel's comic perspective: Emma's desire to be herself, her desire for Mr. Knightley, and her desire to be good all, finally, coincide. Harmony, not sacrifice or division, reigns. In the same way, we soon grasp that Mr. Knightley's concern for principle and for Emma's moral state coincide with his affection for her: to him, she is "faultless in spite of all her faults" (433). Emma's response, in spite of herself, to Mr. Knightley is what enables her to keep our sympathy throughout; it is also what makes her second awakening, unlike that at the end of volume 1, final and convincing. Emma forsakes her fanciful schemes, and can see the vain motives that prompted them, only when she discovers the deepest "source of pleasure to herself" is to be in the real world with the man she respects and loves.

"The perfect happiness of the union," the novel's final words, thus describe a personal integration as well as a wedding (484). Interestingly enough, it is Miss Bates who defines most precisely the connection between psychological and social union; she says during one of her monologues, as if by accident, "It is such a happiness when good people get together—and they always do" (175).

NOTES

1. Darrel Mansell links this remark to Emma's portrait of Harriet, though in somewhat different terms (152). For acute commentary on Box Hill as microcosm, see Mansell 166–70; Tave, *Some Words* 240–46; and Poirier 144–207.
2. For instance, of the critics cited above, Mansell, Wiesenfarth, and Babb all state that the book has a three-part structure.
3. Surprisingly, this patterned play upon the word *friend* has escaped notice. J. F. Burrows is an exception, but he thinks Mr. Knightley's recurring use of the term is meant ironically: Mr. Knightley considers himself to be acting as Emma's friend, but we know differently (107).
4. I am pursuing here a point made by W. J. Harvey: "The world of *Emma* is binary. Around the visible star, Emma herself, circles an invisible planet whose presence and orbit we can gauge only by measuring the perturbations in the world we can see....The written novel contains its unwritten twin whose shape is known only by the shadow it casts" (239).
5. This uncharitable view of Frank, implicit in Mr. Knightley's comments upon his letter, is becoming more evident to the novel's readers. See, for instance, Harvey 240; Tave, *Some Words*; Bush 165; and Duckworth 178.
6. That other major characters embody aspects of Emma herself has been noted by some recent critics: Wiesenfarth, for instance, says of Mr. Woodhouse that he "represents the danger of detachment from reality by way of egoism that she [Emma] is liable to" (114). What I am trying to define here is the function of such correspondences in the comic structure.
7. A. Walton Litz says of the rebuke, "It awakens part of herself, and comes as the voice of her own conscience" (141).
8. Some illuminating comparisons between the two ladies are drawn by Mansell (156–60), Lerner (100–01), Kenneth L. Moler (177), and Mark Schorer (180–81).

 # "The Sentient Target of Death"
Jane Austen's Prayers

JANE AUSTEN'S PRAYERS have a place in her writings that resembles that of some of her own heroines within their fictional worlds. Apparently of little interest, they have been generally ignored. These three short prayers survive in undated manuscripts inscribed "Prayers Composed by my ever dear Sister Jane"; the prayers themselves indicate that one member of the Austen family is reading to the assembled household at night before all retire to bed. Like Elinor Dashwood or Fanny Price or Anne Elliot, the prayers have, in general, not been attended to: biographies and critical studies tend to ignore the prayers (with some striking exceptions, to be mentioned later in this essay). Yet, like those heroines, the prayers have a good deal to say for themselves if one does listen—in this case, a good deal about Jane Austen's life and about the novels. They tell us that Jane Austen was a devout Christian and suggest that the novels are more suffused with religious feeling than we might have thought. Charlotte Brontë's famous disparagement of Jane Austen was written in 1850, and so without the benefit of any biographical knowledge: it is at least possible that, if Brontë had known of Jane Austen's prayers, she might not have considered the novelist "a complete and most sensible lady, but a very incomplete and rather insensible (*not senseless*) woman," one who cannot represent the final truths known by "the sentient target of death" (128).

∞ I

The manuscripts of Jane Austen's prayers, like the prayers they contain, have been overlooked. No accurate scholarly edition of these prayers has yet appeared, and, as we shall see, it is uncertain who actually copied out the prayers.[1] B.C. Southam, justifiably, does not discuss the manuscripts in his authoritative *Jane Austen's Literary Manuscripts*. A clear account of the not-very-clear textual situation may thus be a helpful starting-point.

Jane Austen's sister Cassandra left the manuscripts at her death in 1845 to Cassandra Esten Austen, the eldest daughter of their brother Charles, and two of his granddaughters sold them, along with other Austen papers and memorabilia, at Sotheby's in 1927 (Le Faye 244), for a price of £175 (Gilson, "Auction" 13). They were subsequently acquired by the California book collector William Matson Roth, who produced a limited edition (of 300 copies) of the prayers in 1940. Roth's text of the prayers is a little strange: it is all in capital letters, and the punctuation is frequently modernized. When Chapman included the prayers in the *Minor Works* of 1954, the sixth and final volume of his Oxford Illustrated Jane Austen edition, he relegated them to the volume's final pages and reproduced Roth's text (though reversing his typography, using lower-case throughout). Even the 1993 edition of *Catharine and Other Writings*, edited by Margaret Doody and Douglas Murray, bases its text, not on the manuscripts, but on a "typed transcription made by William Matson Roth" (283).

Roth donated the manuscripts in 1957 to Mills College in Oakland, California; they now reside in the Heller Rare Book Room of the F. W. Olin Library at Mills College. The prayers are found on two sheets of paper of quarto size, each folded into two leaves (or four octavo pages). The inscription "Prayers Composed by my ever dear Sister Jane" appears on the outside of the folded quarto sheet on which the first prayer, with the heading "Evening Prayer," is written. The sheet has a watermark dated 1818. The handwriting of this first prayer is said by Chapman to be "probably—almost certainly?—Cassandra's" (Headnote 453). The inscription appears to be in a different hand (and under the inscription is pencilled lightly the name "Charles Austen"). The second and third prayers appear, without title or number, on the second sheet of manuscript, which lacks a watermark. The second prayer appears on pages 1 and 2 of the four octavo pages, and the third on pages 3 and 4.

A fascinating question emerges here: down to the second-last line of "page 3" of the second sheet (that is, for the first half of the third prayer), one finds what seems to be the same hand as on the first sheet. However, beginning with the last line of that octavo page and on the next occurs a much neater, if still flowing, handwriting that seems fairly clearly to be that of Jane Austen herself. R. A. Austen-Leigh, co-author of *Jane Austen, Her Life and Letters* and editor of *Austen Papers, 1704–1856*, was "quite sure" that it was Jane Austen's handwriting (Roth n.pag.). Chapman, however, considered the handwriting "doubtful" (Chapman, "Jane Austen Collection" 27). If this second sheet does contain Jane Austen's handwriting, it would obviously have to predate both her death in July 1817 and the sheet containing the first prayer. Chapman's headnote in the *Minor Works* volume compounds the confusion. He writes that the second MS sheet "is partly in a hand which I think may be Henry Austen's, partly in a hand which has been thought by experts to be JA's own" (453). The switch from first-person ascription to passive summary underlines the implied doubt.

And yet the confusion is more apparent than actual. What does it matter who copied out the prayers if we continue to believe—and there is no reason not to—their inscribed title, "Prayers Composed by my ever dear sister Jane"? It seems clear that Jane Austen composed the prayers, and that they were copied out, at two different times, by a combination of the Austen brothers and sisters. The manuscripts of Jane Austen's prayers were a family production.

∞ II

This is fitting, because Jane Austen's prayers are communal in nature. Though one person is reading, they are the prayers of the family, not a person, and the third prayer concludes with the petition, "may we by the Assistance of thy Holy Spirit so conduct ourselves on Earth as to secure an Eternity of Happiness with each other in thy Heavenly Kingdom."[2] All three prayers end with those present joining voices to recite the Lord's Prayer; the third prayer thus goes on from the words "Heavenly Kingdom" to conclude, "Grant this most merciful Father, for the sake of our Blessed Saviour in whose Holy Name & Words we further address Thee. Our Father &c."

Furthermore, Jane Austen's prayers, like the *Book of Common Prayer* (the Prayer Book), which they echo in many ways and at many points, speak in a shared voice of a generic predicament (unlike the very personal *Prayers and Meditations* of her mentor Samuel Johnson). The predicament is that outlined in the Prayer Book, the Thirty-Nine Articles, and indeed in the Bible itself: men and women need God's grace and guidance, since human nature is inherently sinful and yet proud, and so prone to self-deception and discontent. A long quotation from Jane Austen's first prayer demonstrates that, as Henry Austen said, "her opinions accorded strictly with those of our Established Church" (8):

> Look with Mercy on the Sins we have this day committed, & in Mercy make us feel them deeply, that our Repentence may be sincere, and our Resolutions stedfast of endeavouring against the commission of such in future.—Teach us to understand the sinfulness of our own Hearts, and bring to our knowledge every fault of Temper and every evil Habit in which we have indulged to the discomfort of our fellow-creatures, and the danger of our own Souls.—May we now, and on each return of night, consider how the past day has been spent by us, and what have been our prevailing Thoughts, Words and Actions during it, and how far we can acquit ourselves of Evil. Have we thought irreverently of Thee, have we disobeyed thy Commandments, have we neglected any known Duty, or willingly given pain to any human Being?—Incline us to ask our Hearts these questions Oh! God, and save us from deceiving ourselves by Pride or Vanity.
>
> Give us a thankful sense of the Blessings in which we live, of the many comforts of our Lot: that we may not deserve to lose them by Discontent or Indifference.[3]

As this passage suggests, the difficulty and yet the necessity of self-knowledge is the principal theme in Jane Austen's prayers. A parallel theme is the struggle for Christ-like forbearance and charity (the "candour" that Jane Bennet exemplifies and Elizabeth acquires in *Pride and Prejudice*). A paragraph from Jane Austen's third prayer is quite explicit:

> Give us grace to endeavour after a truly Christian Spirit to seek to attain that temper of Forbearance & Patience, of which our Blessed Saviour has set us the highest Example and which, while it prepares us for the spiritual happiness of the life to come, will secure to us the best enjoyment of what this World can give. Incline us Oh God! to think humbly of ourselves, to be severe

only in the examination of our own conduct, to consider our fellow-creatures with kindness, & to judge of all they say and do with that Charity which we would desire from them ourselves.[4]

Note that in the prayers morality and religion coincide. In the first passage, the same acts endanger our souls and cause discomfort to fellow creatures, while thinking irreverently of God and disobeying his commandments are equated with neglecting known duties and causing pain to other human beings; in the second passage, spiritual happiness in the life to come and the best enjoyment of this world are gained by the same means.

Given her orthodox beliefs, it is not surprising that Jane Austen's letters reveal her Augustan (and Augustinian) scorn for the new, evangelizing, subjective forms of Christianity: "We do not much like Mr. Cooper's new Sermons;—they are fuller of Regeneration & Conversion than ever—with the addition of his zeal in the cause of the Bible Society" (*Jane Austen's Letters [JAL]* 467). However, she admired the tough-minded sermons preached by Thomas Sherlock, bishop of London, to an audience of lawyers at the Temple Church: "I am very fond of Sherlock's Sermons, prefer them to almost any" (278).

Quite apart from the orthodox beliefs they express, Jane Austen's prayers employ the diction and rhythms of the *Book of Common Prayer*, as Margaret Doody has observed ("Jane Austen's Reading" 347; Austen, *Catharine* 371–72). Indeed, it would be surprising if they did not: she would have heard and said the Prayer Book prayers at least once a week throughout her life. Besides, those prayers were regarded as models: Johnson told Boswell, "I know of no good prayers but those in the *Book of Common Prayer*" (qtd. in Boswell 1292). Jane Austen's prayers are particularly close to the Collects in the *Book of Common Prayer*. Compare, for instance, Jane Austen's prayer for charity, cited above, with the Collect for the Sunday before Lent:

O Lord, who hast taught us that all our doings without charity are nothing worth, Send thy Holy Ghost, and pour into our hearts that most excellent gift of charity, the very bond of peace and of all virtues, without which whosoever liveth is counted dead before thee: Grant this for thine only son Jesus Christ's sake. *Amen.*[5]

Significantly, Jane Austen's petition for self-knowledge (represented in the long excerpt from Prayer I quoted above) does not have such a direct origin in the Prayer Book Collects. Two Collects, however, will serve to suggest its general derivation from the beliefs, stance, and language of the *Book of Common Prayer*:

Almighty and everlasting God, who art always more ready to hear than we to pray, and art wont to give us more than either we desire, or deserve; Pour down upon us the abundance of thy mercy; forgiving us those things whereof our conscience is afraid, and giving us those good things which we are not worthy to ask, but through the merits and mediation of Jesus Christ, thy Son, our Lord. *Amen.* (Collect for the twelfth Sunday after Trinity)

O God, who knowest us to be set in the midst of so many and great dangers, that by reason of the frailty of our nature we cannot always stand upright; Grant to us such strength and protection, as may support us in all dangers, and carry us through all temptations; through Jesus Christ our Lord. *Amen.* (Collect for the fourth Sunday after the Epiphany)

The *collect*, defined in Johnson's *Dictionary* of 1755 as "A short comprehensive prayer, used at the Sacrament," is the form most frequently used in the *Book of Common Prayer* and is "so called because it collects and gathers together the supplications of the multitude, speaking them all with one voice; and because it is a collection and sum of the Epistle and Gospel for the Day" (according to a seventeenth-century dictionary cited in the *Oxford English Dictionary*). In form, the Collect consists of five parts: "Salutation, Ascription, Petition, Reason for Petition, and Conclusion" (Tillotson, Fussell, and Waingrow 1116). These five parts can be seen clearly in the three Collects cited above. In the first quoted, for instance (the prayer for charity), the Ascription begins with the word "who," the Petition with "send," the Reason for Petition with "without," and the Conclusion with "Grant."

The same form can be found in each of Jane Austen's prayers. The long passage from the first prayer beginning with "Look with Mercy" occurs in the second and third paragraphs of the prayer and begins the Petition, after a first paragraph devoted to Salutation and Ascription. Similarly, the paragraph beginning "Give us grace" is the second paragraph of the third prayer and begins the Petition after an opening paragraph of Salutation and Ascription.

The beliefs, language, and form of the Prayer Book prayers were, of course, found in many other books of prayers that Jane Austen knew, including Johnson's *Prayers and Meditations*, published in 1785 and cited frequently and at length in Boswell's *Life of Johnson*, which Jane Austen seems to have known by heart.[6] Another intermediate model for Jane Austen's prayers is one of the twenty surviving books that she owned, *A Companion to the Altar: Shewing the Nature & Necessity of a Sacramental Preparation in Order to Our Worthy Receiving the Holy Communion, to Which Are added Prayers and Meditations*. Apparently written by William Vickers and published in 1793, "this book of devotions always used by Jane Austen," to quote her great-niece Florence Austen, is inscribed with her signature and the date 1794 (qtd. in Gilson, *Bibliography* 445). It is a guide for those about to be confirmed in the Church of England; Jane Austen's copy was probably presented to her at the time of her own confirmation—she was eighteen in 1794

(Tucker 203–04). The prayers appended to the book, as its author points out, paraphrase the Collects in the *Book of Common Prayer*, just as they, in turn, paraphrase the Scriptures ([Vickers] ii).

One interesting difference between Jane Austen's prayers and those of the Prayer Book lies in their language: Austen's is scrupulously conceptual and non-figurative. The Prayer Book, a monument of Renaissance sensibility, is much more "poetic": for instance, "pour into our hearts that most excellent gift of charity, the very bond of peace and of all virtues" (in the Collect for the Sunday before Lent) is much more concrete and metaphorical than the equivalent phrasing in Austen's third prayer, and the same can be said of phrases such as "we cannot always stand upright" in the Collects cited above. Austen concurs with Samuel Johnson in this respect: Johnson notoriously disapproved of Milton's use of "trifling fictions" to convey "the most awful and sacred truths" (Johnson, "Life of Milton" 699), and he tells Boswell roundly, "I do not approve of figurative expressions in addressing the Supreme Being; and I never use them" (qtd. in Boswell 1293).

In general, then, Austen's prayers are meant to be read as the work of the common, generic believer, not the idiosyncratic individual—the first-person plural rather than the first-person singular. Like the Prayer Book, her prayers are not conceived of as literature, though they may have superadded literary interest or value. A passage from *Mansfield Park* dramatizes the point neatly. Henry Crawford is addressing Edmund, but also trying to impress Fanny with his knowledge of religion:

> Our liturgy [Henry says] has beauties, which not even a careless, slovenly style of reading can destroy; but it also has redundancies and repetitions, which require good reading not to be felt. For myself, at least, I must confess being not always so attentive as I ought to be—(here was a glance at Fanny) that nineteen

times out of twenty I am thinking how such a prayer ought to be read, and longing to have it to read myself—Did you speak? (340)

The contrast between "I" and "our" as attitudes to prayer could hardly be sharper, as Fanny's evident, but unarticulated, gesture of dissent suggests.

∞ III

Jane Austen's prayers tell us a good deal about her life. At the same time, they raise some very puzzling questions—which is no doubt why her biographers have by and large left them alone. The most important thing they tell us is also the most obvious: that Austen had a deep and sincere religious faith. Her prayers provide the most telling, if far from the only, evidence of this piety. Proof exists also in her one serious poem, on the death of her friend Mrs. Lefroy (*Minor Works [MW]* 440–42); the comments she made about religious books (for instance, in addition to her disapproval of Dr. Cooper's sermons and her praise of Bishop Sherlock's, her pleasure in Thomas Gisborne's Evangelical conduct-book, *An Enquiry into the Duties of the Female Sex* [*JAL* 112]); the passages of religious consolation in her letters (e.g., *JAL* 13, 96, 146–47); and her attitude of pious submission in the letters written shortly before her death (*JAL* 340–43). And, of course, her grandfather, her father, and two of her brothers were clergymen, as were many others in the family circle, including Cassandra Austen's fiancé Thomas Fowle, who died of yellow fever before they could marry. As Jan Fergus observes in her recent biography, "For Austen, religion was an essential part of daily life" (36).

Austen's prayers also point to the effect that the *Book of Common Prayer* must have had upon her style. Her prayers display the syntactical control and balance, the diction, and the speech rhythms that characterize both the *Book of Common Prayer* and Austen's own prose when she is writing formally. Doody summarizes the case for such an influence:

> The Book of Common Prayer is, to speak profanely, a good influence on style. Its sentiments are emphatic without crudity, and its cadences have the grace of strength rather than of decoration. It is also a language meant to be spoken aloud.... It is here, I believe, that we must look for the origins of Austen's balanced and coordinated sentences rather than to the later and more partial influence of Johnson. ("Jane Austen's Reading" 347–48)

Austen's prayers also pose some difficult biographical questions. Did the Austen family hold evening prayers at home? What is the date at which the prayers were composed? Why do only three short prayers by Austen survive? The answers to these questions must be tentative and incomplete (which is why they have not been treated by her biographers); still, a certain amount can be said.

It *does* seem likely that the Austen family observed evening prayers at home: both Gisborne and *A Companion to the Altar* recommend it, and in *Mansfield Park* Fanny Price says of morning and evening prayers at Sotherton, "A whole family assembling regularly for the purpose of prayer, is fine!" (86). Austen's letters do not allude specifically to evening prayers, but a letter to Cassandra of 1808 refers to evening devotions (which would include prayers) as a matter of course: "In the evening we had the Psalms and Lessons, and a sermon at home" (*JAL* 227).

As for their date of composition, surmise is the best we can do: the prayers themselves contain no hint of their date. It seems quite possible that Austen would have composed the prayers only after the death of her father, an active and devout clergyman, in 1805.

Deirdre Le Faye states, without further explanation, "These prayers are undated, but would seem to be products of JA's later life" (274). Certainly, the three novels that Austen composed during the final years of her life at Chawton (*Mansfield Park*, *Emma*, and *Persuasion*) have a much more overtly religious dimension than the first three, drafted during the 1790s, and Marilyn Butler has made a strong case for viewing the later novels as reflections of "the wartime religious reform movement spearheaded by the Evangelicals...a national mood of self-assessment and regeneration" ("History" 207).

Surmise, again, must suffice as to why only three short prayers by Austen survive. It is possible, but I suspect unlikely, that Austen wrote further prayers that do not survive. Austen's three prayers were probably meant to supplement others that the family would normally use at evening prayers—prayers from the Prayer Book, or from other books of devotion, or indeed prayers composed by other family members, and especially Jane Austen's clergyman father and brothers.

These concrete questions, however, pale beside the overwhelming question raised by Austen's prayers: that of consistency. They seem so different from her letters—chatty and observant, gossipy and often malicious—and from her novels—so worldly in tone, so seemingly silent on spiritual matters. Just as with the specific biographical questions, this question has been generally avoided: it is no easy matter to reconcile the Jane Austen revealed in her prayers with the catty letter-writer and the shrewd comic novelist. Park Honan, in his *Jane Austen: Her Life*, does face the issue and even offers a view of the novels as Austen's resolution of an inner conflict:

> There is no greater contrast in Jane Austen's writings than that between her sharp, comically malicious letters and the Christian prayers she composed.... The effort of reconciling her faith with

her fury was enough to try her, and as happy as she was in green country at Chawton she was to make amends in part through her fictional comedies in which no living being is attacked, but life itself is recreated and appraised for every reader. (255; cf. 124)

One way of tackling this issue is to simplify it. The real problem lies in the apparent discrepancy between the prayers and the novels. The letters are mainly of interest because they are written by Jane Austen the novelist; furthermore, the letters are much more mixed in tone than the most acid (and memorable) excerpts from them suggest—it would not be hard to produce a set of excerpts that would make them seem entirely pious and proper. None of us is, or would like to be, everywhere and always the same. In any case, Austen's letters survive only in part and have the intimate indirectness of writing not meant to be read outside the family circle. What Austen says in her letters can hardly be held against her. The novels, however, are a very different matter.

∞ IV

The contrast between Austen's prayers and her novels brings us back to Charlotte Brontë's insistence on Austen's limitations. Several critics have asserted (and many others have assumed), with Brontë, that the novels are without religious reference or dimension. Lerner states that "Jane Austen the novelist did not believe in God.... [S]he did not arrange, control or interpret her deepest experience in the light of [her piety]" (Lerner 23). Gilbert Ryle observes, "Jane Austen...draws the curtain between her Sunday thoughts, whatever they were, and her creative imagination. Her heroines face their moral difficulties and solve their moral problems without recourse to religious faith or theological doctrines" (Ryle 117).

Of course, there is another view, one that sees Austen as less schizophrenic and the novels as less simply secular. A.C. Bradley put it succinctly in his essay of 1911: "Her inmost mind lay in her religion—a religion powerful in her life and not difficult to trace in her novels, but quiet, untheoretical, and rarely openly expressed" (29). This is the view of the novels taken in the first essay to be devoted to Austen's oeuvre, Richard Whately's 1821 review essay on *Northanger Abbey* and *Persuasion* in the *Quarterly Review*:

> Miss Austin [*sic*] has the merit (in our judgment most essential) of being evidently a Christian writer: a merit which is much enhanced, both on the score of good taste, and of practical utility, by her religion not being at all obtrusive.... The subject is rather alluded to, and that incidentally, than studiously brought forward and dwelt upon....
>
> The moral lessons also of this lady's novels, though clearly and impressively conveyed, are not offensively put forward, but spring incidentally from the circumstances of the story; they are not forced upon the reader, but he is left to collect them (though without any difficulty) for himself; her's is that unpretending kind of instruction which is furnished by real life. (95)

Whately's conception of the interdependence of fiction, morality, and religion is, I believe, shared by Austen herself. Two incompetent readers from her fiction, Catherine Morland of *Northanger Abbey* and Sir Edward Denham of *Sandition*, illustrate the point. Catherine as a girl has a natural tendency to read without thinking: "provided that nothing like useful knowledge could be gained from them, provided they were all story and no reflection, she had never any objection to books at all" (15); Sir Edward is much worse, since he perversely misinterprets Richardson's *Clarissa*: "ill-luck... made him derive only false Principles from Lessons of Morality, & incentives to Vice from the History of it's Overthrow" (*MW* 405).

Austen's prayers confirm this view of Jane Austen as a "Christian writer." Both Bradley and Whately wrote without knowledge of the prayers. Several recent critics of the novels develop roughly the same conception of the novelist, and four of these refer briefly to her prayers: Stuart Tave's *Some Words of Jane Austen* (112–13); Marilyn Butler's *Jane Austen and the War of Ideas* (189, 192, 196); Gene Koppel's *The Religious Dimensions of Jane Austen's Novels* (7–8); and Jan Fergus's *Jane Austen: A Literary Life* (36).

Nevertheless, as I hope to have shown, the relationship between Jane Austen's prayers and her novels deserves fuller treatment than it has yet received; I would like to conclude this discussion of the prayers by outlining three ways in which they might illuminate the novels.

The first way is the most obvious: the beliefs and terms of the prayers inform the novels. One quick way of demonstrating this is to cite from Marianne's speech of contrition in *Sense and Sensibility*: "I wonder at my recovery,—wonder that the very eagerness of my desire to live, to have time for atonement to my God, and to you all, did not kill me at once.... Whenever I looked towards the past, I saw some duty neglected, or some failing indulged" (346). Note that this speech assumes that religious and moral duties coincide ("to my God, and to you all")—the same assumption that we saw earlier in both Austen's prayers and Whately's account of her novels. By far the most striking aspect of the prayers is their insistence on self-knowledge (an insistence based, as we have seen, on a belief in original sin), and of course Austen's novels, particularly the two best of them, *Pride and Prejudice* and *Emma*, are dramas of self-discovery. The prayers also stress "candour" (or charity of judgement). The passage from the third prayer, cited above, shows that Austen considered that it is natural "to think meanly of all the rest of the world, to *wish* at least to think meanly of their sense and worth compared with my own," to use Darcy's words from the concluding pages of *Pride and Prejudice* (369). That is, one can think meanly ("severely" is the word in the prayer) of others and well of oneself, like Emma Woodhouse and Elizabeth Bennet when they are still unreformed, or apply the golden rule and reverse that natural tendency—thereby becoming able to think well of others and severely of oneself (like Miss Bates, or Jane Bennet, or the reformed heroines). Similarly, a conflict between gratitude and discontent is central in both the prayers and the fiction.

These ideas suggest a second way in which Jane Austen's prayers may throw light on her novels. The prayers, as I have argued, speak for a community of believers, rather than as the voice of a particular individual; nevertheless, they do reveal a distinctive emphasis. The central petition of all three prayers is for self-knowledge, with an explicitness that has no model in the *Book of Common Prayer*; similarly, in her third prayer Austen seeks charity *of judgement* (whereas the Prayer Book speaks of charity in "all our doings"). The prayers, thus, must reveal to us the sins to which Austen felt she was most inclined. We can then see the novels as having at their heart the painful struggles that dominated Austen's own inner life: the struggles for self-knowledge, charity of mind, gratitude, and the other virtues of the prayers. This conception of the novels' basis in Austen's experience is very old-fashioned—but it may none the less be true, and it is at least a less lurid formulation than Honan's suggestion (cited above) that in her novels Austen "makes amends" for her spiritual lapses.

Honan does, however, link the prayers to Austen's choice of comedy, which she calls "my own style &...my own Way" (*JAL* 312), and this connection is a third and final way in which the prayers illuminate the novels. In the prayers, as in Christianity as a whole, life is a Divine Comedy: it is good, just, harmonious, and all will turn out well in the end—unless "we..., by our own neglect, throw away the Salvation Thou hast given us," as

Austen's first prayer states. And so it is in the novels: for every Emma there is a Mr. Knightley, for every Elizabeth a Mr. Darcy, for every Anne a Captain Wentworth (and vice versa). Furthermore, good and bad actions, as in Dante's *Divine Comedy*, are not only part of a moral cause-and-effect sequence, so that the good end happily; these actions also bring into being spiritual states that are themselves fitting rewards or punishments. The final and exact reward for Emma (or punishment for Mrs. Elton) is simply to go on being what she has chosen to become. Similarly, nothing could in the end be more harmonious than the disharmony Lucy Steele has achieved at the end of *Sense and Sensibility*:

> [Robert and Lucy Ferrars] settled in town, received very liberal assistance from Mrs. Ferrars, were on the best terms imaginable with the Dashwoods; and setting aside the jealousies and ill-will continually subsisting between Fanny and Lucy, in which their husbands of course took a part, as well as the frequent domestic disagreements between Robert and Lucy themselves, nothing could exceed the harmony in which they all lived together. (377)

Jane Austen's prayers, then, reveal a good deal about both her life and her novels. They show that in her own life she was concerned for the state of her soul, and with an intense awareness that gives the lie to Charlotte Brontë's claim that Austen was ignorant of "the sentient target of death." To be fair, Brontë knew of Austen only what she gathered from reading two novels, *Pride and Prejudice* and *Emma* (126–28). And yet Austen's novels themselves, as her prayers suggest, contain much more than Brontë found there: "ladies and gentlemen, in their elegant but confined houses" (126). Austen's novels *do* tell the stories of ladies and gentlemen; they *are* set in elegant houses. They also, however, present a moral and spiritual terrain that stretches far beyond those dwellings.

NOTES

1. Since the original publication of this essay, Cambridge University Press has released an edition of the prayers based on the manuscripts themselves, rather than Roth's transcription; see Austen, *Jane Austen: Later Manuscripts* (2008).
2. Quotations from Jane Austen's prayers are from the manuscripts at Mills College and are cited by permission of the librarians there.
3. Douglas Murray has suggested, in a letter to me, that the dashes may indicate pauses for the insertion of voiced petitions particular to any given day or of silent petitions.
4. The last sentence here is especially important as a summary of Jane Austen's moral thinking; interestingly, it is in the middle of this sentence that Jane Austen herself (or someone whose hand resembles hers) begins to write out the prayer.
5. The *Book of Common Prayer* was standardized in 1662; quotations here are from the Oxford: Clarendon Press edition of 1803.
6. She alludes to Boswell's *Life of Johnson* at least six times in the *Letters* (*JAL* 32, 33, 49, 181, 363, 368); she paraphrases Boswell's final tribute to Johnson at the end of her poem "To the Memory of Mrs. Lefroy" (cf. Boswell, *Life* 1394–95; Austen, *Minor Works* 442); and Jane Austen's image of "my dear Dr. Johnson" (*JAL* 181) was no doubt derived largely from Boswell's presentation of Johnson—just as Jane Austen uses the phrase, as Chapman points out in his note on the letter, in the course of agreeing with an opinion in a letter from Johnson to Boswell cited by the latter in his *Life* (563).

 # The Genesis of Evelyn Waugh's Comic Vision

Waugh, Captain Grimes, and Decline and Fall

FROM THE VERY START, readers of Evelyn Waugh's first novel, *Decline and Fall* (1928), have found Captain Grimes to be "one of the world's great rogues, one of those whose serenity and bloomy sense of inner rightness almost persuade honest men that there is a strong moral case for roguery," as Rebecca West wrote in her review of the novel (221). Indeed, the novel itself tells us that Grimes is immortal—literally. Even though his hat has been found floating on the most treacherous part of Egdon Mire as the novel closes, we know that he cannot die:

> Lord Tangent was dead; Mr. Prendergast was dead; the time would even come for Paul Pennyfeather; but Grimes, Paul at last realized, was of the immortals. He was a life force. Sentenced to death in Flanders, he popped up in Wales; drowned in Wales, he emerged in South America; engulfed in the dark mystery of Egdon Mire, he would rise again somewhere at some time, shaking from his limbs the musty integuments of the tomb. Surely he had followed in the Bacchic train of distant Arcady, and played on the reeds of myth by

181

forgotten streams, and taught the childish satyrs the art of love? Had he not suffered unscathed the fearful dooms of all the offending gods of all the histories—fire, brimstone and yawning earthquakes, plague and pestilence? Had he not stood, like the Pompeian sentry, while the Citadels of the Plain fell to ruin about his ears? Had he not, like some grease-caked Channel-swimmer, breasted the waves of the Deluge? Had he not moved unseen when darkness covered the waters? (232–34)[1]

Grimes *is* immortal: he does outlive Paul Pennyfeather within the novel, he has survived his creator's death, and he will live on when all of us are gone. And yet this mythical figure had a singularly distinct origin. We now know that Waugh created Captain Grimes by transcribing the career, the personality, and even the idiom of a real person, one Richard Young, a remarkably cheerful and shameless pederast whom Waugh, then twenty-one years old, met while both were teachers at a preparatory school in northern Wales. The relationship between mortal Young and immortal Grimes provides an instance of how Waugh's imagination worked: it seized on observed facts and transformed them into something rich and strange. Even more importantly, it now seems clear that Young played a crucial role in enabling Waugh to achieve the comic outlook on life that characterizes all his best fiction.

Waugh's first public acknowledgement of how much he owed to the real-life model for Grimes combines the idea of transcription with that of transformation. When *Brideshead Revisited* (1945) brought Waugh hundreds of thousands of new American readers and a new experience, fan mail, he replied collectively to this new audience in a *Life Magazine* article entitled "Fan-Fare," published in early 1946. He says there that readers always ask if his characters are drawn from life; to this question he replies:

My problem has been to distill comedy and sometimes tragedy from the knockabout farce of people's outward behaviour. Men and women as I see them would not be credible if they were literally transcribed; for instance,...the character Captain Grimes in *Decline and Fall*. I knew such a man. One of the more absurd escapades of my youth, the result of a debt-settlement conference with my father after which I undertook to make myself financially independent of him, was to take a job as master at a private school. There I met a man who made what has seemed to me the lapidary statement, "This looks like being the first end of term I've seen, old boy, for two years." But had I written anything like a full account of his iniquities, my publishers and I would have been in the police court. (303)

On the one hand, Grimes is a transcription: his lapidary statement sounds like a tuning-fork at the start of his self-exposition in the third chapter of *Decline and Fall*. On the other hand, as we shall see, a great many facts had to be changed in the process of distilling the knockabout farce of Richard Young's life into a comic elixir. Anything like a full account of his iniquities would have been unacceptable for artistic as well as legal reasons.

Waugh's claims of 1946 were borne out in the last book he wrote, his autobiography *A Little Learning* (published in 1964, two years before his death), and in the two posthumous volumes of his *Diaries* (published in 1976) and his *Letters* (published in 1980).[2] Grimes emerges as both an astonishing *objet trouvé* and as someone who, without realizing it, taught Waugh to see life as a comedy.

Certainly Waugh was in need of some help when he met Richard Young in the spring of 1925. Like his anti-hero Paul Pennyfeather (also twenty-one) in *Decline and Fall*, Waugh had been driven by a disgraceful exit from Oxford to become a teacher at a prep school on the seacoast in northern Wales. He had been drinking uncontrollably for three years; he was hundreds of pounds in debt. After coming down from Oxford with a low third-class degree the previous summer, he seemed unable to find a career: he had been an art student for three months and an engraver's apprentice for several days before becoming a schoolmaster at Arnold House School in January 1925 (Arnold House[3] evidently was the inspiration for Llanabba Castle, the fraudulent preparatory school of *Decline and Fall*). Waugh had lost his High Anglican faith in 1921 before leaving his public school and had found nothing to take its place; his conversion from atheism to Roman Catholicism in 1930 suggests that he suffered during his decade as an apostate. Having enjoyed some mild success as a graphic artist and writer of short stories at Oxford, he pottered away at a novel entitled *The Temple at Thatch*, about an undergraduate who lives in an eighteenth-century folly and practises black magic, but the months went by and the novel did not get written. His love life was unhappy as well. Like his own Paul Pennyfeather, Waugh had entered Oxford as a naive, high-minded, and chaste scholarship student, but there he entered into a series of homosexual affairs that he must have found intensely disturbing: although Waugh was a diarist from adolescence until the end of his life, the diaries from his Oxford years are missing—Waugh almost certainly destroyed them.[4] After coming down from Oxford, however, he had fallen in love with his first girl, Olivia Plunket Greene; she was then a fey eighteen-year-old and would later become a religious recluse. In April of 1925, during the month's break after his first term at Arnold House, he had not only had wild times at parties in London and at a house-party held by the Plunket Greenes in a rented lighthouse, but he also came to understand during all-night talks with Olivia that, in Waugh's phrase, "my infatuation had become a matter of only mild interest to her" (*LL* 226).

No wonder, then, that Waugh's diary for 1 May 1925 records that he returned to Arnold House for the summer term "in immeasurable gloom" (210). He notes without comment on the same day, "There is a new usher called Young in Watson's place" (that is, as assistant headmaster) (211). By 5 May, "sunk in Julian apathy," he has been reading a new book of essays by Bertrand Russell and reasoning about suicide: "I debate the simple paradoxes of suicide and achievement, work out the scheme for a new book, and negotiate with the man Young to buy a revolver from him" (211).[5]

The revolver negotiations, never completed, presumably derived from Waugh's suicidal thoughts, and so did the "new book," which turned out to be not *Decline and Fall* but his first serious piece of fiction, a long, avant-garde story called "The Balance" (which he completed in August and which was published in 1926). The story tells of a young man, just down from Oxford, who drunkenly and ineptly tries to commit suicide, but ends by achieving a momentary balance between life and death. If the action of the story is anguished, its narrative method is ingenious and draws attention to itself: the crucial events are presented in the form of a silent-film scenario, and this is only one of the forms of narration used in this tour de force.[6]

Conceiving of this story brought Waugh out of the dumps; by 28 May he records in his diary that he feels inspired and is "writing furiously" (212). Another cause for exhilaration lay in the news that he had finally found a satisfying job. His older brother Alec, already a successful popular novelist living in London, had told him that C. K. Scott Moncrieff, the translator of Proust who lived in Florence, needed a secretary. Waugh applied for the position through Alec, even though he could not type and was not fluent in the languages in which Scott Moncrieff worked. Alec informed Evelyn at the start of June that Scott Moncrieff would take him. Dreaming of an aesthete's life in the sun, Waugh gave notice to the headmaster that he would leave at the end of the term. The headmaster accepted with no show of reluctance (*LL* 226).

June was balmy, but Waugh received two sharp blows at the end of the month. Harold Acton, his friend and aesthetic mentor from Oxford, the man to whom *Decline and Fall* is dedicated "in Homage and Affection," wrote that the opening chapters of *The Temple at Thatch*, which Waugh had sent him, were a precious false start; Waugh acquiesced in this verdict and consigned his manuscript to the school furnace (*LL* 228). The autobiography continues: "Hard on this came a letter from Alec saying that he had misunderstood Scott Moncrieff, who did not need and could not afford a secretary of any kind, least of all one with my deficiencies." During the halcyon days of June, Waugh had not kept his diary, but he returned to it on 1 July; his first entry since 28 May is a long one summarizing his predicament. It concludes:

> It looks rather like being the end of the tether. At the moment I can see no sort of comfort anywhere. I had already decided on a dolorous charabanc expedition that, no doubt justly, the boys—or at least such of them as I liked—had no kind of affection for me. I think the proprietor would be quite unwilling to take me back even if I wanted to return. I can scarcely expect my poor father to give me any more money. The phrase "the end of the tether" besets me with unshakable persistence all the time. (213)

The Captain Grimes concealed within Richard Young now came to Waugh's rescue. Before 1 July, the only mention of Young in the diaries after the initial ones on 1 and 5 May comes on 14 May, when Waugh calculates that "Rather more than a seventh of the term is gone" and adds, "Young the new usher, is monotonously pederastic and talks only of the beauty of sleeping boys" (211). But in the very next entry after 1 July, that for 3 July, we can observe Young leading Waugh out of the Slough of Despond:

> Two things have happened to comfort me a little. Professor Dawkins has come back from Oxford. He arrived on the field the day before yesterday and we spent the afternoon talking in complete neglect of the game which I should have been taking. He told me a pleasing Curzonism [Lord Curzon was Chancellor of Oxford University]. "I myself should deprecate anything in the nature of a beano" (pronounced "bayāno"). The other thing was that Young and I went out and made ourselves drunk and he confessed all his previous career. He was expelled from Wellington, sent down from Oxford, and forced to resign his commission in the army. He has left four schools precipitately, three in the middle of the term through his being taken in sodomy and one through his being drunk six nights in succession. And yet he goes on getting better and better jobs without difficulty. It was all very like Bruce and the spider. (213)

Just as Lord Curzon exists as a comic type in Waugh's imagination (there is a great difference between "He told me a notable remark by Lord Curzon" and "He told me a notable Curzonism"), so, in a much more arresting way, Young becomes to Waugh an emblem of comic persistence and triumph: Young is the spider who refuses to be discouraged, and Waugh is the royal onlooker who finds wisdom in the spider's eventual success. Waugh recounts Young's confession in his autobiography, written almost forty years after the fact, and there Waugh's distillation of a comic type from actual experience has been carried several stages further:

> Grimes sought to enliven me with stories of his own ups and downs; experiences that might have been taken for hallucinations save for his shining candour. Every disgrace had fallen on this irrepressible man; at school, at the university, in the army, and later in his dedicated task as schoolmaster; disgraces such as, one was told, make a man change his name and fly the kingdom; scandals so dark that they remained

secret at the scene of his crimes. Headmasters were loath to admit that they had ever harboured such a villain and passed him on silently and swiftly. Grimes always emerged serenely triumphant. (*LL* 229)

The shocking facts in the diary have given way to richly ironic generalizations about "scandals so dark that they remained secret at the scene of his crimes." Even more significantly, this passage presents not Richard Young, a specific person, but "Grimes," a comic, even mythical figure.[7] In the autobiography, Young is contemplated ironically and from a distance: Waugh now understands the causes for his strangely successful career, whereas the diary simply sees Young as a cause for wonder and consolation. The autobiography makes no mention of the immediate comfort Waugh found in Young's confession; in fact, Waugh concludes this passage in *A Little Learning* with the comment, "The catalogue was diverting rather than consoling" (229). To the man of sixty who wrote the autobiography, the only true consolation lay in the Roman Catholic religion; that consolation was not yet evident to the young man of twenty-one. Furthermore, in the diary Waugh is mainly struck by Young's resilience, his strange ability to "get better and better jobs without difficulty" despite his scandalous behaviour; the autobiography stresses Grimes's freedom from guilt, his "shining candour"—he is not only triumphant, but serenely so. The autobiography implies that any guilt Waugh felt over homosexual relationships with his peers (or over his drinking, for that matter) dwindles to insignificance beside Grimes's grimy proclivities.[8]

The 3 July diary entry recounting Young's confession is the only one that suggests he excited Waugh's imagination. After this, Young reverts to being monotonously pederastic. He is not mentioned significantly in the diary during the rest of July, and Waugh left Arnold House for good at the end of the month. Waugh's next job was at another school, this one in Berkshire, where he taught for a year and a half before he was fired for a drunken assault upon the school matron's virtue. Young visited Waugh there in late March 1926, some eight months after Waugh left Arnold House; the visit lasted for some days, suggesting that Young, at least, considered them to be good friends. Young was the same as ever. Waugh writes in his diary on 26 March, "Today I have been entertaining Young—the lecher from Denbighshire. He came on a marvellous bicycle—a Sunbeam. We lunched at the Bell and went to see the children at football. He fell in love with R—" (249). Five days later, he records, "Young of Denbighshire came down and was rather a bore—drunk all the time. He seduced a garage boy in the hedge" (250).

The diary, however, tells a good deal less than the whole truth. Waugh's genius was for detached observation, rather than introspection, and his voluminous diaries contain no entries covering the four most intense periods of his life: his Oxford years, 1922–1924; his first wife's infidelity and the collapse of their marriage in 1929; his decision to convert to Roman Catholicism in 1930; his mental breakdown due to paranoid delusions in 1954. He either refused to record his own innermost feelings or simply found himself unable to do so.[9] Thus, it is not really surprising that Waugh omits from his diary two remarkable incidents involving Young (or, more properly, Grimes: Young as a comic type). Both events hinge upon Grimes's pederasty, both had an electrifying and decisive effect upon Waugh's imagination, and both only became known when Waugh recounted them in his autobiography. Young is the central figure in the concluding pages of *A Little Learning*: Waugh's story ends with the Grimes in himself triumphant and facing the future with resolve.

Young's first appearance in the autobiography, in contrast to his entrance in Waugh's diary, is dramatic: he is, in fact, an embodiment of life's capacity to astonish and delight. Returning to school for the summer term of 1925 was bitter, Waugh recounts: "There seemed no prospect of surprise. In this foreboding I was wrong.

A very surprising man, about ten years my senior, had come to take the place of the disgruntled Scotchman as second master; a dapper man of sunny disposition who spoke in the idiom of the army" (*LL* 227). These initial sentences describe a Captain Grimes, rather than a Richard Young. In fact, to paraphrase Waugh's author's note to *Brideshead Revisited*—"I am not I; thou art not he or she; they are not they"—Young is not Young in the autobiography: Waugh follows this description by saying that the newcomer was the model for Captain Grimes, and from this point on in *A Little Learning* the new teacher who spoke in the idiom of the army is referred to as "Grimes," a comic figure infinitely more fascinating than the lecher from Denbighshire had been in actuality.

Waugh then recreates in us the shock and delight which he felt upon first encountering Grimes; he does so by recounting an aspect of the "dolorous charabanc expedition" not mentioned in the diary entry for 1 July:

> I was puzzled why he should choose to exile himself among us. But he was a man without deceit. His weakness (or strength) was soon revealed. After a week or two a whole holiday was ordained in honour of [the headmaster's] birthday. It was no holiday for the assistant masters. The whole school was packed into charabancs in the early morning and driven to the slopes of Snowdon, where games were played and a picnic luncheon devoured and scrupulously cleared up. Great licence was allowed; boys and masters chased one another and scuffled on the turf. At length at nightfall we returned wearily singing. When it was all over and the boys in bed we sat in the common-room deploring the miseries of the day. Grimes alone sat with the complacent smile of an Etruscan funerary effigy.
>
> "I confess I enjoyed myself greatly," he said as we groused. We regarded him incredulously. "*Enjoyed* yourself, Grimes? What did you find to enjoy?"

"Knox minor," he said with radiant simplicity. "I felt the games a little too boisterous, so I took Knox minor away behind some rocks. I removed his boot and stocking, opened my trousers, put his dear little foot there and experienced a most satisfying emission."

A memorable confession which, meeting him in after life, I found he had entirely forgotten. Such episodes were not rare in his chosen career. (*LL* 227–28)

Grimes is comic in this passage, and more than a figure of knockabout farce, because, in Waugh's words, his weakness is also his strength: Grimes feels no guilt, nor even any sense of the momentousness of his act. Rebecca West's account of Grimes's "serenity and bloomy sense of inner rightness" hits exactly the right note (221). Waugh gave a striking definition of Grimes's comic impact upon him when his aristocratic friend Katharine Asquith wrote to him in 1964 asking why he had told such an obscene story in his autobiography. He replied:

Simply because I find it a richly comic incident. Forget the moral implications of Grimes's vicious life. I may have told it badly but the point was that here was a new, senior master more or less in command of all of us who had given no hint of his sexual proclivities nor had any indication that any of us would have any sympathy with them. He suddenly electrified us with an unsought & unexpected confession told with complete aplomb. The grotesque details make the point. If I had written: "He confessed to sexual irregularity," there would have been no point. I still find it an enormously comic moment but I know there are fastidious people who won't like it & I am sorry to offend them. (*Letters* 623–24)

If Richard Young's confession about Knox minor was memorable, perhaps so memorable that Waugh felt he did not need to record it at the time, Waugh's autobiography closes with an even more electrifying episode also left out of the diary: on the night of July 1, Waugh tried to commit suicide and failed. *A Little Learning* ends with Waugh's account of his triumph over his wish for easeful death:

> We had a deserted beach where we had to conduct the boys for morning bathes, but from which we could swim alone at night.... One night, soon after I got the news from Pisa, I went down alone to the beach with my thoughts full of death. I took off my clothes and began swimming out to sea. Did I really intend to drown myself? That certainly was in my mind and I left a note with my clothes, the quotation from Euripides about the sea which washes away all human ills. I went to the trouble of verifying it, accents and all from the school text:
>
> Θάλασσα κλύζει πάντα Τανθρώπων χαχά
>
> At my present age, I cannot tell how much real despair and act of will, how much playacting, prompted the excursion.
>
> It was a beautiful night of a gibbous moon. I swam slowly out but, long before I reached the point of no return, the Shropshire Lad was disturbed by a smart on the shoulder. I had run into a jellyfish. A few more strokes, a second more painful sting. The placid waters were full of the creatures.
>
> An omen? A sharp recall to good sense such as Olivia would have administered?
>
> I turned about, swam back through the track of the moon to the sands which that morning had swarmed under Grimes's discerning eye with naked urchins. As earnest of my intent I had brought no towel. With some difficulty I dressed and tore into small pieces my pretentious classical tag, leaving them to the sea, moved on that bleak shore by tides stronger than any known to Euripides, to perform its lustral office. Then I climbed the sharp hill that led to all the years ahead. (228–30)

Waugh has swum out as the Shropshire Lad, but returns to a world enjoyed with Grimes's discerning eye. The sea, rather than washing Waugh clean of all human ills, carries away his foolish claim that he can separate himself from the world of Grimes. Waugh further stresses Grimes's role in this comic triumph of life over death in the autobiography by relating his attempted suicide immediately *after* the account of Grimes's drunken confession: in real life, the confession came after the suicide attempt and not before it, as the diary entry for July 3 reveals. In reality, Young's unbosoming unwittingly consoled a desperate young man; in the autobiography, Grimes's cv epitomizes all that drives Waugh to swim out to sea and all that he accepts when he turns back to the shore.

That Waugh chose to conclude his autobiography with this comic vignette underlines its significance. The last chapter of *A Little Learning* is entitled "In Which Our Hero's Fortunes Fall Very Low," and Waugh's image of a steep uphill climb suggests that, if the confusions and difficulties of Waugh's post-Oxford period were far from over (Waugh had two more turbulent years ahead of him before he would begin his first novel, *Decline and Fall*), still, the failed suicide attempt brought him to a new state of awareness and resolve. In the first paragraph of "A Little Hope," his unfinished and unpublished continuation of *A Little Learning*,[10] Waugh says, "I was unaware of change.... My prospects were as empty, my character as feckless as before my encounter with the jelly-fish. I had nevertheless unknowingly passed a climacteric. After that night everything about me began by small degrees to ameliorate" (qtd. in Stannard, *Evelyn Waugh: The Early Years* 113). Waugh could see in retrospect that the jellyfish had killed the Paul Pennyfeather within him: the single-minded self-absorption that lay behind the suicide attempt, and behind the verified Greek quotation and the resolve to leave this world towel-less, had been dissolved in the sea of life and replaced by a richer, comic outlook. The hill the young Waugh was now ready to climb was Parnassus: he would go on to create a remarkable series of comic novels about the adventures of earnest, innocent young men—Paul Pennyfeather, Tony Last, William Boot, Charles Ryder, and Guy Crouchback. Yet, once the young Waugh had himself left this charmed company of innocents and become their creator, his autobiography became a story that Waugh could not tell. He worked off and on for more than two years, from early 1964 until his death in April 1966, upon the second volume (of a projected three) of his autobiography, and all he managed to complete were five heavily revised pages of manuscript. He had never been able to recount the adventures of a sophisticated, self-aware protagonist, let alone recount them in the first person.[11]

If Waugh actually had a brilliant future before him in 1925, Richard Young's life, from that time onward, had an eccentric glory of its own. Grimes, as well as Richard Young, lived on. As the autobiography suggests, with its comment that in later life Grimes had entirely forgotten the incident that the young Waugh found so electrifying, Waugh looked up Young in 1963 in order to ask his permission to tell about the origins of Captain Grimes. Waugh wrote in some glee to his agent in December 1963: "Captain Grimes had third thoughts about his vicious past and has given me written license to print what ten years ago could not have been printed about the dead let alone the living" (*Letters* 616). In their exchange of letters in 1963, Young told Waugh that he had soon tired of schoolteaching as a profession and tried becoming an author. His first and only novel was entitled *A Preparatory School Murder*, published in 1934 under the name Richard MacNaughton; it was a detective story set, like Waugh's own first novel, in a disguised version of Arnold House. (Young did not inform Waugh, but the prime suspect in the novel's murder is a young, confused, self-divided teacher who is clearly a portrait of Waugh himself. The Waugh figure, who had been sacked for disrespect before the novel begins, is eventually proved innocent.¹²) Not having found great success as an author, Young became a solicitor, but, as he told Waugh, "I was then too old to start a learned profession and took little interest in it" (qtd. in Waugh, *Letters* 116). When Waugh found him in 1963, Young was living in an institution that Anthony Trollope—or Waugh himself—might have created: the Saint Cross Alms Houses, meant for old men in "noble poverty," at Winchester. Young said that he was living there "owing to some unfortunate speculations," but that conditions were very pleasant (qtd. in Waugh, *Letters* 116). "It might be an ideal place for you," he told Waugh, "if you were not married and were a trifle older" (qtd. in *Letters* 116). Young died in 1972, leaving 58,000 pounds and a collection of German and Chelsea porcelain to the Ashmolean Museum in Oxford.¹³

Clearly, then, the Captain Grimes of *Decline and Fall* had his origins in and represents a "climacteric" in the young Waugh's own experience. At least four more conclusions can be drawn from this meeting point of biography and fiction. One is that Grimes carries out in the novel the same factitious suicide that Waugh had attempted—except that Grimes's increasing despair, pile of clothes, hopeless final note, and self-drowning are all deliberately staged.¹⁴ The sea, after all, if full of stinging creatures, is Grimes's natural element: far from drowning in the Irish Sea or Egdon Mire, he has been breasting the waves like some grease-caked Channel-swimmer since the world was created. Waugh's own doubt, despair, and self-castigation exist in poor, dim Prendergast, who is Grimes's opposite, who wrestles with Doubts (with a capital D), and who is murdered by the novel's end: "'Funny thing,' said Grimes,…'but I've never had any Doubts. When you've been in the soup as often as I have, it gives you a sort of feeling that everything's for the best, really'" (45). In fact, as Stannard points out, *Decline and Fall* is "[i]n many respects…a comic version" of "The Balance" (*Evelyn Waugh: The Early Years* 138).

A second conclusion is that we can now understand more fully why the figure of Grimes carries a particular imaginative charge in the novel: he has a special significance for its author. This short, balding, one-legged, and very surprising man, no captain but very grimy, plays virtually no part in the plot of the novel, but he dominates *Decline and Fall*, as Jeffrey Heath says (64).[15] He gives the novel its comic exuberance, its outrageous playfulness. In his death and resurrection, and the example they provide for Paul Pennyfeather, Grimes is a parody-Christ, at once a satiric and a comic figure: he points up the blasphemous materialism of the novel's society and, perhaps more importantly, allows a psychic holiday to all of us who are not, like Grimes, "singularly in harmony with the primitive promptings of humanity" (Waugh, *Decline and Fall* 45).[16] Certainly, almost all readers of *Decline and Fall* have loved Grimes. Many of the first reviewers of the novel joined Rebecca West in singling out Grimes for praise; J. B. Priestley, for instance, said, "Mr. Waugh has done something very difficult to do, he has created a really comic character. This is Captain Grimes" (84). In 1966, John Willett considered Grimes the mainstay of *Decline and Fall* and claimed he "is now part of our heritage" (93).[17] Kingsley Amis, in a retrospective essay written in 1978 on the fiftieth anniversary of the first publication of *Decline and Fall*, considered that it is Waugh's one truly great novel, that it is incidentally satiric and essentially comic, and that Grimes is at the heart of its success ("Fit to Kill" 384).

A third conclusion is that, to the surprise of many readers, the Grimes of the novel is clearly, upon close examination, a pederast. That Grimes is always in the soup because of his "sexual proclivities" (*Letters* 624) is evident from a great many small hints, beginning with Grimes's remark early in the third chapter: "'Temperament,' said Grimes, with a far-away look in his eyes—'that's been my trouble, temperament and sex'" (Waugh, *Decline and Fall* 37). A subordinate series of hints suggests that Young

Clutterbuck is the Knox minor of the novel (see 32, 47, 49, and *passim*). Waugh discloses Grimes's criminal predilection obliquely for the same reason that he uses sly indirection elsewhere in this novel and throughout his other novels: the contradiction between the decorous social surface and its actual meaning, between Grimes's blithe lack of inhibitions and his sordid activities, heightens the comedy and sharpens the satiric attack. Grimes's flourishing life is presented in the same way as Little Lord Tangent's gratuitous death—by tone and implication rather than direct narration. And, in fact, the book is more "richly comic" if we do not "Forget the moral implications of Grimes's vicious life" (*Letters* 624). The chapter entitled "The Agony of Captain Grimes," presenting Grimes's despair at his approaching marriage to the headmaster's daughter, becomes all the more agonized; his subsequent suicide note ("THOSE THAT LIVE BY THE FLESH SHALL PERISH BY THE FLESH") becomes sharper-edged (*Decline and Fall* 134). Many funny moments become even funnier: for instance, the envoi describing Grimes as an immortal life-force, a travesty of Pater's celebrated description of the enigmatic smile of Leonardo's Mona Lisa, gains added point when we realize that Grimes's capacity to teach the childish satyrs the art of love and to stand while Sodom and Gomorrah fall to ruin replaces Pater's conception of a mysterious, eternal knowledge that women possess and men desire.[18] Waugh's revised edition of the novel restores several manuscript readings that he had altered in 1928; Grimes's pederasty is more noticeable in the revised version, but his crime and the indirect narration of it are the same in both versions. The difference between the two editions is one of degree and not of kind.[19]

A final, and more speculative, conclusion emerges from an additional and rather surprising fact: not one reviewer of the novel, and there were at least twenty-five of them between 1928 and 1930, including West, Priestley, Arnold Bennett, and Cyril Connolly (see Davis et al. 156–63), acknowledged Grimes's pederasty, nor did any critic of the novel up to 1973. Early that year, abundant excerpts from Waugh's *Diaries* began appearing in the *Observer*; the entry containing Young's confession of sodomy was published on 1 April 1973 (Waugh, "Private Diaries" 25). Interestingly, the revised edition of 1962 and even the account of Grimes in *A Little Learning* in 1964 had had little effect: for instance, to Stephen Jay Greenblatt in 1965, Grimes is simply "a bigamist and a scroundel [sic]," (9) and to Thomas Friedmann in 1972 he is "a lovable bounder" (5).[20] As we have seen, Waugh presents Grimes in the autobiography as a comic, fictional character, not a real man; once the facts about Richard Young became public knowledge in 1973, however, Grimes is perceived by critics as "a shameless deviate" and a "sodomist," and since then critics have stressed his brutishness (McAleer 2; Phillips 11).[21] How can one explain the fluctuating perception of Grimes by reviewers and critics (as opposed to the common reader) over the past sixty years? Perhaps the obvious explanation suffices: for the first time in British history, public mores in the 1970s allowed frank acknowledgement of homosexuality in print—a change represented by P. N. Furbank's discussion of E. M. Forster's homosexuality in his 1977 biography of the novelist. Another way of accounting for Grimes's ups and downs among the critics is to say that Waugh miscalculated: he made Grimes so enormously charming, on the one hand, and the hints about his proclivities so veiled, on the other, that readers simply did not see what Waugh meant them to see—until publication of his diaries forced them to do so. It is just possible, however, that the critical response to Grimes points to a central fact about Waugh's art and about comic art in general: the distinction between what the reader of *Decline and Fall* knows and does not know is not absolute. The action is presented so externally, the wit is so coruscating and effervescent, the suggestions are so deft, the implications are so shockingly subversive, that the reader half-knows a great deal. A reviewer of the novel in 1928 notes, "There is a steady stream running through the book of salacious innuendoes, which seem perpetually about to break out into something which one would not expect to see in print" (J.M.S.G. 83). This state of semi-awareness, of always being on the edge of being surprised by something one already knows, is exactly the state of mind that led to *Decline and Fall*, since Young/Grimes served as Waugh's mentor without realizing it, and Waugh himself passed his climacteric unknowingly. Like the elder Waugh trying to decide just what was in the mind of the Shropshire Lad, Waugh's reader cannot tell how much is conscious knowledge and how much is play-acting.

NOTES

1. As Waugh explains in his preface, the second edition restores several manuscript readings that Waugh altered when the novel was first published in 1928 (with the title *Decline and Fall: An Illustrated Novelette*); his editors, fearing that the book might seem too licentious, suggested that several passages be toned down, and Waugh complied.
2. The facts in the following paragraph are drawn from *A Little Learning* (henceforth *LL*), *The Diaries of Evelyn Waugh* (*Diaries*), and *The Letters of Evelyn Waugh* (*Letters*).
3. Arnold House no longer exists; a detailed description of it by Derek Verschoyle, who was a student there during Waugh's seven months at the school, can be found in Christopher Sykes (93–95). Another account of the school is given in Ronald Harwood and John Selwyn Gilbert (528–29). Photographs of Arnold House and of the headmaster and his wife were included when the *Observer* printed excerpts from Waugh's diaries in 1973 ("The Private Diaries of Evelyn Waugh" 16–17).
4. This is Michael Davie's judgement in his edition of the *Diaries* (vi). Martin Stannard, Waugh's most recent biographer, concurs (*Evelyn Waugh: The Early Years* 66–68).

5. The volume of essays was probably Russell's *Mysticism and Logic and Other Essays*; this influential collection of skeptical essays went through its sixth impression in 1925.
6. For detailed description and commentary, see Davis (*Evelyn Waugh, Writer* 32–38).
7. Ian Littlewood also contrasts Waugh's accounts of Young in the diary with that of Grimes in the autobiography (185–87).
8. In his later life, now a successful man of letters, country squire, and paterfamilias, Waugh spoke openly of his homosexual phase; for instance, in a letter to Nancy Mitford of December 1954, he describes Richard Pares as "my first homosexual love" (*Letters* 435; cf. *LL* 191–92).
9. It seems that two of the flagrant gaps in the diaries (the Oxford period and the breakdown) are the result of Waugh's later destruction of an existing diary and that the other two (the marriage collapse and the conversion) simply represent Waugh's inability or refusal to record such experience; see Davie's comments in Waugh's *Diaries* (vi–vii, 157, 305, 328, 724), and Stannard's biography, *Evelyn Waugh: The Early Years* (66, 153, 215).
10. The manuscript itself is in the Humanities Research Center, at the University of Texas at Austin.
11. As Robert Murray Davis points out, in "The Failure of Imagination: Evelyn Waugh's School Stories," Waugh "did not complete any serious attempt to portray anything like his own character" (97).
12. Young's novel and its relationship to *Decline and Fall* were brought to light in T. M. Higham, "Captain Grimes's Revenge" (65–73).
13. The facts in this paragraph are drawn, in part, from Higham's article.
14. Littlewood makes much the same point (187). The resemblance is also noted by Gene D. Phillips (10).
15. See also the comments by Willet and Amis later in this paragraph.
16. The conception of Grimes as a parody of Christ is stressed by Jerome Meckier, though Meckier sees Grimes only as a vehicle for bitter satire (51–75). A similar view is advanced by Heath, who sees Grimes as an embodiment of barbarism (*Picturesque* 65).
17. Willett observes, "there is only one memorable episode in which Grimes does not take part: the convicts in chapel making their gory *ad hoc* adaptation of hymns A. &. M." (93).
18. The travesty of Pater is noted by Edward C. McAleer (1–2) and by Heath (64). Pater's description of Mona Lisa in *The Renaissance* (1873)—"She is older than

the rocks among which she sits"—gave English aesthetes their credo and prize specimen: W. B. Yeats, for instance, chose the passage, laid out as verse, as the first poem in his anthology of modern poetry, *The Oxford Book of Modern Verse, 1892–1935*, chosen by W. B. Yeats (1).

19. In his 1962 preface, Waugh himself describes the 1928 changes as "negligible" (11). For a survey of the changes, see Paul A. Doyle (4–5). Stannard is incorrect when he implies that the manuscript was bowdlerized in 1928 to remove all reference to "an overt homosexual relationship between Captain Grimes and the boy Clutterbuck" (*Evelyn Waugh: The Early Years* 156; also J.M.S.G. 83–84). For a description of the manuscript, which is also in the Humanities Research Center of the University of Texas, see Davis (*Evelyn Waugh, Writer* 39–50) and Jeffrey Heath, "Waugh's *Decline and Fall* in Manuscript" (523–30).

20. James F. Carens offers both a partial exception to this generalization and an explanation for it when he observes, "The...account of 'Grimes' that Waugh gives in the first volume of his autobiography, *A Little Learning* (1964), is extraordinary, indeed. Even in this nonfictional treatment, however, Waugh's sense of 'Grimes,' who might have been rendered as a pathetic victim of aberrant appetites, is that of the satirist" (60).

21. Meckier and Heath, among others, see Grimes as bestial.

 # Traditional Comedy and the Comic Mask in Kingsley Amis's *Lucky Jim*

READERS OF ALL SORTS continue to find *Lucky Jim* exhilarating. Anyone who has taught Amis's novel recently to North American undergraduates knows that it still has a unique energy and immediacy, though the social controversies that swirled around it in the years following its publication in 1954 are now history. Yet there have been few attempts to account for the intensity of laughter *Lucky Jim* produces. The prevailing view is, as Rubin Rabinovitz maintains, that "Amis' humor is mainly satirical" (59). An alternative is to acknowledge gratefully that Amis's funny business is very funny indeed and leave the matter at that: Ralph Caplan remarks, "Have we forgotten how to take humor straight? Unable to exit laughing, the contemporary reader looks over his shoulder for Something More. The trouble is that by now he knows how to find it. So Amis' prodigious gifts were regarded from the first as instrumental, a kit for exploring social problems, and fairly restricted social problems at that" (4). I would like to outline here a third position: *Lucky Jim* is neither satire nor high-spirited farce (nor a uniquely adroit fusion of the two[1]), but, like its eighteenth-century progenitor, *Tom Jones*, absorbs satire and farce into a broader comic structure and vision. David Lodge, in his penetrating chapter on Amis in his *Language of Fiction*, approaches the novel in just these terms; but because Lodge's subject is the creative use of language in English fiction, he concentrates, as do several other critics, on the wordplay so evident in the texture of Amis's novels.[2]

Lucky Jim, then, has itself become a strangely neglected topic. In all that has been written on the novel, for instance, nobody has observed that its title alludes to its comic structure and perspective as surely as do, say, *Much Ado about Nothing* and *Pride and Prejudice*. Similarly, Jim's face-making, the funniest single device in the novel and the one that stays in the reader's mind as its great comic invention, gets very little critical attention.[3] I will argue here that Jim's faces function as a modern version of the comic mask: they create the holiday world of comedy, just as the masquerade—the donning of masks—does in traditional comedy.

First, though, we should note how artfully Amis has recreated in narrative form the conflicts, patterns, devices, and vision of traditional stage comedy, just as his literary hero, Henry Fielding, had done two centuries earlier in *Tom Jones*.[4] Both novels have a fast-paced, external action: scenes succeed each other with accelerating speed as the comic hero hurtles toward a disaster that he miraculously—luckily—escapes at the last minute. Both have the age-old plot of young lovers rebelling against an obstructing society of foolish elders that has power—in *Lucky Jim*, both psychological and social power—over each of the lovers. The lovers are ideal in their very normality; Jim is a comic everyman (as Tom Jones is by his very name) and wins his job at the end, not because he is qualified for it, but because, he is told, "You haven't got the disqualifications, though, and that's much rarer" (Amis, *Lucky Jim* 234). The spontaneous desire of Jim and Christine, the healthy young lovers, is strong enough to impose a happy ending on the story, overcoming not only the drab logic of reality, but also their own considered objections to their union.

My point is that our laughter is not so much at individual moments in *Lucky Jim* as at the conflicts and movement of the whole action. Suzanne Langer argues that comedy presents the rhythm of life overcoming obstacles and renewing itself; since laughter itself, according to Langer, is a surge of vital feeling, our laughter while reading or seeing a comedy is the crest of a wave of intensified vitality, the rising to a breaking-point of our response to the work as a whole (119–40, esp. 131–36). This notion allows us to understand Jim's luck. It is not, in fact, chance or coincidence, but the providence that rules in comedy, where the predictable happy ending is heightened and enriched by the playfully unpredictable quirks of circumstance that produce that ending. If the dammed-up energy and high spirits in Jim bring him horrendously bad luck from the first stone he kicks as Welch's subordinate, the same energies finally bring him, as a counterbalance, astonishingly good luck. Furthermore, Jim's comic providence, like that of Tom Jones, is voluntarist, not predestinarian: luck will save Jim, but only if and when "[f]or once in his life Dixon resolved to bet on his luck" (Amis, *Lucky Jim* 136).

The external source of Jim's luck, Gore-Urquhart, is frequently criticized as a gratuitous character imported from the realms of romance. But such a character is the traditional agent of fortune in comedy, the genial older man whose authority overrules the obstructing society (Jonson's Lovewit, or Sheridan's Uncle Oliver). Northrop Frye considers such a figure inherent in the three-phase movement of comedy, where "we have a stable and harmonious order disrupted by folly, obsession, forgetfulness, 'pride and prejudice,' or events not understood by the characters themselves, and then restored" (*Anatomy* 171).[5]

The action of the novel, then, is the essential comic one: the struggle of two social orders. Professor Welch is not merely a classic instance of Henri Bergson's mechanical man (155–56, 79–80), solemn, unaware of himself, slow-witted, absent-minded ("Faulkner"!), unable to use rudimentary social conventions like syntax, and predictable in all these traits; the professor is also the centre of power in his own constricted, absurd, and life-stifling society. His vague invitations to tea or dinner, and his wife's more pointed threats, have an absolute power over Jim. Allied with the Welches are those they sponsor among the younger people, Bertrand and Margaret. These would-be lovers, another comic convention, are also mechanical: their manipulative behaviour is as predictable as their mannerisms—Margaret's laugh as of tiny silver bells, Bertrand's "you sam" and his hackneyed witticisms.

Set against the Welches and their spy, Johns, is a comically diverse group: Jim, Christine, Carol, Gore-Urquhart, and Atkinson. The characters are grouped symmetrically, as in traditional comedy: for every Margaret, there is a Bertrand; for every Atkinson, a Johns. Jim tells Christine on the way home from the dance that she and Bertrand represent "the two great classes of mankind, people I like and people I don't" (Amis, *Lucky Jim* 143). Those whom Jim likes share Christine's "more normal, i.e. less unworkable, character" (242); Margaret and Bertrand, Jim realizes, are radically different, and, unlike them, Jim has no "desire to range himself with children, neurotics, and invalids by thus specializing his needs" (141).

Another important comic convention in the novel grows out of the struggle of social orders: the double plot. Bertrand, like Fielding's Blifil or Congreve's Fainall, is the hero's rival both for the girl he loves and for a higher place in society. This double struggle anchors the comic action in the world of actual satisfactions; more importantly, it creates an intricate, rapid train of events that can finally be resolved into a complex and balanced harmony.

This counterpointed plotting forces comic detachment on us, as we must stand back to grasp the multiplying complexities and the patterns that emerge through them. For instance, a reflective reader notices that Gore-Urquhart is a comic *deus ex machina* in both plots, not only offering Jim a new job, but also freeing Carol to tell Christine about her secret relationship with Bertrand.

As in traditional comedy, the characters, without realizing it, trace a symmetrical, dance-like pattern. Just as, in Fielding's *Tom Jones*, we see Sophia pursue Tom Jones to Upton, and then emerge, hurt and indignant, with Tom in pursuit of her, so Jim's eager compliance with Christine's message that she will be at the railway station if he cares to join her is the exact counterpart of her acceptance, halfway through the novel, of his offer to wait outside the dance for twenty minutes if she cares to join him. The book begins with Welch adding to Jim's trials by confusing an appointment; it ends with Welch saving Jim by confusing train departures. Just as Christine surprises Margaret and Jim at Margaret's door as he is being indignantly bundled out, so Margaret surprises Christine and Jim laughing together outside the same door the next morning. Only we can see how apt Carol's reply to Jim on the dance floor is; as he tries to understand why she is angry, why she wants him to pursue Christine, and why she attacks Margaret's hold over him, Carol says, "it's all connected, all connected" (Amis, *Lucky Jim* 121). The union of Carol and Gore-Urquhart, implied in the final pages, is an important part of this comic design.

This conception of *Lucky Jim* as a comedy has been far from obvious to critics of the novel.[6] It seems, then, an idea worth pursuing in further detail, and I would like to do so by looking in turn at four characteristics of traditional comedy that figure centrally in *Lucky Jim*: the happy ending, the use of festivity, the mood of play, and the pervasive comic irony.

The end of comedy, both its goal and its conclusion, is the achievement of what might be called a morality of desire. That is, what the central characters want to do coincides in the end with what they ought to do. Fielding makes this the theme as well as the pattern of *Tom Jones*: Tom's impulses lead him inevitably into foolish errors, but they are also a necessary part of the beneficent pattern of growth into maturity. Comedy presents a conflict of morality and desire, but resolves that conflict into a larger harmony. Jim's desire for Christine is "as natural to him, as unimportant and unobjectionable, as reaching out to take a large ripe peach from a fruit-dish" (73). By the same token, Jim's conscience eventually leads him *to*, not away from, Christine: Carol repeatedly tells him, "you've got a moral duty to perform. Get that girl away from Bertrand" (125). Jim's truth is more than a truism when he affirms "his theory that nice things are nicer than nasty ones" (140).

The happy ending of traditional comedy usually results from immersion in a festive, carnival world: the characters, freed from everyday constraints, sort themselves out into new and truer relationships. *Lucky Jim* concentrates its action in and through three scenes of spurious festivity, which Jim turns into genuine saturnalia. These scenes—the arty weekend, the midsummer ball, and the Merrie England lecture—take up about half the novel's length. In the first and last, Jim gets wildly drunk; at the ball, he drinks freely and enthusiastically. In all, he experiences a violent, childlike desire that the adult world should be more as he wants it to be. The important point is that Jim's saturnalia grow increasingly communal, marking his progress from misfit and secret rebel in one society to central figure in another, fitter one. Jim's carnival is, at first, private: the "festive, Yule-tide pop" of the Welch port bottle, makes him alone feel splendid (59), even if his drunkenness does clarify his relations with Margaret (not to mention Mrs. Welch) and set in motion a new relationship with the "dignant"

Christine (68). Jim is one of six lovers at the ball, which tries out all possible pairings and sorts the lovers into proper partnerships as surely as a Shakespearean revel. By the Merrie England lecture, Jim is the Lord of Misrule, turning a pious tribute to folk custom into a living celebration of merrymaking. Fittingly, Jim's final face, the farewell to face-making he uses to celebrate happiness, is his "Sex Life in Ancient Roman face" (250). This pattern is amplified by Jim's growing participation in another, more mundane festivity—laughter. Bergson points out that laughter expresses and demands shared delight, complicity: we are uncomfortable laughing alone (64–65). Thus the action of comedy—the creation of a new community—is a formal counterpart of the communal impulse in laughter. Surprisingly, right up until Christine's laughter over his bed forces Jim to laugh with her, we have never seen Jim laugh, and even then it is "not because he was much amused but because he felt grateful to her for her laughter" (Amis, *Lucky Jim* 73). But his subsequent explanations to Margaret finally allow him to reach a comic detachment: "As he talked, his incendiarism and the counter-measures adopted struck him for the first time as funny" (74). From this point on, Jim and Christine are brought together again and again by her healthy and contagious laughter.

The ending and the festive scenes are structural features; equally important, perhaps, in creating traditional comedy is the comic mood. Unlike modern comedy, in which no person or act can be merely or finally ridiculous, the traditional sort assumes, like children at play, that there is a larger realm of serious reality that, in turn, allows the creation of a special, holiday world of mock-seriousness.[7] The very title page establishes this mood: there we find the epigraph-cum-title of serious works of fiction like *The Sun Also Rises* or *The Sound and the Fury* or *Tender Is the Night*, but we are directed for metaphorical significance, not to the Bible or Shakespeare or Keats, but to an unknown and suspiciously appropriate OLD SONG. And Amis keeps us aware from the start (for instance, by Jim's memories and dreams of London) that there is a larger frame of reality, in relation to which the university world is a separate mock-world with its own arbitrary rules. Jim at least knows that he is playing games, unlike Welch, Bertrand, and (particularly) Margaret: even when his fortunes are lowest, he knows that he is "jobless, Christineless, and now grand-slammed in the Margaret game" (220). Comedy maintains this playful mood by assuring us implicitly throughout that good will eventually triumph. Just as no sensible reader doubts whether Tom Jones will win his Sophia or be hanged, no matter how much artful suspense accumulates, so we are assured that Jim will triumph by the good luck that, symmetrically and emblematically, consoles him and us for every stroke of bad luck. If he is acutely uncomfortable opening and closing his mouth in silence while madrigals are sung, Bertrand and Christine arrive just in time to prevent his exposure (38). If Welch makes a particularly irritating demand on his "time and integrity" (173) by asking Jim to do his busywork, luck throws Jim the vignette, emblematic in itself, of Welch struggling to enter a revolving door the wrong way: Jim "felt it was things like this that kept him going" (174). In such a play world, there can be no real or lasting suffering: Margaret's neuroticism is so melodramatic and widely advertised as to seem unreal, while Jim's humiliation at his lecture is the means to his final reward. Similarly, evil is ultimately powerless: the Don Johns and Blifils can be laughed off or even forgiven. Jim comes to see that Welch is actually decent enough, for all his self-absorbed stupidity: Jim regrets, once he has been fired, "having spent so much of his time and energy in hating Welch" (229).

It is worth pausing over my final characteristic, irony, since it plays such a central, yet subtle, role in *Lucky Jim*. Irony is inherently comic. Not only does the shock of ironic awareness always engender detachment, but the movement of traditional comedy is itself an ironic process. Irony exists when there is a clash of ostensible and real meanings in a speech or situation; traditional comedy dramatizes the clash between fossilized forms and energies hidden within or beneath those forms. Consequently, the movement of a comedy like *Lucky Jim* is ironic, since we can see the familiar comic action fulfilling itself, without the knowledge and even against the will of the main actors in it. Jim, like the heroes and heroines of Shakespeare or Congreve or Jane Austen, unconsciously resents the power over him of his need for Christine: when he taunts Bertrand into personal combat over her, he *thinks* he does so solely for the pleasure of giving Bertrand what he deserves. Furthermore, the narrative method is ironic. Jim is himself an ironist: the contrast between his public mask—conventional, mild, subservient—and the violent energies within is Amis's chief ironic, and so comic, device. Confronted with Margaret's avowals at the ball, Jim manages "a remark both honest and acceptable: 'You mustn't say things like that'" (111). The novel itself is told not simply from Jim's point of view, but in a concise, understated style that corresponds exactly to Jim's own ironic way of communicating. For instance, we last see Welch's car "parked slightly nearer one kerb than the other" (250).

This ironic vision becomes richest when it is trained upon Jim himself, something that Jim is unable to do, since Jim is as self-deceived as the other major characters. Critics think of Jim—just as he thinks of himself—as a clear-sighted penetrator of other people's folly; but, as Anthony Burgess points out, "[a]lthough we are meant to be on Dixon's side, we are also intended to laugh at him, to pity his ignorance" (142). Jim's ignorance is mainly of himself: if he is unwilling to admit to his love for Christine, his feelings about Margaret are even more tangled and obscure. Margaret has Jim hoodwinked, though he thinks he is in control of the Margaret game. Note, for instance, how Jim refuses to acknowledge to himself Margaret's brazen desertion of him for Gore-Urquhart at the ball. After Jim and Margaret agree to call off everything between them, "[h]e thought of his appointment with Christine the next day but one, and regarded it entirely without pleasure. Some part of what had happened in the last half-hour had spoilt all that, though he didn't know which part. Somewhere his path to Christine was blocked; it was all going to go wrong in some way he couldn't foresee" (164). It is part of himself that spoils the break with Margaret, the part that welcomes humiliation and enjoys grievances, the part that Margaret, and Margaret alone, knows and addresses as "James." Jim is like Beatrice and Benedick, or Elizabeth Bennet and Emma Woodhouse, in that the obstacles between him and his love are internal, mental blocks, rather than simply blocking characters. We may suspect that more than nobility lies behind Jim's refusal to tell Christine of Bertrand's affair with Carol: Jim confesses as much to Christine at the novel's end.

Jim's conscience is a source of irony. It is both his scourge and his salvation: "He'd been drawn into the Margaret business by a combination of virtues he hadn't known he possessed" (10), yet his conscience is also Margaret's ally and the source of her power. Again and again, Jim tries chivalrously not to notice her manipulating poses and blames himself when he does. His conscience is always telling him he must try harder, be more understanding: he mustn't "allow his irritation with some of the things about her to do what it always did, to obscure what was most important: she was a neurotic who'd recently taken a bad beating" (77). Jim's patronizing concern allows him to remain independent and invulnerable. After inviting Christine to join him outside the dance, Jim thinks, "She wouldn't come, of course, but at any rate he'd made his gesture. In other words, he'd thought of a way of hurting himself more severely than usual, and in public" (128).

The note of self-pity is typical: if Margaret holds Jim by "pity's adhesive plaster" (243), that pity is partly self-pity for his own constant sacrifices. We see the pattern at the ball when Margaret addresses Jim as "Poor James." Jim bristles inwardly, but then goes through the familiar cycle of guilt for his resentment, self-castigation for his callousness and neglect, and renewed pity for her loneliness. Within ten lines he is thinking, "Poor old Margaret.... He must try harder" (111). Just as Christine is, ironically, a mirror image of Jim's split nature, so Margaret and Jim echo each other. She secretly despises Jim; the mask falls for a moment the day after the ball when she bursts out with "You don't think she'd have you, do you? A shabby little provincial bore like you" (158).

Analysis of the psychological ironies is misleading. Comedy has no time for such introspection: inner conflicts and changes are conveyed in extroverted form (Tom wins his Sophia, Jim leaves Margaret for Christine). But the conflicts and changes are nonetheless there. Jim's comic liberation is finally the freeing of himself from himself. His anxiety throughout over his job is more complex than it seems: he does not really want the post (or, more precisely, the success by Welch standards necessary to win it).[8] His nervousness as the lecture approaches is partly nervousness lest he should be able to go through with such a complete prostitution of his talents as this exercise in ventriloquism clearly is (see the three snippets from it: 166, 195, 204–05). Jim's split response to both Christine and Margaret is similarly, if much more subtly, ironic. Certainly Jim's real luck is Catchpole's sudden reappearance, though Jim begins to feel that he needs even more than Catchpole's evidence: "Failing some other purgative agent than facts, he could foresee himself coming to disbelieve this lot altogether" (238). That agent immediately appears when Jim learns of Christine's offer to meet him halfway, so to speak, at the station. Jim's own acts, culminating in his lecture, win him Gore-Urquhart's favour and Christine's love, but only comic providence can extricate him from Margaret.

This context of traditional comedy enables us to understand more precisely how Jim's fantasies, and particularly his secret faces, work within the novel. Jim's faces have two functions: they establish him as the comic hero, bursting with frustrated and misdirected vitality; they also create an inward version of the masquerade, the carnival interregnum, of comedy. If we look at any one of Jim's faces, we see it creates sympathy with him, yet keeps that sympathy detached and comic. When Jim makes his shot-in-the-back face on being hailed by Michie (27), or his lemon-sucking face in the darkness on hearing Christine express Bertrand's philosophy that artists are special (141), the image allows us to experience from within Jim's inner repudiation. At the same time, we join in transforming his life into the "intensified, speeded-up, exaggerated" world of comic types described by Langer (135). Yet Jim must outgrow his secret and self-pitying faces by sharing them, by communicating his vital powers.[9]

Jim's face-making, more than anything else, conveys to us these heroic powers. Jim's public mask, the one he wears in hopes of succeeding in Welch society, is completely untrue to his inner nature. He must "flail his features into some sort of response to [Welch's] humour" (Amis, *Lucky Jim* 8); though he struggles to complete his lecture by the evening of delivery, he must pretend to Welch that he has long since finished it (172) and that "I guarantee I could read that script blindfold, I've been through it so many times" (212). Jim compensates for his hypocrisy by an ever-erupting volcano of inner revolt. Face-making is merely his main outlet: his hands surreptitiously form fists, and he makes mocking, obscene gestures (12, 56, 175, 241); he mumbles "a long string of swear-words" to himself (81) and hums his derisive Welch music (87, 147, 174); he imagines abusive analogies, seeing Welch as "an African savage being shown a simple conjuring trick" (12), a "broken robot" (79), "some obsolete howitzer" (84), possessed of a "sexual maniac's smile" (175), and, as the moment of judgement nears, "an old boxer, given to a bit of poaching now and then, standing with his ex-kitchenmaid wife" (220). And every reader must be struck by Jim's fantasies of attacking the Welches. Each instance of dithering absurdity or affectation ignites a precise fantasy of physical revenge. Jim not only sees through the Welch crowd; he also rebels against them violently, if secretly, with dammed-up moral, emotional, and imaginative energy. Jim is, after all, a rough and ready poet of the moral life. His faces are metaphors: his Edith Sitwell face, for example, concretizes his triumphant disdain after the disguised telephone interview with Bertrand (102).

It is worth remarking that Jim's face-making draws its power from a condition in everyday life. Faces are, by far, the most expressive part of our bodies—so expressive, in fact, that we are trained not to allow this expressiveness its free play. Ernst Kris argues that laughter is so satisfying a release because it is the one time in social intercourse that adults allow their faces their natural expressiveness (217–39). The physical constraints, like the moral ones Freud stressed in his discussions of humour, no longer rule. George Santayana's reflections on the comic mask, which he considers the primitive spirit of comedy, offer a suggestive parallel:

> Objections to the comic mask—to the irresponsible, complete, extreme expression of each moment—cut at the roots of all expression. Pursue this path, and at once you do away with gesture: we must not point, we must not pout, we must not cry, we must not laugh aloud; we must not only avoid attracting attention, but our attention must not be obviously attracted; it is silly to gaze, says the nursery-governess, and rude to stare. (75)

Jim and his creator are both keenly aware of the sensitive, magnifying power of facial features. Jim not only makes faces to himself, but he exuberantly transforms the face on the cover of Johns's magazine with a few pencil strokes. Welch's small eyes and "large, open-pored tetrahedron" of a nose (86), Margaret's removing her glasses, Bertrand's flattened eyeballs, all convey dramatic meaning. Jim even sees that Christine's face "touched upon other sorts of face by a kind of physiognomical allusion"—but, unlike Margaret, whose face reminds him of a man he once knew, Christine's facial analogues are all female (154). Welch's face, like his personality, is to Jim a mechanism running on without human intervention: "Welch went on talking, his own face the perfect audience for his talk, laughing at its jokes, reflecting its puzzlement or earnestness, responding with tightened lips and narrowed eyes to its more important points" (178).

Jim's faces are, by contrast, "the irresponsible, complete, extreme expression of each moment" (Santayana 75); they have the power to, and eventually do, create a joyous carnival, as Santayana says the comic mask does. We can describe the action of traditional comedy—of Shakespearean comedy, for example—as a masquerade, a playful, fantasticated donning of masks, which leads to a final clarification or restoration of true identity. The comedy ends when masks no longer need be worn. Yet here the masks are internalized; they can only create festivity when Jim shares them, and so the action of the novel traces Jim's gradual freeing of his inner resources in overt, communal action. Leslie Fiedler has claimed that Jim's faces are more significant than the plot of the novel (420); the truth is that the faces reflect, and create, the curve of Jim's movement from isolation to community.

Jim's faces are, at first, a venting of his concealed antagonism. When making his Sex Life in Ancient Roman face at the end, he reflects, "what a pity it was that all his faces were designed to express rage or loathing" (250). But once he leads Christine onto the dance floor, he feels a positive counterpart to his usual face-making: "Dixon felt like a special agent, a picaroon, a Chicago war-lord, a hidalgo, an oil baron, a mohock" (113). No longer is Jim secretly a crazy peasant, a consumptive, a tragic mask, or a Martian invader. Christine draws Jim into public, rather than merely private, independence, into offensive and not simply defensive manoeuvres, into war against Bertrand, rather than mere rebellion.

It is Jim's physical triumph over Bertrand, in fact, that sets in motion, as if magically, the upward swing of his fortunes—and it is in this scene that his faces are first made for others. Until now, Jim has never made his faces publicly, just as he has never declared openly his own feelings (his "Well, hard luck" to Margaret is a momentary dropping of his public mask, which he quickly repairs [158]). Only once, two days before the lecture (and the fight), have others seen one of his faces: his grimace at his ripped pants is inadvertently witnessed by Christine, Bertrand, Mrs. Welch, and Margaret (179). Now, though, his faces come into the open. Bertrand enters in the middle of Jim's cathartic ape imitation and takes it as a personal affront. Jim makes their fight inevitable when he shrieks, "I'm not Sam, you fool," at once exposing Bertrand's mask and revealing his own secret mockery: "this was the worst taunt of all." And, after the battle, Jim finally utters what is inside him, in ritual manner, over the prostrate Bertrand: "The bloody old towser-faced boot-faced totem-pole on a crap reservation, Dixon thought. 'You bloody old towser-faced boot-faced totem-pole on a crap reservation,' he said" (209). Michie immediately knocks on Jim's door "[a]s if discreetly applauding this terminology" and quickly enters.[10]

From this point on, Jim's comic masks are more and more openly, and more and more publicly, displayed. He puts on, and speaks through, the mask of American mobster with Christine and Bertrand at the sherry party: "Better do as he says, lady, otherwise he's liable to kick your teeth in" (216). Jim is surprised in the washroom by Gore-Urquhart while making a more savage version of his Evelyn Waugh face; Gore-Urquhart sympathizes and helps create Jim's carnival by plying him with whisky (220–21).

The lecture shows Jim's comic invention, as well as the novelist's, at its most brilliant. Jim creates a carnival by putting on a medley of funny faces. At first, his masks are unconscious imitations of Welch and the principal, but they soon turn to voluntary assertions. Jim decides to go down fighting, if go down he must: "He'd do some good, however small, to those present, however few. No more imitations, they frightened him too much, but he could suggest by his intonation, very subtly of course, what he thought of his subject and the worth of the statements he was making" (225). Jim finally shares his face-making genius: "Within quite a short time he was contriving to sound like an unusually fanatical Nazi trooper in charge of a book-burning reading out to the crowd excerpts from a pamphlet written by a pacifist, Jewish, literate Communist" (226). Jim completes the lecture by dropping his masks entirely: he comes around to the front of the lectern and denounces Merrie England and Merrie Englanders *in propria persona*.

Jim's faces keep their comic functions until the very end. On the one hand, his expressiveness is his distinctive power as a comic hero: he catches the crucial bus by winning over the bus conductor with "the best-known obscene gesture" (241). At the same time, now that he can make his faces publicly, Jim releases his dammed-up energies and no longer needs his faces. When he discovers that Caton has stolen his article, "[a]t a loss for faces, he drew in his breath to swear, then cackled hysterically instead" (229).

The final tableau summarizes both the comic action and Jim's changing use of his faces. Structurally, Jim, with Christine on his arm, stands in the centre of this little dumb-show, laughing with manic energy at the Welches, revealed for what they are—waxwork dummies. Jim's face is at the centre of this scene: he first puts on "a fruity comic-butler voice" and nods indulgently to Mrs. Welch, since "[h]e remembered something in a book about success making people humble, tolerant, and kind." But this mask is soon replaced by simple, total, open delight: "With Christine tugging at his arm he halted in the middle of the group, slowly doubling up like a man with the stitch, his spectacles misting over with the exertion of it, his mouth stuck ajar in a rictus of agony. 'You're...' he said. 'He's...'" (251). Northrop Frye suggests that the three-phase action of comedy is "like the removal of a neurosis or blocking point and the restoring of an unbroken current of energy and memory" (*Anatomy* 171). The action of *Lucky Jim* is not simply like such a removal—it *is* that removal.

NOTES

1. See R. B. Parker's "Farce and Society: The Range of Kingsley Amis."
2. Some brief but illuminating comments on *Lucky Jim* as comedy occur in Gerard Strauch (57–66). Several critics have stressed Amis's wordplay; James Gindin, for instance, speaks of Amis's "quick verbal incongruities" (*Postwar* 38).
3. Lodge is a notable exception (254–55). Two sober existentialist interpretations of Jim's faces are offered by Ted E. Boyle and Terence Brown and also by Naomi Lebowitz.
4. During the fifties, Amis frequently proclaimed his admiration for Fielding. The most striking instances are the tribute paid in the climactic scene of Amis's third novel, *I Like It Here*, and Amis's essay, "Laughter's to Be Taken Seriously."
5. Frye's views have influenced my discussion of comedy throughout this essay.
6. For instance, Amis is alternately taken to task by F. R. Karl (224) and praised by James Gindin for lacking an artful structure in *Lucky Jim* (Karl 224; Gindin, "Reassertion" 128).
7. Elder Olson makes a relaxation of seriousness essential to comedy in his *The Theory of Comedy* (see especially 16, 36). Robert W. Corrigan has some suggestive remarks in "Comedy and the Comic Spirit" (4–7). Both develop the implications of Aristotle's definition of the ludicrous (*Poetics* ch. 5).

8. John D. Hurrell argues that Jim is trying subconsciously throughout to get himself fired (39–53).
9. This point is made in rather different terms by Alan Kennedy (272–73).
10. Lodge discusses the fight scene in similar terms: "The issues of the novel can only be resolved when Jim wills his inner life to coincide with his outer life" (255). Jim's declamation finally expresses his initial response to Bertrand: "He thought of a sentence in a book he'd once read: 'And with that he picked up the bloody old towser by the scruff of the neck, and, by Jesus, he near throttled him'" (50). Amusingly, Jim's sentence is from the Cyclops episode of Joyce's *Ulysses*.

∞ Afterword   ISOBEL GRUNDY

THE EPIGRAPH for this collection might well be a sentence that Bruce Stovel uses as he approaches the topic of Walter Scott's allusions in *Waverley* to Homer's *Aeneid*: "We have some hope of reward, then," in examining these allusions. Every one of these essays is written in hope of reward, and every one is rewarding to read in several ways. The reading itself is a pleasure, partly because Bruce is so attuned to the pleasures of reading, partly because he always has something specific to say, something of value for the understanding and enjoyment of the text or texts he discusses, and partly because of the lucidity and friendliness, often the humour, of his style.

    His topics are specific, but they illuminate broad issues. Examining those allusions to the *Aeneid* enables a brilliant reading of the depth and sadness, the epic qualities, of *Waverley*, which is particularly salutary at a time when intense interest in the romance has directed critical comment on *Waverley* to favour that aspect over others.

    This collection ranges widely, back in time to Homer and forward to Kingsley Amis's *Lucky Jim* (1954). The central genre here is not romance but comedy, and the central author is Jane Austen. To read Austen's novels as comedy, as Bruce astutely points out, is to align them for comparison not only with their novelistic contemporaries or immediate predecessors, but also with Shakespearean romantic comedy and Restoration comedy of manners. Such breadth of reference is well fitted to Bruce's catholic interests.

Commitment to the genre of comedy sustains the marvellous "*Tom Jones* and the *Odyssey*," which makes a case for complex and enriching intertextuality—a reading against the grain of most comment on *Tom Jones*, which tends to minimize or overlook the structural and thematic relationship with the *Odyssey* in favour of the specific, mock-heroic use of passages from the *Iliad*. It sustains, too, the piece on *Lucky Jim*, whose anti-hero's habit of pulling funny faces Bruce reads as analogous to the masks of traditional comedy. This essay convincingly demonstrates the tight comic structure of a novel often read as unstructured.

The individual essays deploy a wide range of tools. "The Genesis of Evelyn Waugh's Comic Vision" is a model of biographical criticism, using actual events and characters variously presented in Waugh's diary and letters to illuminate their creative transformation in his first published novel. "Asking versus Telling," which observes Jane Austen distinguishing these two roles in conversation and what they imply about their users, ends with a confession that the genre of literary criticism finds asking difficult or impossible. Value judgement, too, has its place. In his essay on Austen's prayers, Bruce observes categorically, in passing, that her best novels are *Pride and Prejudice* and *Emma*. Who, reading his discussions of those novels here, would have the temerity to disagree?

Many of these essays grew out of Bruce's teaching. "Female Difficulties" is an early and wonderfully perceptive analysis of Charlotte Lennox's *The Female Quixote* and Frances Burney's *Camilla*, both novels that were featured on the syllabus of the graduate course that Bruce and I team-taught at the University of Alberta in 1990–1991. It reflects the excitement of reading eighteenth-century novels by women at a date when hardly anyone was yet doing that, and it reflects also the sobering discovery that these authors were using the genre of comedy, or romance, or courtship novel, to point the narrowness and barrenness of the choices open in their day to marriageable young women.

That graduate syllabus culminated with Austen, and it is a particular joy to read Bruce's ruminations on her work. "Jane Austen and the Pleasure Principle" points out "the happy coincidence of pleasure and duty" in most of her novels (so very different from the focus on self-sacrifice so common in the fiction of the time). What an insight that Austen's prayers, which seem so generic, so little individual, such close relations to the *Book of Common Prayer*, nonetheless centre just like the novels on the issue of self-knowledge, its necessity and its difficulty.

That brings me, finally, to the moral implications of these essays. Samuel Johnson held that to think rationally is to think morally. To read this book is to be reminded just why the study of English literature, to which Bruce devoted his working life, matters so much. Reading good books does not, alas, make people better, as history has painfully taught us. But studying, meditating, and discussing such books is sure to increase the individual's opportunities for self-knowledge, for exchanging ideas, and for learning how other people's minds and imaginations work. By such means does literary study enrich the individual life and increase at least its potential for goodness in action.

∞ Works Cited

Abrams, M. H. *A Glossary of Literary Terms*. 7th ed. Fort Worth, TX: Harcourt Brace, 1999.
Alter, Robert. *Fielding and the Nature of the Novel*. Cambridge: Harvard UP, 1968.
———. *Partial Magic: The Novel as a Self-Conscious Genre*. Berkeley: U of California P, 1975.
Amis, Kingsley. *I Like It Here*. London: Victor Gollancz, 1958.
———. "Fit to Kill." *New Statesman* 22 September 1978: 384.
———. "Laughter's to Be Taken Seriously." *New York Times Book Review* 7 July 1957: 1, 13.
———. *Lucky Jim*. London: Penguin, 1961.
Amory, Anne. "The Reunion of Odysseus and Penelope." *Essays on the Odyssey: Selected Modern Criticism*. Ed. Charles H. Taylor, Jr. Bloomington: Indiana UP, 1963. 100–21.
Aristotle. *Poetics*. Trans. Stephen Halliwell. Cambridge: Harvard UP, 1995.
Armstrong, Isobel. *Jane Austen: Mansfield Park*. Penguin Critical Studies. London: Penguin, 1988.
Austen, Henry. "Biographical Notice of the Author." *Northanger Abbey*. Vol. 5. *The Novels of Jane Austen*. Ed. R.W. Chapman. 3rd ed. 6 vols. London: Oxford UP, 1953. Rpt. with revisions, 1969. 3–9.
Austen, Jane. *Catharine and Other Writings*. Ed. Margaret Anne Doody and Douglas Murray. Oxford: Oxford UP, 1993.
———. *Emma*. Vol. 4. *The Novels of Jane Austen*. Ed. R.W. Chapman. 3rd ed. 6 vols. London: Oxford UP, 1953. Rpt. with revisions, 1969.

———. *Jane Austen: Later Manuscripts.* Ed. Janet Todd and Linda Bree. Cambridge: Cambridge UP, 2008.

———. *Jane Austen's Letters.* Ed. Deirdre Le Faye. 3rd ed. Oxford: Oxford UP, 1995.

———. *Mansfield Park.* Vol. 3. *The Novels of Jane Austen.* Ed. R.W. Chapman. 3rd ed. 6 vols. London: Oxford UP, 1953. Rpt. with revisions, 1969.

———. *Minor Works.* Vol. 6. *The Novels of Jane Austen.* Ed. R.W. Chapman. 3rd ed. 6 vols. London: Oxford UP, 1954. Rpt. with revisions, 1969.

———. *Northanger Abbey.* Vol. 5. *The Novels of Jane Austen.* Ed. R.W. Chapman. 3rd ed. 6 vols. London: Oxford UP, 1953. Rpt. with revisions, 1969.

———. *Persuasion.* Vol. 5. *The Novels of Jane Austen.* Ed. R.W. Chapman. 3rd ed. 6 vols. London: Oxford UP, 1953. Rpt. with revisions, 1969.

———. *Pride and Prejudice.* Vol. 2. *The Novels of Jane Austen.* Ed. R.W. Chapman. 3rd ed. 6 vols. London: Oxford UP, 1953. Rpt. with revisions, 1969.

———. *Sense and Sensibility.* Vol. 1. *The Novels of Jane Austen.* Ed. R.W. Chapman. 3rd ed. 6 vols. London: Oxford UP, 1953. Rpt. with revisions, 1969.

Babb, Howard S. *Jane Austen's Novels: The Fabric of Dialogue.* Columbus: Ohio State UP, 1962.

Baker, Sheridan. "Fielding and the Irony of Form." *Eighteenth-Century Studies* 2.2 (December 1968): 138–54.

———. "Fielding's Comic Epic-in-Prose Romances Again." *Philological Quarterly* 58 (1979): 63–81.

———. "Henry Fielding's Comic Romances." *Papers of the Michigan Academy of Science, Arts, and Letters* 45 (1960): 411–19.

———, ed. Note. *Tom Jones.* By Henry Fielding. New York: W.W. Norton, 1973. 4.

Bakhtin, M.M. "Epic and Novel." *The Dialogic Imagination: Four Essays.* Ed. Michael Holquist. Trans. Caryl Emerson and Michael Holquist. Austin: U of Texas P, 1981. 3–40.

Battestin, Martin C. *The Providence of Wit: Aspects of Form in Augustan Literature and the Arts.* Oxford: Clarendon, 1974.

Bergson, Henri. "Laughter." *Comedy.* Ed. Wylie Sypher. Baltimore: Johns Hopkins UP, 1956. 61–190.

Blake, William. *The Marriage of Heaven and Hell. The Complete Poetry and Prose of William Blake.* New rev. ed. Ed. David V. Erdman. Berkeley: U of California P, 1982. 33–45.

The Book of Common Prayer. Oxford: Clarendon, 1803.

Boswell, James. *Life of Johnson.* 1791. Ed. R.W. Chapman. Oxford: Oxford UP, 1980.

Boyle, Ted E., and Terence Brown. "The Serious Side of Kingsley Amis's *Lucky Jim*." *Critique* 9 (1966): 100–07.

Bradley, A. C. "Jane Austen." *Essays and Studies by Members of the English Association* 2 (1911): 7–36.

Brontë, Charlotte. "Charlotte Brontë on Jane Austen, 1848, 1850." *Jane Austen: The Critical Heritage, 1811–1870.* Vol. 1. Ed. B.C. Southam. New York: Barnes and Noble, 1968. 126–28.

Brooks, Douglas. "Abraham Adams and Parson Trulliber: The Meaning of Joseph Andrews, Book II, Chapter 14." *Modern Language Review* 63.4 (October 1968): 794–801.

———. "Fielding: Tom Jones and Amelia." *Number and Pattern in the Eighteenth-century Novel: Defoe, Fielding, Smollett and Sterne.* London: Routledge and Kegan Paul, 1973. 92–122.

Brown, David R. *Walter Scott and the Historical Imagination.* London: Routledge and Kegan Paul, 1979.

Brown, Homer O. "The Errant Letter and the Whispering Gallery." *Genre* 10 (1977): 573–99.

Budgen, Frank. *James Joyce and the Making of Ulysses.* Bloomington: Indiana UP, 1960.

Burgess, Anthony. *The Novel Now: A Student's Guide to Contemporary Fiction.* London: Faber and Faber, 1967.

Burney, Frances. *Camilla, or A Picture of Youth.* 1796. Ed. Edward A. Bloom and Lillian D. Bloom. Oxford: Oxford UP, 1983.

———. *Evelina, or The History of a Young Lady's Entrance into the World.* 1778. Ed. Edward A. Bloom. Oxford: Oxford UP, 1968.

———. *The Wanderer, or Female Difficulties.* 1814. Introd. Margaret Drabble. London: Pandora, 1988.

Burrows, J. F. *Jane Austen's "Emma."* Sydney: Sydney UP Press, 1968.

Bush, Douglas. *Jane Austen.* New York: Collier, 1975.

Butler, Marilyn. "History, Politics, and Religion." *The Jane Austen Companion.* Ed. J. David Grey, A. Walton Litz, and Brian Southam. Macmillan: New York, 1986. 190–208.

———. *Jane Austen and the War of Ideas.* Oxford: Oxford UP, 1975.

Byrne, Paula. *Jane Austen and the Theatre.* London: Hambledon, 2002.

Caplan, Ralph. "Kingsley Amis." *Contemporary British Novelists.* Ed. Charles Shapiro. Carbondale: Southern Illinois UP, 1965.

Carens, James F. *The Satiric Art of Evelyn Waugh.* Seattle: U of Washington P, 1966.

Chapman, R.W. Headnote to "Prayers." *Minor Works.* Vol. 6. *The Novels of Jane Austen.* By Jane Austen. 3rd ed. Oxford: OUP, 1953. Rpt. with revisions, 1969. 453.

———. "Introductory Note to *Pride and Prejudice.*" *Pride and Prejudice.* Vol. 2. *The Novels of Jane Austen.* By Jane Austen. 3rd ed. Oxford: OUP, 1953. Rpt. with revisions, 1969. xi–xiii.

———. "A Jane Austen Collection." *Times Literary Supplement* 14 January 1926: 27.

Chaucer, Geoffrey. *The Works of Geoffrey Chaucer.* Ed. F.N. Robinson. 2nd ed. Boston: Houghton Mifflin, 1957.

Cockshut, A.O.J. *The Achievement of Walter Scott.* New York: New York UP, 1969.

The Concise Oxford Dictionary of Current English. 9th ed. Oxford: Clarendon, 1995.

Congreve, William. *The Way of the World.* New York: Norton, 1971.

Cook, Albert. *The Dark Voyage and the Golden Mean: A Philosophy of Comedy.* Cambridge: Harvard UP, 1949.

Corrigan, Robert W. "Comedy and the Comic Spirit." *Comedy: Meaning and Form.* Ed. Robert W. Corrigan. San Francisco: Chandler, 1965. 1–11.

Dalziel, Margaret. Introduction. *The Female Quixote.* By Charlotte Lennox. London: Oxford UP, 1970. xiii–xviii.

Davie, Donald. *The Heyday of Sir Walter Scott.* London: Routledge and Kegan Paul, 1961.

Davis, Robert Murray. "The Failure of Imagination: Evelyn Waugh's School Stories." *London Magazine* 25.1–2 (April–May 1985): 88–97.

———. *Evelyn Waugh, Writer.* Norman, OK: Pilgrim, 1981.

Davis, Robert Murray, Paul A. Doyle, Donat Gallagher, Charles E. Linck, and Winnifred M. Bogaards. *A Bibliography of Evelyn Waugh.* Troy, NY: Whitston, 1986.

Devlin, D.D. *The Author of Waverley: A Critical Study of Walter Scott.* Lewisburg: Bucknell UP, 1969.

Doody, Margaret Anne. *Frances Burney: The Life in the Works.* New Brunswick, NJ: Rutgers UP, 1988.

———. "Jane Austen's Reading." *The Jane Austen Companion.* Ed. J. David Grey, A. Walton Litz, and Brian Southam. New York: Macmillan, 1986. 347–63.

Doyle, Paul A. "*Decline and Fall*: Two Versions." *Evelyn Waugh Newsletter* 1.2 (Autumn 1967): 4–5.

Drew, Elizabeth. *The Novel: A Modern Guide to Fifteen English Masterpieces.* New York: W.W. Norton, 1963.

Duckworth, Alastair M. *The Improvement of the Estate: A Study of Jane Austen's Novels.* Baltimore: Johns Hopkins, 1971.

Duffy, Joseph M. "Emma: The Awakening from Innocence." *ELH: English Literary History* 21 (1954): 39–53.

Dyson, A. E. *The Crazy Fabric: Essays in Irony*. London: Macmillan, 1965.

Ehrenpreis, Irvin. *Fielding: Tom Jones*. London: Edward Arnold, 1964.

Epstein, Julia. *The Iron Pen: Frances Burney and the Politics of Women's Writing*. Madison, WI: U of Wisconsin P, 1989.

Farrer, Reginald. "The Book of Books." *Jane Austen: Emma*. Ed. David Lodge. London: Macmillan, 1968. 64–69.

———. "[Truth, Reality, and Good Sense in Jane Austen.]" *Pride and Prejudice: An Authoritative Text, Backgrounds, Reviews and Essays in Criticism*. Ed. Donald J. Gray. New York: W.W. Norton, 1966. 342–45.

Fergus, Jan. *Jane Austen: A Literary Life*. London: MacMillan, 1991.

Fiedler, Leslie. "Class War in British Literature." *The Collected Essays of Leslie Fiedler*. Vol. 1. New York: Stein and Day, 1971. 409–27.

Fielding, Henry. *Covent-Garden Journal* 28 January 1752. Ed. Gerard Edward Jensen. Vol. 1. New York: Russell and Russell, 1964.

———. *The History of Tom Jones, A Foundling*. Ed. Fredson Bowers. Introd. and notes by Martin C. Battestin. Wesleyan ed. 2 vols. Oxford: Oxford UP, 1974.

———. *Joseph Andrews*. Ed. Martin C. Battestin. London: Oxford UP, 1967.

Friedmann, Thomas. "*Decline and Fall* and the Satirist's Responsibility." *Evelyn Waugh Newsletter* 6.2 (Autumn 1972): 3–8.

Frye, Northrop. *Anatomy of Criticism: Four Essays*. Princeton: Princeton UP, 1957.

———. *A Natural Perspective: The Development of Shakespearean Comedy and Romance*. New York: Columbia UP, 1965.

Furbank, P. N. *E. M. Forster: A Life*. 2 vols. London: Secker and Warburg, 1977.

Gilson, David. "Auction Sales." *The Jane Austen Companion*. Ed. J. David Grey, A. Walton Litz, and Brian Southam. Macmillan: New York, 1986. 13–15.

———. *A Bibliography of Jane Austen*. Oxford: Clarendon, 1982.

Gindin, James. *Postwar British Fiction: New Accents and Attitudes*. Berkeley: U of California P, 1963.

———. "The Reassertion of the Personal." *Texas Quarterly* 1.4 (Winter 1958): 126–34.

Gottfried, Leon. "The Odysseyan Form: An Exploratory Essay." *Essays on European Literature in Honor of Liselote Dieckmann*. Ed. Peter Uwe Hohendahl, Herbert Lindenberger, and Egon Schwarz. St. Louis: Washington UP, 1972. 19–43.

Greenblatt, Stephen Jay. *Three Modern Satirists: Waugh, Orwell, and Huxley*. New Haven: Yale UP, 1965.

Halliday, E. M. "Narrative Perspective in *Pride and Prejudice*." *Nineteenth-Century Fiction* 15.1 (1960): 65–71.

Hart, Francis R. *Scott's Novels: The Plotting of Historic Survival*. Charlottesville: UP of Virginia, 1966.

Harvey, W. J. "The Plot of *Emma*." *Jane Austen:* Emma. Ed. David Lodge. London: Macmillan, 1968. 232–47.

Harwood, Ronald, and John Selwyn Gilbert. "A Sense of Loss: The Ordeal of Evelyn Waugh." *Listener* 26 October 1978: 528–30.

Heath, Jeffrey. *The Picturesque Prison: Evelyn Waugh and His Writing*. Kingston: McGill-Queens UP, 1982.

———. "Waugh's *Decline and Fall* in Manuscript." *English Studies* 55 (1974): 523–30.

Higham, T. M. "Captain Grimes's Revenge." *London Magazine* 17.1 (April–May 1977): 65–73.

Hilles, Frederick W. "Art and Artifice in *Tom Jones*." *Imagined Worlds: Essays on Some English Novels and Novelists in Honour of John Butt*. Ed. Maynard Mack and Ian Gregor. London: Methuen, 1968. 91–110.

Homer. *The Odyssey*. Trans. E. V. Rieu. Harmondsworth: Penguin, 1946.

Honan, Park. *Jane Austen: Her Life*. London: Weidenfeld and Nicolson, 1987.

Horativs Flaccvs, Q. *Opera*. Ed. D. R. Shackleton Bailey. Monachii: In Aedibvs K. G. Saur, 2001.

Hunter, J. Paul. *Occasional Form: Henry Fielding and the Chains of Circumstance*. Baltimore: Johns Hopkins UP, 1975.

———. "Response as Reformation: *Tristram Shandy* and the Art of Interruption." *Novel* 4 (1971): 132–46.

Hurrell, John D. "Class and Conscience in John Braine and Kingsley Amis." *Critique* 2 (1958): 39–53.

Isles, Duncan. Appendix: "Johnson, Richardson, and *The Female Quixote*." *The Female Quixote*. By Charlotte Lennox. London: Oxford UP, 1970. 418–27.

Jeffrey, Francis. "*Waverley*—a Novel." *Edinburgh Review* 24 (November 1814): 203–43.

J. M. S. G. Rev. of *Decline and Fall* by Evelyn Waugh. *Evelyn Waugh: The Critical Heritage*. Ed. Martin Stannard. London: Routledge and Kegan Paul, 1984. 82–83.

Johnson, Maurice. "Some Minute Wheels." *Fielding's Art of Fiction: Eleven Essays on* Shamela, Joseph Andrews, Tom Jones, *and* Amelia. Philadelphia: U of Pennsylvania P, 1961. 115–38.

Johnson, Samuel. *A Dictionary of the English Language*. London, 1755.

———. *The History of Rasselas, Prince of Abyssinia.* 1759. *Samuel Johnson.* Ed. Donald Greene. Oxford: Oxford UP, 1984. 335–418.

———. "Life of Milton." 1779. *Samuel Johnson.* Oxford Authors ed. Ed. Donald J. Greene. New York: Oxford UP, 1984.

———. *Prayers and Meditations.* London: H. R. Allenson, 1785.

Karl, F. R. *A Reader's Guide to the Contemporary English Novel.* London: Thames and Hudson, 1962.

Kennedy, Alan. *The Protean Self: Dramatic Action in Contemporary Fiction.* New York: Columbia UP, 1974.

Konigsberg, Ira. *Narrative Technique in the English Novel: Defoe to Austen.* Hamden, CT: Archon, 1985.

Koppel, Gene. *The Religious Dimension of Jane Austen's Novels.* Ann Arbor, MI: UMI P, 1988.

Kris, Ernst. *Psychoanalytic Explorations in Art.* New York: International Universities, 1952.

Lamont, Claire. Editor's Notes. *Waverley; Or, 'Tis Sixty Years Since.* By Sir Walter Scott. Oxford: Clarendon, 1981. 419–70.

Langer, Suzanne. "The Comic Rhythm." *Comedy: Meaning and Form.* Ed. Robert W. Corrigan. San Francisco: Chandler, 1965. 119–40.

Lanham, Richard A. *Tristram Shandy: The Games of Pleasure.* Berkeley: U of California P, 1973.

Leavis, F. R. *The Great Tradition: George Eliot, Henry James, Joseph Conrad.* Harmondsworth, UK: Penguin, 1966.

Lebowitz, Naomi. "Kingsley Amis: The Penitent Hero." *Perspective* 10 (1958): 129–36.

Le Faye, Deirdre. *Jane Austen: A Family Record.* London: The British Library, 1989.

Lennox, Charlotte. *The Female Quixote, or The Adventures of Arabella.* Ed. Margaret Dalziel. London: Oxford UP, 1970.

Lerner, Laurence. *The Truthtellers: Jane Austen, George Eliot, D. H. Lawrence.* New York: Shocken, 1967.

Littlewood, Ian. *The Writings of Evelyn Waugh.* Oxford: Basil Blackwell, 1983.

Litz, A. Walton. *Jane Austen: A Study of Her Artistic Development.* New York: Oxford UP, 1965.

Lodge, David. "The Modern, the Contemporary, and the Importance of Being Amis." *Language of Fiction: Essays in Criticism and Verbal Analysis of the English Novel.* New York: Columbia UP, 1966. 243–67.

Lukács, Georg. *The Historical Novel*. Trans. Hannah and Stanley Mitchell. London: Merlin, 1962.

Mack, Maynard. Introduction. *Joseph Andrews*. By Henry Fielding. New York: Holt, Rinehart and Winston, 1948. vii–xvi.

Mansell, Darrel. *The Novels of Jane Austen: An Interpretation*. London: Macmillan, 1973.

Maresca, Thomas E. *Epic to Novel*. Columbus: Ohio State UP, 1974.

McAleer, Edward C. "*Decline and Fall* as Imitation." *Evelyn Waugh Newsletter* 7.3 (Winter 1973): 1–4.

McCarthy, Mary. "The Fact in Fiction." *On the Contrary*. New York: Farrar, Straus, and Cudahy, 1961. 249–70.

McMaster, Juliet. "The Secret Languages of *Emma*." *Persuasions: The Journal of the Jane Austen Society of North America* 13 (1991): 119–31.

———. "The Silent Angel: Impediments to Female Expression in Frances Burney's Novels." *Studies in the Novel* 21 (1989): 235–52.

Meckier, Jerome. "Cycle, Symbol, and Parody in Evelyn Waugh's *Decline and Fall*." *Contemporary Literature* 20.1 (Winter 1979): 51–75.

Miller, Henry Knight. *Henry Fielding's* Tom Jones *and the Romance Tradition*. Victoria: English Literary Studies, U of Victoria, 1976.

Moler, Kenneth L. *Jane Austen's Art of Allusion*. Lincoln: U of Nebraska P, 1968.

Monaghan, David. *Jane Austen: Structure and Social Vision*. London: Macmillan, 1980.

Morgan, Susan. *In the Meantime: Character and Perception in Jane Austen's Fiction*. Chicago: U of Chicago P, 1980.

Olson, Elder. *The Theory of Comedy*. Bloomington: Indiana UP, 1968.

Oxford English Dictionary. 2nd ed. Oxford: Oxford UP, 1989.

Parker, R. B. "Farce and Society: The Range of Kingsley Amis." *Wisconsin Studies in Contemporary Literature* 2 (Fall 1961): 27–38.

Phillips, Gene D. *Evelyn Waugh's Officers, Gentlemen, and Rogues: The Fact behind His Fiction*. Chicago: Nelson-Hall, 1975.

Poirier, Richard. "Transatlantic Configurations: Mark Twain and Jane Austen." *A World Elsewhere: The Place of Style in American Literature*. New York: Oxford UP, 1966. 144–207.

Priestley, J. B. Rev. of *Decline and Fall* by Evelyn Waugh. *Evelyn Waugh: The Critical Heritage*. Ed. Martin Stannard. London: Routledge and Kegan Paul, 1984. 84.

Rabinovitz, Rubin. *The Reaction against Experiment in the English Novel, 1950–1960*. New York: Columbia UP, 1967.

Rawson, C. J. *Henry Fielding and the Augustan Ideal under Stress: "Nature's Dance of Death" and Other Studies*. London: Routledge and Kegan Paul, 1972.

Ross, Deborah. "Mirror, Mirror: The Didactic Dilemma of *The Female Quixote*." *Studies in English Literature* 27 (1987): 455-73.

Roth, William Matson. Introduction. *Three Evening Prayers*. By Jane Austen. San Francisco: Colt, 1940. n.pag.

Rozema, Patricia, dir. *Mansfield Park*. Alliance Atlantis Communications; Miramax Films, 1999.

Ryle, Gilbert. "Jane Austen and the Moralists." *Critical Essays on Jane Austen*. Ed. B.C. Southam. London: Routledge and Kegan Paul, 1968. 106-22.

Santayana, George. "The Comic Mask." *Comedy: Meaning and Form*. Ed. Robert W. Corrigan. San Francisco: Chandler, 1965. 73-76.

Schiller, Friedrich von. *On the Naive and Sentimental in Literature*. Anonymous trans. London: n.pag., 1851.

Schorer, Mark. "The Humiliation of Emma Woodhouse." *Jane Austen: Emma*. Ed. David Lodge. London: Macmillan, 1968. 170-87.

Scott, Sir Walter. *Waverley; Or, 'Tis Sixty Years Since*. Ed. Claire Lamont. Oxford: Clarendon, 1981.

Selwyn, David. *Jane Austen and Leisure*. London: Hambledon, 1999.

Simon, Richard Keller. *The Labyrinth of the Comic: Theory and Practice from Fielding to Freud*. Tallahassee: Florida State UP, 1985.

Shakespeare, William. *Much Ado about Nothing*. Oxford: Clarendon, 1978.

Smollett, Tobias. *The Expedition of Humphry Clinker*. 1771. Ed. Lewis M. Knapp. Oxford: Oxford UP, 1984.

Southam, B.C., ed. *Critical Essays on Jane Austen*. London: Routledge and Kegan Paul, 1968.

———. *Jane Austen: The Critical Heritage, 1811-1870*. Vol. 1. New York: Barnes and Noble, 1968.

Spacks, Patricia Meyer. "Gossip: How It Works." *Yale Review* 72 (1983): 561-80.

———. *Imagining a Self: Autobiography and Novel in Eighteenth-Century England*. Cambridge: Harvard UP, 1976.

———. "In Praise of Gossip." *Hudson Review* 35 (1982): 19-38.

Spencer, Jane. *The Rise of the Woman Novelist: From Aphra Behn to Jane Austen*. Oxford: Basil Blackwell, 1986.

Stanford, W. B. *The Ulysses Theme: A Study in the Adaptability of a Traditional Hero*. 2nd ed. Oxford: Basil Blackwell, 1963.

Stannard, Martin, ed. *Evelyn Waugh: The Critical Heritage*. London: Routledge and Kegan Paul, 1984.

———. *Evelyn Waugh: The Early Years 1903-1939*. London: Dent, 1986.

Sykes, Christopher. *Evelyn Waugh: A Biography*. Rev. ed. Harmondsworth: Penguin, 1977.

Sterne, Laurence. *The Life and Opinions of Tristram Shandy, Gentleman*. 1759-1767. The Florida Edition of the Works of Laurence Sterne. 3 vols. Ed. Melvyn New and Joan New. Gainesville: UP of Florida, 1978.

Strauch, Gerard. "Calendar, Construction, and Character in Kingsley Amis's *Lucky Jim*." *Recherches Anglaises et Americaines* 3 (1970): 57-66.

Swedenberg, H.T., Jr. *The Theory of the Epic in England*. New York: Russell and Russell, 1972.

Tave, Stuart M. *The Amiable Humorist: A Study in the Comic Theory and Criticism of the Eighteenth and Early Nineteenth Centuries*. Chicago: U of Chicago P, 1960.

———. *Some Words of Jane Austen*. Chicago: U of Chicago P, 1973.

Tillotson, Geoffrey, Paul Fussell, and Marshall Waingrow, ed. *Eighteenth-Century Literature*. New York: Harcourt, Brace, Jovanovich, 1969.

Torrance, Robert M. *The Comic Hero*. Cambridge: Harvard UP, 1978.

Tucker, George Holbert. *Jane Austen the Woman: Some Biographical Insights*. New York: St. Martin's, 1994.

Twain, Mark. *The Adventures of Tom Sawyer*. Hartford, CT: American Publishing; San Francisco: A. Roman, 1876.

"Unsigned review, *British Critic*: August 1814, ns ii, 189-211." *Scott: The Critical Heritage*. Ed. John O. Hayden. London: Routledge and Kegan Paul, 1970. 67-74.

"Unsigned review, *Critical Review*: March 1813, 4th series, iii, 318-24." *Jane Austen: The Critical Heritage 1811-1870*. Ed. B.C. Southam. London: Routledge, 1968. 43-47.

Varey, Simon. *Henry Fielding*. Cambridge: Cambridge UP, 1986.

[Vickers, William.] *A Companion to the Altar: Shewing the Nature & Necessity of a Sacramental Preparation in Order to Our Worthy Receiving the Holy Communion, to Which Are Added Prayers and Meditations*. London: Scatcherd and Whitaker, [1793?].

Virgil. *Eclogues, Georgics, Aeneid, Appendix, and Vergilliana*. Trans. H.R. Fairclough. 2 vols. Cambridge: Harvard UP, 1960.

Watt, Ian. *The Rise of the Novel: Studies in Defoe, Richardson and Fielding*. Berkeley: U of California P, 1957.

Waugh, Evelyn. "The Balance: A Yarn of the Good Old Days of Broad Trousers and High Necked Jumpers." *Evelyn Waugh, Apprentice: The Early Writings, 1910-1927*. Ed. Robert Murray Davis. Norman, OK: Pilgrim, 1985. 155-85.

———. *Brideshead Revisited: The Sacred and Profane Memories of Captain Charles Ryder.* Boston: Little, Brown, 1946.

———. *Decline and Fall.* 2nd ed. London: Chapman and Hall, 1962.

———. *The Diaries of Evelyn Waugh.* Ed. Michael Davie. Harmondsworth: Penguin, 1979.

———. "Fan Fare." *The Essays, Articles, and Reviews of Evelyn Waugh.* Ed. Donat Gallagher. Harmondsworth: Penguin, 1986. 300–04.

———. *The Letters of Evelyn Waugh.* Ed. Mark Amory. Harmondsworth: Penguin, 1982.

———. *A Little Learning: The First Volume of an Autobiography by Evelyn Waugh.* Harmondsworth: Penguin, 1983.

———. "The Private Diaries of Evelyn Waugh." *Observer* 1 April 1973: 16–17.

Welsh, Alexander. Rev. of *The Laird of Abbotsford: A View of Sir Walter Scott,* by A. N. Wilson; *Sir Walter Scott: Landscape and Totality,* by James Reed; *Landscapes of Memory: Turner as Illustrator to Scott,* by Gerald Finley; and *Waverley; or, 'Tis Sixty Years Since,* by Walter Scott, ed. Claire Lamont. *Nineteenth-Century Fiction* 36.3 (December 1981): 358–63.

West, Rebecca. "Evelyn Waugh." Rev. of *Decline and Fall* and *Vile Bodies,* by Evelyn Waugh. *Ending in Earnest.* Garden City, NY: Doubleday, Doran, 1931. 217–26.

Whately, Richard. "Whately on Jane Austen." Unsigned rev. *Jane Austen: The Critical Heritage 1811–1870.* Ed. B. C. Southam. London: Routledge and Kegan Paul, 1968. 87–105.

Whitman, Cedric H. *Homer and the Heroic Tradition.* Cambridge: Harvard UP, 1958.

Wiesenfarth, Joseph. *The Errand of Form: An Assay of Jane Austen's Art.* New York: Fordham UP, 1967.

Willett, John. Rev. of *Decline and Fall,* by Evelyn Waugh. *Evelyn Waugh: The Critical Heritage.* Ed. Martin Stannard. London: Routledge and Kegan Paul, 1984. 92–94.

Woolf, Virginia. *A Room of One's Own.* 1929. London: Grafton, 1977.

Wright, Andrew H. *Jane Austen's Novels: A Study in Structure.* New ed. London: Chatto and Windus, 1967.

Yeats, W. B., ed. *The Oxford Book of Modern Verse.* Clarendon: Oxford UP, 1936.

OTHER BOOKS FROM THE UNIVERSITY OF ALBERTA PRESS

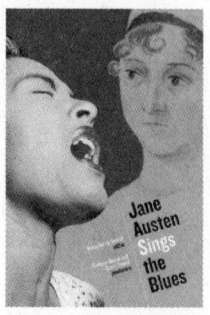

Jane Austen Sings the Blues
NORA FOSTER STOVEL, *Editor*
GRAHAM GUEST AND GRANT STOVEL, *Producers*
304 pages ‖ Audio CD, *notes*
$26.95 paper
ISBN-13: 978-0-88864-510-4
Literature/Music

The Talk in Jane Austen
BRUCE STOVEL & LYNN WEINLOS GREGG, *Editors*
296 pages ‖ *Notes, bibliography, index*
$29.95 paper
ISBN-13: 978-0-88864-374-2
Literary Criticism